# THE BIG BOOK  of
# CANADIAN TRIVIA

**Thomas Beer**
46194 Mellard Ave
Chilliwack BC  V2P 2Y9

# THE BIG BOOK of CANADIAN TRIVIA

## Mark Kearney and Randy Ray

### DUNDURN PRESS
TORONTO

Editor: Allison Hirst
Design: Erin Mallory
Printer: Webcom

Library and Archives Canada Cataloguing in Publication

Kearney, Mark, 1955-
     The big book of Canadian trivia / Mark Kearney and Randy Ray.


ISBN 978-1-55488-417-9


     1. Canada--Miscellanea.  I. Ray, Randy, 1952-  II. Title.

FC61.K425 2009              971.002          C2009-900285-X

1  2  3  4  5    13  12  11  10  09

  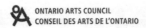

We acknowledge the support of the **Canada Council for the Arts** and the **Ontario Arts Council** for our publishing program. We also acknowledge the financial support of the **Government of Canada** through the **Book Publishing Industry Development Program** and **The Association for the Export of Canadian Books**, and the **Government of Ontario** through the **Ontario Book Publishers Tax Credit** program, and the **Ontario Media Development Corporation**.

Care has been taken to trace the ownership of copyright material used in this book. The author and the publisher welcome any information enabling them to rectify any references or credits in subsequent editions.

*J. Kirk Howard, President*

Front cover (left to right): Top: Barbara Ann Scott (*courtesy Library and Archives Canada, PA-165291*); the *Bluenose II* (*courtesy LAC, PA-30803*); Elizabeth Arden (*Alan Fisher/Wikimedia Commons*). Middle: postage stamp remembers Canadian women who helped with the war effort (*courtesy Canada Post Corporation, 1991. Reproduced with permission*); Seagram's VO (*Randy Ray*); Marilyn Bell (*courtesy City of Toronto Archives, f1244_it2128*). Bottom: A.E. LePage (*courtesy Royal LePage Real Estate Services, Ltd.*); Canadian four-dollar bill; the Last Spike, **November 7, 1885** (*courtesy LAC, C-003693*).

Printed and bound in Canada.
www.dundurn.com

Dundurn Press
3 Church Street, Suite 500
Toronto, Ontario, Canada
M5E 1M2

Gazelle Book Services Limited
White Cross Mills
High Town, Lancaster, England
LA1 4XS

Dundurn Press
2250 Military Road
Tonawanda, NY
U.S.A. 14150

For a Big Book allow us a big list of family and friends
to dedicate our latest trivial pursuit to


Janis

Catherine

The Ray boys: Chris, Andrew, Marcus (and Duffy, of course) and
the Ray grandchildren: Aryana, Sydney, and Hazel

Shirley Kearney and the late Basil Kearney

Various publications in Canada and the U.S. that have faithfully published our
trivia over the years, including *Forever Young, Boomer Life Magazine* and *Chill Magazine*.

# TABLE OF CONTENTS

# INTRODUCTION

When you have stories about everything from Tim Hortons doughnuts to the Halifax explosion, Molson beer to the introduction of the loonie, Joni Mitchell to Simon Whitfield, and Red Green to CCM bicycles, you know it's going to take a big book to cram in all that amazing Canadiana.

The Big Book of Canadian Trivia contains all that and much more.

From history and sports to music and business, this book will enlighten you about the many threads that weave through the tapestry that is Canada. For fans of our previous books, this new collection takes some of the best items from our more than 20 years of research into this country and blends them with an array of new information we've dug up since our last book *Whatever Happened To...? Catching Up with Canadian Icons.*

Think of this book as something of a Greatest Hits CD of Canadian trivia. We've gathered together some of the most surprising, delightful, and stirring moments from Canada's long history and added in as bonus tracks an array of new, compelling Canadiana.

And as a tip of the hat to all those Canadians who grew up as keen observers of the culture and history of our neighbours to the south, we've added a sprinkling of American trivia that should be a fun test of your knowledge about goings on across the border.

Many of you grew up watching the Oscars, listening to American rock and roll, or indulging in Sunday afternoons with NFL football on the tube, and we've got some quizzes on those topics and others to test your brainpower.

Of course, even *The Big Book of Canadian Trivia* can't encompass everything, so if you want to continue to dabble please visit our website www.trivaguys.com for more factual fun and tantalizing trivia tidbits.

Whether you read our Canadian trivia in this, our latest book, or on our website, we're pleased to have you along for the ride as we take you on a trip that explores the lighter side of Canada.

Enjoy!

# CHAPTER 1
# Blast from the Past: Historic Canada

## 🍁 HISTORY HODGEPODGE

- The word *Canada* is derived from the Huron-Iroquois word *Kanata*, which means "village" or "settlement." The term was used to describe Stadacona (the current site of Quebec City) by two Amerindians who accompanied Jacques Cartier on his 1535 return voyage from France.

- Although we ended up with the name Dominion of Canada, there were several others discussed at the time, in the press as well as among politicians and citizens.

    Some of the favourite suggestions were New Britain, Laurentia, and Brittania. A union of the Maritimes has also been discussed, and Acadia was the front-runner name for that. It was also considered a possibility for the entire country.

    Other suggestions included Cabotia, Columbia, Canadia, and Ursalia. By agreeing to the name Canada, both Lower and Upper Canada had to change their names, to Quebec and Ontario respectively.

- Several thousand people living in what is now Canada participated in the U.S. Civil War. The soldiers fought mostly for the North and the cause of opposing slavery, but others fought on the South's side. Some who fought from Canada were former slaves who had escaped into southwestern Ontario.

- Oh, by the way, did we tell you the war is over? The Battle of New Orleans, made famous in the 1959 song by American singer Johnny Horton, took place a month after the War of 1812 ended. The British and Americans had

### They Said It!

"The acquisition of Canada this year, as far as the neighbourhood of Quebec, will be a mere matter of marching, and will give us experience for the attack of Halifax the next, and the final expulsion of England from the American continent."

– *Thomas Jefferson, circa 1812, in a letter to Colonel William Duane*

signed the Treaty of Ghent, officially ending the war, on December 24, 1814. But it took several weeks for the news to reach military officials, and this final battle took place in January 1815.

• Canada's first overseas war was the Boer War, fought from 1899 to 1902. According to Fred Gaffen, former senior historian at the Canadian War Museum, approximately 8,000 Canadians served during that war, with about 7,000 of them seeing action in South Africa. The rest performed garrison duty in Halifax.

   The soldiers served as part of the British army but as Canadian soldiers. During the war 89 were killed, 135 others died by accident or disease, and 252 soldiers were injured.

• Ever wonder why Canadian fighter pilots wore silk scarves during the First World War? Well, military historian Ben Greenhouse explained that pilots wore the flowing scarves around their necks to prevent discomfort caused by swivelling their heads to check for trailing enemy aircraft. The open-cockpit aircraft they flew at the time did not have rearview mirrors so the pilots had to turn their heads regularly from side to side in order to look out for enemy planes coming from the rear. The constant head-turning caused chafing when the pilots' coat collars rubbed on their necks, so they donned the scarves to prevent irritation.

• When the Second World War was declared in 1939, Canada was completely unready, having no tanks, aircraft, or machine guns. While the government placed orders for uniforms and rifles, volunteers trained in their "civvies," sometimes carrying broomsticks instead of guns.

• The community of Swastika, Ontario, had no connection to the Nazis, but rather was named for a good luck symbol after gold was found in the area in the early 1900s. Despite efforts by the provincial government during the Second World War to change the name to Winston, in honour of Winston Churchill, the citizens of Swastika resisted. They argued that the name had been around long before Adolf Hitler appropriated the symbol.

**They Said it!**

"A sub-arctic lumber village converted by royal mandate into a political cockpit."
– essayist Goldwin Smith after Ottawa was picked as Canada's new capital city.

• The Red Ensign was Canada's recognized flag for many years in the 20th century, but it was never our country's official banner. The flag was approved for use on government buildings in 1924, and after a lengthy debate the current maple leaf flag replaced it in 1965.

#  TEN CANADIAN FIRSTS: 1900 TO 1950

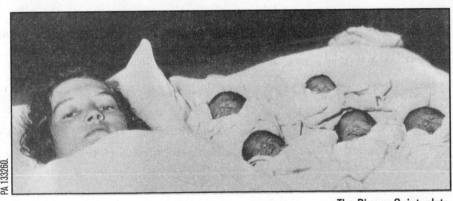

### They Said it!

"I'm a Quebecker, I was born alienated."

– *Laurier LaPierre, Canadian historian and broadcaster*

1. The first dial telephones came into use at Sydney Mines, Nova Scotia: 1907.

2. The first Canadian service station opened in Vancouver: 1908.

3. John Alexander Douglas McCurdy flew the Silver Dart at Baddeck, Nova Scotia in the first powered flight in Canada: 1909.

4. The first parachute jump in Canada was made by Charles Saunders at Vancouver: 1912.

5. Thomas Wilby became the first person to drive across Canada in a fifty-two-day trip between Halifax and Victoria: 1909.

6. Canada's first feature film, *Evangeline*, premiered in Halifax: 1913.

7. First radio transmission of music took place between Montreal and the Chateau Laurier Hotel in Ottawa: 1918.

8. First exhibition of Group of Seven, Art Gallery of Toronto: 1920.

9. The Dionne Quintuplets were born, the first surviving quintuplets in Canada and the world: 1934.

10. Canada's first drive-in movie theatre opened in the Hamilton area: 1946.

Photo courtesy of the National Archives of Canada
PA 133260.

The Dionne Quintuplets.

## 🍁 TEN CANADIAN FIRSTS: 1950 TO 2009

1. CBFT, Canada's first television station, began transmitting in Montreal: 1952.

2. The Yonge Street subway opened in Toronto, the first underground public transit system in Canada: 1954.

3. Canada's new Maple Leaf flag was flown for the first time on Parliament Hill: 1965.

4. The Cat's Whiskers, Canada's first strip bar, opened in Vancouver: 1966.

5. Dr. Pierre Grondin of the Montreal Heart Institute performed Canada's first heart transplant operation: 1968.

6. Prime Minister Pierre Trudeau married Margaret Sinclair in North Vancouver, becoming the first prime minister to marry while in office: 1971.

7. Canada's first astronauts were chosen, including Marc Garneau, Canada's first man in space and Roberta Bondar, Canada's first woman in space: 1983.

8. Pope John Paul II made first papal visit to Canada: 1984.

9. New Democratic Party Member of Parliament Svend Robinson was the first MP to publicly declare his homosexuality: 1988.

10. Heather Erxleben became the first female combat soldier in the Canadian Armed Forces: 1995.

## 🍁 CANADA'S TEN WORST KILLER DISASTERS
(ranked by number of fatalities)

1. **Spanish Influenza Outbreak:** Between 1918 and 1925 this viral infection affected all regions of the country, killing more than 50,000 Canadians.

2. **Halifax Explosion:** On December 6, 1917, the French munitions ship *Mont Blanc* collided with the Belgian relief ship *Imo* in Halifax Harbour causing an explosion that

killed more than 1,600 people and seriously injured 9,000 more. Six thousand people were left homeless and property damage was estimated at $50 million.

3. **St. Lawrence River Collision:** On May 29, 1914, 1,012 people died when Canadian Pacific steamer *Empress of Ireland* collided with the Norwegian ship *Storstad* in the Gulf of St. Lawrence. It was the worst peacetime maritime disaster in Canadian history.

4. **Matheson Fire:** A devastating fire broke out in this town northwest of North Bay, Ontario, on July 29, 1916, taking the lives of between 200 and 250 men, women, and children and destroying six towns, including Matheson and Cochrane. Property damage was estimated at more than $2 million.

5. **Hillcrest Explosion:** A dust explosion at a coal mine in Hillcrest, Alberta, on June 19, 1914, killed 189 miners.

6. **Noronic Fire:** On September 14, 1949, the *Noronic,* the largest Canadian passenger ship on the Great Lakes, was destroyed by fire at Toronto, claiming 118 lives.

7. **Newfoundland Fire:** During a dance at the Knights of Columbus Hotel in St. John's, Newfoundland, on December 12, 1942, a fire killed 99 people.

> **They Said It!**
>
> "I must say, however, that although Florida may have a more favourable climate than anything I've seen and its soil may be more fruitful, you could hardly hope to find a more beautiful country than Canada."
>
> — *Samuel de Champlain in 1603*

8. **Quebec Bridge Collapse:** Part of the Quebec Bridge in Quebec City collapsed on August 29, 1907, killing 75 workers and injuring 11 others.

9. **Frank Slide:** On April 29, 1903, at 4:10 a.m. 70 million tons of limestone from Turtle Mountain crashed onto the town of Frank, Alberta, and a nearby valley, killing at least 70 people. It was Canada's most destructive landslide.

10. **Train Derailment in Spanish River, Ontario:** On January 21, 1910, a Canadian Pacific Railways passenger train en route to Minneapolis hit a bridge causing the back half of the train to leave the tracks. Sixty-three people died and twenty others were injured.

# 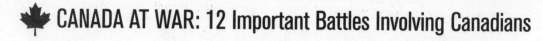 CANADA AT WAR: 12 Important Battles Involving Canadians

1. **Paardeberg:** The first battle and first victory for Canadians on foreign soil in the twentieth century took place in February 1900 during the Boer War. Fighting alongside the British, the Canadians played a key role in what has been described as a turning point in that war.

2. **Second Battle of Ypres:** Canadian soldiers survived the first major gas attack in modern war and helped hold off an attack by German soldiers in April 1915.

3. **Vimy Ridge:** Arguably Canadian soldiers' finest hour. The four divisions involved in the fighting in April 1917, captured an enemy position many thought was impregnable. The battle marked not only the first major victory for the Canadian Corps in the First World War, but the first significant Allied advance on the Western Front.

4. **Moreuil Wood:** The Canadian Cavalry Brigade slowed down a German offensive in the spring of 1918. A decisive German victory here could well have prolonged the war for many more months.

5. **The Battle of the Atlantic:** Throughout the Second World War, it was crucial to get supplies to Britain. The Royal Canadian Navy and Canadian merchant sailors overcame fierce storms, German submarines, and heavy losses to transport much-needed supplies across the ocean to Allied soldiers.

6. **The Battle of Britain:** Hundreds of Canadians took part in this key battle in the summer of 1940 and helped destroy much of the German Luftwaffe. This key battle prevented the Germans from conquering Britain.

7. **The Battle of Hong Kong:** Some two thousand mostly unseasoned Canadian troops valiantly fought off the Japanese for more than two weeks before surrendering in December 1941. More than a third were killed and wounded; the rest suffered horrible conditions in prison camps.

8. **Dieppe:** Considered by some to be a dress rehearsal for D-Day, Dieppe proved disastrous for Canadians. Almost 5,000 Canadian troops took part in an almost suicidal raid on France in August 1942, where they came under heavy fire from German troops. More than 900 were killed and nearly 2,000 taken prisoner.

9. **The Battle of Ortona:** The December 1943 battle against elite German paratroopers saw Canadians involved in one of the toughest clashes in the Italian campaign of the Second World War. The Canadian victory helped take the sting out of the defeat at Dieppe a year earlier.

10. **D-Day:** Some fifteen thousand Canadians took part in the largest invasion in the world on June 6, 1944. Along with British and American soldiers, they turned the tide of the Second World War. The Canadians were the first troops to reach their planned objective.

11. **Battle of the Scheldt:** Canadian soldiers battled through coastal towns of France and Belgium in late 1944 removing the Germans. There were more than 6,000 Canadian casualties, but they succeeded in freeing the port of Antwerp and opening a supply route for the Allies to make a final onslaught against the Nazis.

12. **Kap'yong:** In April 1951, during the Korean War, Canadian soldiers prevented the Chinese from occupying Seoul, and for their action received the United States Presidential Distinguished Unit Citation for gallantry and heroism under fire.

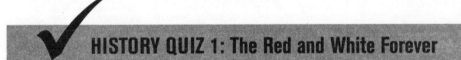

## HISTORY QUIZ 1: The Red and White Forever

1. In what year did the federal government first begin searching for a new Canadian flag?

   a) 1963
   b) 1959
   c) 1925
   d) 1960

2. At Confederation in 1867, which flag was considered Canada's official flag, the Union Jack or the Red Ensign?

3. At game two of the 1992 World Series between Toronto and Atlanta and during Canada Day ceremonies on Parliament Hill

on July 1, 1999, the Canadian flag was flown improperly. What was wrong?

    a) both flags were the wrong color
    b) the flags were flown upside down
    c) improper flagpoles were used
    d) the flags were flown too low

4. Two members of the Group of Seven submitted designs to a Parliamentary committee that was examining proposed designs for Canada's new flag. Which one of the following three artists did not suggest a design?

    a) A.Y. Jackson
    b) Lawren Harris
    c) A.J. Casson

5. Which national organization condemned Prime Minister Lester B. Pearson's promise in the mid-1960s to give Canadians a flag of their own?

    a) Canadian Automobile Association
    b) Royal Canadian Legion
    c) Canadian Medical Association
    d) Canadian Chamber of Commerce

6. How many red maple leaves were on Pearson's preferred design for a new Canadian flag, unveiled in May 1964?

    a) two
    b) one
    c) three
    d) five

7. What was the nickname given to Pearson's proposed flag design?

    a) Pearson's Pennant
    b) Red Cabbage

c) the Maple Leaf Rag

d) all of the above

8.  Which of the following reasons were cited to condemn Pearson's plan to include the maple leaf on Canada's new flag, according to *I Stand for Canada* by Rick Archbold?

> a) The maple leaf did not represent the existence of English and French Canada
>
> b) The sugar maple tree didn't grow anywhere west of the Ontario/Manitoba border
>
> c) The Communist Party of Canada supported the flag
>
> d) The sugar maple was the official tree of New York State
>
> e) All of the above

9.  Fill in the name on this declaration: I, _____, Prime Minister of Canada, declare that February 15 will be celebrated henceforth as National Flag of Canada Day. Let us be proud of our flag!

10. What was the final alteration before the maple leaf flag selected by a Parliamentary committee was adopted?

Photo by Randy Ray.

The red and white maple leaf.

> a) the maple leaf was enlarged by one inch
>
> b) a deeper shade of red was used
>
> c) two points were removed from the base of the maple leaf
>
> d) the stem of the maple leaf was shortened

11. What was the occupation of George Stanley in 1965 when he proposed the basic design that became Canada's red and white maple leaf flag?

> a) a senator in Manitoba

b) a Halifax-based graphic artist

c) a National Hockey League defenceman

d) dean of the arts at Royal Military College in Kingston

12. What was flying atop the Peace Tower at Parliament Hill on February 15, 1965, before the first official raising of Canada's maple leaf flag took place?

a) Union Jack

b) nothing

c) Red Ensign

d) the governor general's standard

13. When former prime minister John Diefenbaker died, two flags were draped over his coffin as his body lay in state at Parliament Hill in August 1979. Which two?

a) Canadian flag

b) Saskatchewan provincial flag

c) Red Ensign

d) Union Jack

14. How does the federal government recommend Canadians dispose of a worn out Canadian flag?

a) mail it to the Department of Canadian Heritage in Ottawa

b) burn it

c) shred it into tiny pieces

d) take it to a landfill site

15. A version of the Union Jack is still found on the provincial flags of which four Canadian provinces?

a) Ontario, Manitoba, Nova Scotia, and Saskatchewan

b) Ontario, Manitoba, British Columbia, and Newfoundland

c) Ontario, Alberta, Prince Edward Island, and Quebec

d) Ontario, Alberta, Nova Scotia, and British Columbia

16. The national flag is one of three of Canada's symbols of sovereignty. Pick the other two.

    a) the national coat of arms
    b) the Great Seal of Canada
    c) the House of Commons Mace
    d) the governor general's standard

➥ **Answers on pages 339–340**

# CHAPTER 2
# Bon Appétit: A Fascination with Food

**M**any great entrepreneurs got their start in Canada, and many of them were in the business of food production, distribution, and service. Here are a few who will be familiar to you:

## 🍽 Tim Horton (Tim Hortons Doughnuts)

To many hockey fans, Tim Horton was a legendary National Hockey League defenceman whose name is etched onto the Stanley Cup four times as a member of the Toronto Maple Leafs. To those who couldn't care less about hockey, he is a name on a sign and a synonym for a regular coffee and a Dutchie to go.

"Mr. Horton will be famous long after most Timbit dunkers have forgotten what he did for a living," *Globe and Mail* reporter John Saunders once wrote.

In fact, Horton supported himself and his family by playing professional hockey in the 1950s, 60s, and 70s, not by peddling Timbits, doughnuts, and coffee. During his hockey career, the Tim Hortons doughnut chain was merely a sideline, but one that would earn millions of dollars for others long after he was killed in a 1974 car accident.

Miles Gilbert "Tim" Horton was born in the northern Ontario mining community of Cochrane on January 12, 1930, about 18 months before Conn Smythe opened Maple Leaf Gardens. He was a quiet but muscular kid who played his early hockey in Copper Cliff near Sudbury before heading south to play for Toronto's St. Michael's Majors in 1947.

As a youngster, his dream was to be a fighter pilot. As a young hockey player, his focus changed to pro hockey and he developed into a tough but capable rushing defenceman. Shortly after joining the Majors, his penchant for penalties earned him the nickname "Tim the Terrible."

After a promising junior career, Horton played for the Pittsburgh Hornets of the American Hockey League before he and his trademark Marine Corps brush cut joined Toronto as a regular rearguard in 1952.

Horton wore number 7 for the Leafs until the 1969–70 season when he was traded to the New York Rangers. In 1971–72 he joined the Pittsburgh Penguins before being acquired by Punch Imlach's Buffalo Sabres in 1972. He was in his second season with Buffalo when he died.

Despite being shortsighted and nearly blind in his left eye (he was nicknamed Mr. Magoo and Clark Kent for the thick, dark-rimmed glasses he wore away from the rink), Horton was a rock-steady rearguard who left a legacy in the NHL. Playing for much of his career with fellow defensive stalwarts Allan Stanley, Bobby Baun, and Carl Brewer, Horton's Leafs won the Stanley Cup in 1962, 1963, 1964, and 1967. He was voted to the NHL's first all-star team three times and in 1977 was inducted into the Hockey Hall of Fame.

"He was one of those steady defencemen who never set many fires but was always around to put them out," sports columnist Dick Beddoes once wrote about Horton, who was known for his powerful slapshot, extraordinary strength, and his love for doughnuts, fast cars, and booze. Teammates remember him as modestly confident about his abilities, approachable, generous, and considerate, although he had his share of off-ice temper tantrums.

The night of his death, the 44-year-old Horton was named third star after the Sabres fell 4–2 to the Leafs at Maple Leaf Gardens. He died at 4:30 a.m., when he was thrown from his high-performance Ford Pantera as it flipped several times after leaving the Queen Elizabeth Way in St. Catharines, Ontario. The car was a signing bonus when Horton inked his second contract with the Sabres.

During his NHL career, Horton logged 1,446 regular season games, scored 115 goals and 403 assists, and registered 1,611 minutes in penalties. Another impressive statistic was the success of his doughnut business, which in its first decade had grown from a single franchise to 35 outlets.

The business was launched in February 1964 when Horton and two partners formed Tim Donut Ltd., which licensed Horton's name for use in their proposed chain of doughnut shops. Two months later, they opened the first Tim Hortons franchise on Ottawa Street in Hamilton, Ontario, where a dozen doughnuts cost 69 cents and a cup of coffee was a dime. As doughnuts filled with cream or jelly and coated with sugar and honey glaze flew off the shelves that spring, Horton was helping the Leafs capture their third successive Cup.

**Food BITE!**

Doughnuts were not Horton's first business venture. In the late 1950s, he ran a service station and car dealership in Toronto. In 1963, he was a partner in an unsuccessful chain of drive-in chicken and burger restaurants in the Toronto area. He also ran a burger outlet in North Bay in partnership with his brother Gerry.

Why did Horton get into the doughnut business? As an investment and because he had a sweet tooth, according to *Open Ice: The Tim Horton Story* by Douglas Hunter. "I love eating doughnuts and that was one of the big reasons that I opened my first doughnut shop. Buying doughnuts was costing me too much money," Horton said in 1969. Until the mid-1980s, the logo found on Tim

Hortons signs, coffee cups, bags, and doughnut boxes was Horton's signature and an oval depicting a stack of four doughnuts, one for each of his daughters. Today, the doughnuts are gone from the company's advertising but his signature is still on the signs that dot neighbourhoods across Canada.

In the mid-1960s, Horton took over his partners' shares in the company and soon after met ex-police officer Ron Joyce, who became owner of two Hamilton franchises, including the first one opened by the company. In 1967, Joyce became Horton's business partner and eventually built the company into one of Canada's most popular and successful food chains. In 1975, he bought control of the company from Horton's wife Lori for $1 million and a Cadillac. Twenty years later, the company, then known as TDL Group Ltd., merged with Ohio-based Wendy's International Inc.

Tim Hortons is a registered trademark of the TDL Marks Corporation. Used with permission.

Tim Horton, who launched his successful venture in 1964.

Today, the name that brought hockey fans to their feet in the 1950s, 60s, and 70s is the fourth largest publicly-traded quick service restaurant chain in North America based on market capitalization, and the largest in Canada. As of December, 2008, the chain had 3,437 locations in North America, 2,917 in Canada and 520 in the United States. In 2006, Tim's opened up a location in a 40-foot trailer on a Kandahar, Afghanistan, military base to give the Canadian troops a taste of home. The company has also entered into a partnership with the SPAR convenience store chain in the United Kingdom and Ireland, where customers that likely include a few ex-pat Canadians can get a Tim Hortons coffee and doughnut from one of the small self service kiosks located in many SPAR stores.

## 🍽 Bruce Druxerman (Druxy's)

For Bruce Druxerman, the recipe for a successful deli was buns, salami, and experience in banking.

When Bruce Druxerman graduated with a degree in science, commerce, and business administration, he worked in the New York office of the Mercantile Bank of Canada. But later, after he switched his attention to the restaurant business, the Belleville, Ontario, native decided that owning a chain of delis was the way to make his riches. According to *The New Entrepreneurs* by Allan Gould, Druxerman tried to rent some space in the Royal Bank Plaza in Toronto in 1976, but was told by a realtor that it couldn't happen because he had no track record.

Druxerman then phoned the bank's chairman, who was an acquaintance of his father, and the deal was made within a day. The first Druxy's (Druxerman's dad had been given the nickname by a neighbour) opened in the fall of 1976, and a profusion of pumpernickel has been served up ever since. Within three years there were 13 Druxy's in Toronto. Druxerman's brothers joined the firm, and by the mid-1980s Druxy's was doing about $20 million in business. There are currently more than 50 Druxy's locations, mostly in Ontario, with a few in Calgary.

Who was the mysterious Harvey?

## 🍽 Harvey _____? (Harvey's)

The man who inspired the name of one of Canada's leading hamburger and fast food chains likely didn't know about his claim to fame. And we'll never be sure if this mysterious Harvey, whoever he was, even bit into one of the juicy burgers that bear his name.

Harvey's was the brainchild of Toronto-area restaurateur Rick Mauran, who brought charbroiled burgers to Canada in 1959. Although there is something of an urban myth that the chain was named after the title character in the famous Jimmy Stewart movie *Harvey*, the real story is simpler. Mauran chose the Harvey name after seeing it in a newspaper story. Company history doesn't provide the context of what the story was even about, but Mauran thought the name had personality, was easy to spell, and memorable. And it was short. Mauran had hired a sign painter for his first restaurant who charged by the letter.

The first Harvey's opened at 9741 Yonge Street in Richmond Hill, Ontario, where burgers, fries, and onion rings are still hot sellers. Since then, the chain has grown enormously across Canada. Its first franchised restaurant opened in 1962 in Sarnia, Ontario, and by the time CARA Operations Ltd. bought the company in 1979, there were more than 80 Harvey's restaurants. In 1980, Harvey's opened Canada's first drive-thru restaurant in Pembroke, Ontario, and today there are 273 outlets nationwide. More than 7,000 employees serve up close to a million burgers each week.

A few other Harvey's tidbits to chew on:

- Harvey's has served up more than one billion burgers since 1959.
- Four out of five guests order pickles on their burger.
- The most frequently requested Harvey's topping is mustard.
- The northernmost Harvey's is in Edmonton.
- In 1999, Harvey's became the first national chain to introduce a veggie burger to its permanent menu.

 ## CANADIAN NAMES IN THE KITCHEN

Canadians spend long hours in the kitchen whipping up favourite dishes for family and friends.

And as they've steamed, stirred, and sautéed their way into the hearts and stomachs of their loved ones, they've encountered names such as Catelli, Goudas, Redpath, Schneider, and Loblaw.

Familiar monikers to be sure, but did you know there were real people behind them with fascinating tales to tell?

Next time you open the cupboard, buy groceries, or reach into the refrigerator, think of the stories of a handful of innovative Canadians who have been putting food on Canadian tables for many years.

**Food BITE!**

A road in Barrington, Illinois, is the source for the name of one of Canada's most popular restaurant chains. Back in the 1970s, when Paul Jeffery and his brother were visiting a friend in Barrington, they frequented a bar on Kelsey's Road. Jeffery liked the name "Kelsey's" enough to slap it onto the front of the first roadhouse-style eatery he opened in Oakville, Ontario, in 1978. These days there are over 140 Kelsey's locations, stretching from Ontario to British Columbia.

## 🍽 Carlo Catelli

Pasta lovers can twirl their forks in thanks to Carlo Catelli. Born in Vedano, Italy, Catelli came to Canada in 1866, and one year later started the Catelli Macaroni Company in Montreal. At first, he needed just three bags of flour a day to satisfy his customers' palates for pasta, but by the end of the 19th century the business was flourishing and he was a respected leader of the country's Italian-Canadian community.

Catelli was also a founder of the Chamber of Commerce in Montreal and was its president from 1906 to 1908. He was also created a chevalier of the Crown of Italy in 1904 for his work in building Italian-Canadian relations. Once described as "a respectable gentleman who has achieved commercial success," Catelli was chosen the Honorary Canadian Representative to the International Exposition in Milan in 1906.

He retired from business in 1910, but continued to be a key figure in the city. At the outbreak of the First World War, the firm was controlled by Tancredi Bienvenu, and by the start of the Second World War, the company not only dominated the pasta and tomato paste market in Canada but had a tremendous presence in Britain, too. In fact, after the war, Catelli and other companies were exporting macaroni to Italy!

During his life, Catelli also helped found an orphanage in the city. The prosperous pasta pioneer died on October 3, 1937, at his home in Montreal on City Hall Avenue and was survived by a son, Leon, and a daughter, Marguerite. He was an important enough business figure beyond Canada to have received a brief obituary in the *New York Times*.

After Catelli was gone, the company that continues to bear his name dominated the pasta and tomato paste market in Canada. After the Second World War, Catelli products were even being exported to Italy, the home of great pasta. In June 1989, Borden Inc., an American firm, purchased Catelli, and two years later spent $20 million to double production capacity at the Montreal plant.

The Catelli business was sold to H.J. Heinz Inc. in 2001 and they continue to run the division.

## 🍽 William Mellis Christie (Christie, Brown & Company)

Mr. Christie, the man who has filled millions of tummies with cookies, crackers, and snacks, is a Canadian who changed the course of the baking industry in North America. In 1848, at age 19, William Mellis Christie came to Canada from Huntley, Aberdeenshire, Scotland, where he had apprenticed as a baker. He soon formed a partnership with James Mathers and Alexander Brown, working as an assistant baker and travelling salesman. When Mathers retired in 1850, Brown took Christie into the partnership, and 28 years later, Christie became the sole owner of Christie, Brown & Company.

Around that time, Christie attended the Philadelphia Centennial Exhibition with samples of his biscuits and returned with silver and bronze medals. He became known throughout Canada for his high quality biscuits that today are found in kitchen pantries from St. John's to Victoria. In 1900, Christie died of cancer in Toronto and his son Robert took over the business, which at the time employed 375 people and had offices in Montreal and Toronto. In 1928, Christie, Brown & Company was sold to National Biscuit Company (Nabisco) of the United States and has been in American hands ever since.

The company William Mellis Christie founded is now owned by Kraft Foods North America. It operates five biscuit bakeries in Toronto and Montreal, producing such well-known products as Oreo and Chips Ahoy! cookies, Premium Plus and Ritz crackers, and Peek Freans and Dad's biscuits.

## ¡©¡ Charles H. Doerr (Dare Foods)

In 1892, Charles Doerr sold everything from soup to nuts at his grocery store in Berlin, Ontario (now Kitchener). But after meeting Ted Egan, a baker from nearby Guelph, Doerr and his associate focussed on making biscuits and candies.

With the opening of C.H. Doerr and Company, the seeds were sown for what would become Dare Foods, a Canadian company with a worldwide reputation for innovation and quality.

Egan eventually left the company and Doerr worked tirelessly to take advantage of the expanding Canadian market from the turn of the century until the First World War. Numerous expansions enlarged the original store on the corner of Weber and Breihaupt streets.

In the early years, Doerr did everything but bake the products. Because there were no supermarket chains or centralized buying groups, biscuits and candies were sold in bulk to individual neighbourhood stores, each visited personally by Doerr. Twice a year he embarked on sales trips to allow local grocers to sample his products.

Popular items were traditional English drop cookies and stamped biscuits; sugar, molasses, and shortbread cookies; and soda crackers. Customers also loved Doerr's individually hand-stencilled sandwich creams and his marshmallow cookies. The company's candy line included humbugs, toffees, gum drops, and seasonal specialties such as chocolate-coated marshmallow Easter eggs and Christmas cut rock candy. Many were handmade.

As word of Doerr quality spread, salespersons were hired and sales multiplied across Ontario. Soon, major national retail chains such as Woolworth and Kresge were distributing Doerr products across Canada. In 1919, the company landed a major contract with Hamblin Metcalf (later Smiles and Chuckles) to produce chocolate candies for export to

England, added 40,000 square feet of space, and soon after bought modern chocolate-making equipment.

During his life, Doerr was known as responsible and sensible with few extravagances, other than ownership of two cars. He was cheerful and had a pleasant personality and lots of friends, many of whom were also businessmen. He was a commissioner of the Kitchener Public Utilities Commission for 17 years, liked dancing, and was generous to his nine siblings, employing a number of them in his business and supporting the distant ones with annual gifts of money.

Doerr had three wives. The first died at age 58; he then married a long-time family friend who passed away two years later. Doerr's third wife worked for him in the company office and lived for many years after his death.

The period 1920 to 1945 was among the company's toughest. The Great Depression caused sales to stagnate; in June 1941, Doerr died at age 72, leaving his firm to his 24-year-old grandson Carl, who had been raised by Doerr and his wife Susannah after his parents died in the great influenza epidemic. In February 1943, Carl watched helplessly as fire destroyed the company factory in the largest blaze in Kitchener's history.

Using facilities at the Howe Candy Company in Hamilton, Ontario, which had been acquired prior to the fire, Carl Doerr was able to continue production and finance a new plant on Kitchener's southern outskirts.

## Food BITE!

In the tough Depression years, newly hired 16-year-old workers at Dare's Kitchener factory were paid 17 cents an hour. At the time, Ontario's minimum wage for adults was 22 cents an hour.

In 1945, the company and family names were legally changed to Dare because it was easier to pronounce and was an approximate equal of Doerr in sound.

Since then, the company has been responsible for several innovations in the biscuit and cookie industry, including cellophane packaging; assorted cookie packs, which contain several Dare favourites in the same package; and cookie bags sealed with a wire tie, which enables customers to reseal the bag to retain freshness. Such bags became the standard for biscuit packaging.

Also unique was the way Dare salespersons were trained to be merchandisers. To help retailers improve sales, they regularly arranged Dare products on store shelves and set up in-store product displays, the first in the industry to take such a hands-on approach.

In 1982, Dare introduced its Breton line of crackers; in 2001, the company completed an acquisition which added Wagon Wheels, Viva Puffs cookies, Grissol Melba Toast, Whippet chocolate-coated mallow cookies, and Loney dried soups and bouillon to its lineup.

In 2002, Dare was chosen as exclusive supplier of cookies for the Girl Guides of Canada, and in 2003 became one of North America's first major food manufacturers to declare all of its manufacturing facilities "peanut free."

The company that Charles Doerr founded was run by fourth generation members of the Dare family, led by president Carl Dare and his sons Graham, executive vice-president, and Bryan, senior vice-president, until 2002. At that time, the first non-family member, Frederick Jacques, was appointed president of operations. Graham and Bryan remain as co-chairmen of the Board of Directors.

The company operates bakeries in Kitchener, Ontario; Montreal, St-Lambert, and Ste-Martine, Quebec; Denver, Colorado; and Spartanburg, South Carolina, and candy factories in Toronto and Milton, Ontario. Its products are sold in more than 25 countries and it employs more than 13,000 people.

**Charles Doerr.**
Photo courtesy of Dare.

## Peter Goudas

Lovers of ethnic foods can toast Peter Goudas, the brains behind dozens of different canned and bagged goods that bear the Mr. Goudas name. Born in Greece in 1942, Goudas came to Toronto in 1967 with 100 dollars in his pocket and no job prospects. He learned English by watching television and slept on the city's streets on occasion.

But an idea stirred him that would endear Goudas to cooks everywhere. "There was nobody packaging ethnic food at the time. I knew there was a demand for it. So I said, why not?"

Goudas built an empire of chickpeas, spices, beans, and a wide array of Chinese, Indian, and Caribbean specialties. Today his company services more than 20 chain food stores and 3,000 independent grocers. Food wasn't his only passion. Goudas also bought a nightclub in 1970, where he played deejay and earned the nickname "Mr. Wu" from patrons who thought he looked "Oriental."

## John Redpath

Cooks who use sugar might want to know the sweet tale of John Redpath, who immigrated to Canada from Scotland in 1816 as a skilled stonemason. One of his early jobs was digging outhouses in Montreal, but he later earned a fortune as a building contractor who helped to construct several buildings at McGill University and portions of the Rideau Canal, among other projects. After the Rideau Canal opened in August 1831, Redpath cooked up a scheme to construct a sugar refinery next to the Lachine Canal in Montreal; it became a city landmark and made him famous. More than 150 years later, Redpath sugar is a mainstay in restaurants, pantries, and grocery stores. A Toronto refinery bearing the founder's name produces more than 2,000 tons of sugar used for baking and in processed foods, explosives, gasoline additives, paints, and cosmetics. All of their products are made from pure cane sugar.

The Redpath Sugar Museum was established in 1979 to celebrate the 125th anniversary of the company's sugar refining operation. The free museum is located at 95 Queen's Quay East in Toronto, Ontario.

The Redpath logo is believed to be the oldest continuously used trademark in Canada.

## 🍽 John McIntosh (McIntosh Apple)

In the spring of 1811, John McIntosh stumbled upon a handful of apple tree seedlings while clearing land near Prescott, Ontario, where he planned to establish a farm. Instead of tossing the tiny trees onto a pile of brush that would later be burned, he transplanted them to a nearby garden. McIntosh and his farm in Dundas County south of Ottawa were about to take their place in Canada's history books.

By the following year all but one of the trees had died. He nursed it and it slowly grew, eventually producing a red, sweet, and crisp fruit with a tart taste.

So began the story of the McIntosh apple, which by the 1960s, accounted for nearly 40 percent of the Canadian apple market and continues to be the most widely grown and sold Canadian fruit. In fact, the Mac has become accepted worldwide and is responsible for much of Canada's domestic and export apple growing industry. Today, more than three million McIntosh apple trees flourish throughout North America, all stemming from the single tree discovered by McIntosh.

Fifteen years earlier, McIntosh, the son of Scottish Highland parents, had immigrated to Upper Canada from New York State. Eventually he married Hannah Doran and set out to tame the land he had traded with his brother-in-law.

McIntosh's discovery, near what would eventually become the village of Dundela, would not have been significant if John, and later his son Allan

**Food BITE!**

To this day no one is certain how the orphan tree discovered by McIntosh arrived on his property. Experts speculate that it likely grew from the seeds of an apple core tossed onto the ground by a passerby.

and grandson Harvey, had not nurtured, propagated, and marketed the apple named after his family. In 1835, Allan McIntosh learned the art of grafting and the family began to produce the apples on a major scale.

Despite Allan and his brother Sandy's efforts, it was many years before the McIntosh Red became prominent. In fact, not until 1870, nearly a quarter of a century after John's death, was it officially introduced and named. The Mac made its first appearance in print six years later (in *Fruits and Fruit Trees of America*) and began to sell in large numbers after 1900. The Mac's hardiness, appearance, and taste made it a contender from birth, but it was only when turn-of-the-century advances in the quality and availability of sprays improved its quality that it realized its incredible commercial potential.

By that time things had changed at the McIntosh farm near Dundela, Ontario. In 1894, a fire burned down the family home and badly damaged the original tree. Though Allan made extensive efforts to nurse it back to health, the historic tree produced its last crop in 1908 and died two years later. Allan died in 1899 and Sandy in 1906, leaving grandson Harvey at the helm when the family apple became world-famous.

Early in the 21st century, the Mac accounted for more than half of the 17 million bushels of apples produced in Canada every year, making it Canada's most commonly grown fruit. In the U.S. it ranked behind only the two Delicious varieties and has a personal computer named for it; overseas it is one of the few successful North American varieties.

## 🍽 Rose-Anna and Arcade Vachon (Vachon Cakes)

The company that brought Canadians Jos. Louis snack cakes and a variety of other tasty pastries was launched by a modest family with a dream, a bank loan, and a brood of hard-working children.

From its beginnings as a mom and pop bakery operated by Arcade and Rose-Anna in Quebec's Beauce Region, Vachon Cakes evolved into a multi-million dollar operation, which was referred to by one media commentator as a "treasured morsel of the province's food industry heritage."

In 1923, Arcade, 55, and his wife, who was 10 years his junior, left Saint-Patrice de Beaurivage, Quebec, after spending 25 years as farmers there. Under the direction of Rose-Anna, the couple borrowed $7,000 and bought the Leblond Bakery in Sainte-Marie de Beauce, about 60 kilometres from Quebec City. They had 15 dollars in the bank at the time.

Their first employee was their son Redempteur, who made bread, and with his father criss-crossed the surrounding area in a buggy selling loaves for six cents apiece.

As a way to boost sales, Rose-Anna two years later diversified into other baked goods, including doughnuts, sweet buns, shortbread, cakes, pies, and even baked beans, which she made in the wood oven in the kitchen of the family home. Simone, one of two daughters, helped sell the tasty treats after school. In 1928, two of the Vachons' six sons, Louis and Amédée, returned from the United States to help out. The business prospered when it began exporting to Quebec City.

By 1932, sons Joseph, Paul, and Benoit had also joined the company, which by then had 10 employees and had introduced the Jos. Louis, which soon became its most popular cake. As business grew, trucks were purchased to make deliveries, and trains transported goods to more distant customers. By 1937, the company was peddling its products in Ontario and the Maritimes.

Several significant events occurred between 1938 and 1945: On January 15, 1938, at age 70, Arcade Vachon died. His wife and sons kept the company running and moved to a former shoe factory, where an 8,000-square-foot extension was built and modern production equipment installed. In 1940, the family decided to focus exclusively on snack cakes.

**Food BITE!**

Some snack lovers believe the Jos. Louis is named after the legendary American boxer Joe Louis. In fact, the chocolate cake's moniker is a combination of the names of two Vachon sons – Joseph and Louis.

In 1945, at the age of 67, Rose-Anna retired and sold her interest in the company to her sons Joseph, Amédée, Paul, and Benoit, who broadened the product line to 111 different items. Rose-Anna died on December 2, 1948. Two years later a new company, Diamond Products Limited was founded to produce jams for the bakery. It was later sold to J.M. Smuckers of the United States.

In 1961, with its sinfully sweet pastries being sold in most of Canada, the company changed its name to Vachon Inc. By 1970, following several expansions and an acquisition, the company had 12,000 employees. That year, 83 percent of Vachon shares were sold to Quebec banking co-op Mouvement des Caisses populaires Desjardins, leaving 17 percent in the Vachon family's hands.

Montreal-based food giant Culinar Inc. bought the company in 1977; in 1999, Culinar and Vachon were acquired by dairy and grocery products company Saputo Inc., of Montreal. Despite the corporate shuffle, the Vachon family name is still found on a handful of products made famous by Arcade, Rose-Anna, and their children, including Jos. Louis and May West snack cakes.

The Vachon home in Sainte-Marie de Beauce, Quebec, where Rosa-Anna did her bookkeeping and used her own recipes to bake breads and snack cakes, is a historic monument and museum.

## ¡⦿¡ Walter and Jeanny Bick (Bick's Pickles)

Walter and Jeanny Bick never intended to get into the pickle business. But when warm and humid weather in the summer of 1944 produced a glut of cucumbers, the couple was desperate to salvage tons of cukes before they rotted in their fields.

The Bicks dug out a family recipe from their native Holland and began producing dill pickles in a barn at Knollview, their 116-acre farm in the former suburb of Scarborough, now part of the Greater Toronto Area. "We got into pickles by sheer accident," said Walter.

The rest, as they say, is condiment history.

The family sold the cattle, chicken, and pigs they'd been raising since Mr. Bick's parents George and Lena Bick bought the farm in 1939 after coming to Canada from Amsterdam. Instead of selling their cucumbers to stores and markets, they turned them into pickles, said Walter, who apprenticed in the Dutch banking industry before coming to Canada at age 22.

During the first few years, the Bicks packed their cucumber crop in 50-gallon barrels of brine that were sold to restaurants, butcher shops, and army camps in the Toronto area. In 1952, they entered the retail trade when they packaged whole dills in 24-ounce jars under the Bick's name, with the now-familiar cucumber in place of the letter *i* on the labels.

Soon after, the business expanded into a renovated barn on their farm and Canada's fastest-growing manufacturer of pickles and relishes was on its way to leadership in the Canadian pickle business.

As their business prospered, the Bicks saw many changes: Their product line expanded to include sweet mixed pickles, gherkins, cocktail onions, hot peppers, pickled beets, relishes, and sauerkraut; in 1958 their barn burnt in a fire and was replaced with a modern building. Gradually, sales of their products spread from Ontario to western and eastern Canada and around the world.

In 1966, with a staff that ranged between 125 in the summer and 65 in the winter, the

### Food BITE!

Like a cucumber on a cutting board, the Bicks' farm in the former Toronto borough of Scarborough was sliced in two when Highway 401 was built in the mid-1950s.

BICK'S...THE PICK OF PICKLES

*Courtesy of Walter Bick.*

Bick's Pickles brochure.

Bicks made their biggest change when they sold their company, their farm, and their home to Robin Hood Flour Mills.

"We sold because the company was bigger than we could handle," said Walter. "I was never a great delegator. In the beginning, I never realized we needed a sales manager, a purchasing agent but as business increased we had to hire these people … however the family run business way did not disappear."

Until 2004, Bick's was a wholly-owned subsidiary of International Multifoods of Wayzata, Minneapolis, whose products included 50 different varieties of Bick's pickles and relishes, Habitant Pickles, Gattuso Olives, Woodman's Horseradish, Robin Hood Flour, Monarch Cake & Pastry Flour, and Red River Cereals.

It is now owned by American food company J.M. Smucker Co, which produces Smucker Jams and Jif peanut butter and also owns such iconic brands at Crisco, Robin Hood, Folgers, Pillsbury and Eagle Brand condensed milk.

In addition to more than 30 different varieties of Bick's pickles and relishes, its consumer products lineup includes pickled hot peppers, beets, and sauerkraut.

**Food BITE!**

According to Pickle Packers International, Inc., the perfect pickle should exhibit seven warts per square inch for North American tastes – Europeans prefer wartless pickles.

**Food BITE!**

Pickles date back 4,500 years to Mesopotamia, where it is believed cucumbers were first preserved. Cleopatra, a devoted pickle fan, believed pickles enhanced her beauty.

## ¶◎| J.M. Schneider (Schneider Foods)

From button manufacturing to the butchering business.

It's a strange shift in careers, but for J.M. Schneider, whose name today is found on hot dogs, cold cuts, sausages, and other products, it was the route to fame and fortune. John Metz Schneider was born February 17, 1859 in Berlin (now Kitchener), Ontario. He grew up on a farm, looked after the livestock, and helped his parents slaughter and dress the hogs.

As an adult, he found work on the assembly line of the Dominion Button Works earning a dollar a day and working six days a week. When he was 24, he married Helena Ahrens, and they began raising a family. In 1886, Schneider had an accident at the button factory that kept him away from work for about a month. With his hand in a bandage, Schneider, his wife, and his mother began grinding up meat and creating German sausages in their kitchen as a way of earning extra money.

Schneider sold those first sausages door to door, and though he went back to work making buttons, he began building up loyal customers who liked the taste of his sausages. After his long days at the factory, J.M. and Helena would work well into the night trying to make their new venture successful. Eventually J.M. started selling sausages to market butchers and grocers until he reached a point at which he had to choose between the security of buttons and the uncertainty of a new business venture.

When he decided to plunge into the meat business, Schneider turned his house into company headquarters and had a wooden shanty built in the backyard for butchering hogs. By 1891, he had saved enough to build a storey-and-a-half structure in which to operate his business and paid an annual licence fee of 20 dollars to run it. Schneider's timing was good. Berlin was booming and described around that time as "the most rapidly growing and liveliest town west of Toronto."

But the early days were still tough, leading Schneider to offer his business for sale. He changed his mind, however, and in 1895 hired a skilled German-trained butcher named Wilhelm Rohleder, who would play a significant role in the company's growth over the next 45 years. The hard-working Rohleder developed several recipes for Schneider products that made them popular, and he was so secretive about the ingredients that he didn't even tell J.M.

Schneider, meanwhile, was a hands-on owner from the beginning. He sold his products personally and took the lead in purchasing livestock. When not working, he led a quiet social life playing cards, devoting time to church activities, and enjoying his family. He knew all his workers by their first names and was not one for putting on airs or dressing ostentatiously.

Schneider's sons followed him into the business when they were old enough and watched it expand in the early 20th century as electricity and refrigeration became essential to the industry. By 1910 Schneider was a wealthy man, but it was the years around the First World War that saw the company expand twentyfold to become a million-dollar business. Despite his wealth, Schneider continued to show up for work every day into his early 80s. He died in 1942, and his epitaph reads "to live in the hearts we leave behind is not to die."

These days Schneider Foods Inc. remains a mainstay of the Kitchener economy and is a multi-million-dollar enterprise producing a wide range of products across Canada. Its sign on Highway 401 near Guelph, known as the "wiener beacon," is one of the most recognizable advertising landmarks in southern Ontario.

## 🍽 James Lewis Kraft (Kraft Foods)

In the world of food products, J.L. Kraft was certainly the big cheese.

His name has become synonymous in Canada and around the world with such famous products as Jell-O, Miracle Whip, and that staple of university students everywhere, Kraft Dinner.

Born in the Niagara region community of Stevensville, Ontario in the 1870s, Kraft was one of 11 children in a Mennonite family who grew up on a dairy farm. When he was 18, he landed a job at Ferguson's grocery store in Fort Erie, Ontario before investing in a cheese company in Buffalo. In 1903, Kraft moved to Chicago with $65 to his name and decided to rent a wagon and a horse named Paddy. According to company history, Kraft bought cheese every day from the city's warehouses and resold it to local merchants who didn't want to make the trip themselves. From this humble beginning, Kraft built up his business to the point that he decided to manufacture cheese and brought in four of his brothers to help him with his enterprise.

### Food BITE!

One of Kraft's hobbies was to make rings with semi-precious stones and give them to employees as awards for their hard work. He had to abandon the idea as the number of workers began to grow.

In 1909, JL Kraft and Brothers Co. began importing cheeses from Europe, but it was Kraft's dream to make cheese that would keep longer, cook better, and be packaged in convenient sizes. At the time, cheddar cheese, the most popular variety in the U.S., moulded or dried quickly and was difficult to ship long distances. As Kraft continued to sell different cheeses, however, he experimented with ways of making cheese a more marketable commodity. Kraft sold $5,000 worth of pasteurized cheese in 1915, and the next year sales jumped to $150,000.

The year 1916 would be the key one in Kraft's life. He received a patent for what would become known as processed cheese, narrowly beating out another company that was working on a similar process. To his credit, Kraft would later share the patent rights with the company.

Four years later, Kraft entered the Canadian market selling processed cheese and bread on a national scale. The famous Kraft kitchens were also started in the 1920s, and some of the products resulting from this approach were Miracle Whip in 1933 and Kraft dinner in 1937. It was said that by the 1930s, Kraft was selling three million pounds of cheese a day. Per capita cheese consumption in the U.S. increased by 50 percent between 1918 and 1945, largely because of Kraft's efforts and innovations.

Kraft was also an innovator when it came to advertising. As early as 1911, he was advertising on Chicago's elevated trains, using billboards, and mailing circulars to retailers. He was among the first to use coloured ads in magazines, and in 1933 the company began using radio to advertise its products by sponsoring the Kraft Musical Review. Though he was in his seventies by the time television arrived, Kraft embraced the new medium and created the Kraft Television Theatre.

The company prospered throughout his life, and by the time Kraft died in 1953, the firm had become one of the most recognizable brand names in the world. The company merged with General Foods in 1989 and continues to produce an array of famous products including Minute Rice, Cool Whip, Maxwell House coffee, and Tang.

Not bad for a young man who started out with less than 100 dollars in his pocket.

# CHAPTER 3
# Canadian Women: Ladies of the North

 MAKING HISTORY

- Approximately 50,000 Canadian women served their country during the Second World War. Eighty-one were killed: six from the Royal Canadian Navy, 25 from the army, 32 from the Royal Canadian Air Force, 10 with nursing services, and eight from the Canadian Merchant Navy.

Postage stamp remembers Canadian women who helped with the war effort.

- Though women first got the right to vote in Manitoba in 1916, it took some time for other provinces to follow suit. Women in Newfoundland (not then a province) had to wait until 1925, while their counterparts in Quebec didn't get the right until 1940.

- Adelaide Hunter Hoodless of St. George, near Brantford, Ontario, helped establish the Victorian Order of Nurses, Women's Institutes, the National Council of Women of Canada, the National Council of the YWCA, the Macdonald Institute in Ontario, and Macdonald College in Quebec. She was motivated to help women take good care of their children after one of her children, an infant son, died in 1889 after drinking infected milk.

- The first woman to attend a University of Toronto lecture was Catherine Brown, youngest daughter of George Brown, founder of *The Globe* newspaper and a prominent politician. Catherine and her older sister Margaret were among the University of Toronto's first five women graduates in 1885. Both received Bachelor of Arts degrees in modern languages.

- Anna Sutherland Bissell, a native of River John, Nova Scotia, helped design, build, and market the Bissell carpet sweeper that would become a friend to homeowners everywhere. Bissell and her husband, Melville, patented the sweeper in 1876 in Grand Rapids, Michigan, where she often became frustrated when sawdust became embedded in the carpet of her crockery shop.

- Although Ottawa's Charlotte Whitton gained fame in 1951 as the first female mayor of a major Canadian city, she wasn't the first woman to sit on a municipal council. That honour goes to Mary Teresa Sullivan, who was sworn in as a Halifax city councillor in 1936.

- As the publisher and editor of the *Provincial Freeman*, a black newspaper in Chatham, Ontario, from 1853 until 1859, Mary Ann Shadd was the first black woman to be an editor in North America. She was also a respected educator and abolitionist.

- Elsie Gregory MacGill was Canada's first female electrical engineer, the only woman in the world to hold a graduate degree in aeronautical engineering in the early 1930s, and the first woman to become a corporate member of the Engineering Institute of Canada.

- In 1787, Frances Barkley, married to Charles Barkley, captain of the *Imperial Beagle*, became the first white woman to arrive in British Columbia.

## Trivia BITE!

Women typically outlive men by an average of six years. The average age of a widow in North America is 58. If a woman was born between 1945 and 1965, she can expect to live into her eighties.

- Mary Ellen Smith became a minister without portfolio in the British Columbia government in 1921, making her the first woman to hold a cabinet post in the British Commonwealth.

- Ellen Louks Fairclough became secretary of state in 1957, the first woman to be appointed to the Cabinet in Canada.

# 🍁 LADIES FIRST: FIRSTS FOR CANADIAN WOMEN: 1900–1950

Canadian women in the 20th century broke new ground in many aspects of society. Here are some of their achievements.

1. **Clara Brett Martin:** First woman barrister in Canada, 1901.

2. **Carrie Derick:** First woman to become a full professor in Canada, 1912, McGill University, Montreal.

3. **Alys McKey Bryant:** First woman to pilot an airplane in Canada, 1913, Vancouver.

4. **Annie Langstaff:** First woman to graduate with a law degree in Quebec, 1914. Forced to work as a legal clerk because the Quebec bar refused to admit her.

5. **Elizabeth Smellie:** First woman appointed a colonel in the Canadian Army, 1915, as head of the Canadian Army nurse corps.

6. **Emily Murphy, Alice Jamieson:** Murphy of Edmonton and Jamieson of Calgary were the first women in the British Empire to be appointed police magistrates, 1916.

7. **E.M. Hill:** First woman architect in Canada graduated from University of Toronto, 1920.

8. **Lydia Emelie Gruchy:** First woman ordained in the United Church, 1923.

9. **Cecil Smith:** First woman to represent Canada in any Olympic event. She competed in figure skating at the 1924 Winter Olympics in Chamonix, France.

10. **Eileen Volick:** First Canadian woman to earn a pilot's licence, 1928. She also became the first female pilot to fly a ski-plane.

11. **Ethel Catherwood:** Canada's first woman gold medalist. She won the high jump at the Amsterdam Olympics with a jump of five feet three inches, 1928.

12. **Canada's Olympic Team:** The first time the track and field team included women, Amsterdam Olympics, 1928.

13. **Mona Campbell:** First woman veterinarian in private practice, 1948.

# 🍁 FIRSTS FOR CANADIAN WOMEN: 1950–2009

1. **Winnie Roach Leuszler:** First Canadian to swim the English Channel, 1951.

2. **Addie Aylestock.** Canada's first female Black minister she was ordained in 1951, and served with the British Methodist Episcopal Church until her death in 1998.

3. **Jean Sutherland Boggs:** First woman in the world to head a national art gallery, National Gallery of Canada, Ottawa, 1966.

4. **Lorraine Carrie:** First woman elected president of a wing of the Royal Canadian Air Force, Wing No. 1, composed of women enlisted in the RCAF, 1969.

5. **Ada Mackenzie, Marlene Stewart Streit:** First women elected to the Canadian Golf Hall of Fame, 1970.

6. **Rosella Bjornson:** First North American woman jet pilot, Transair, Winnipeg, 1973.

7. **Dr. Lois Wilson:** First woman to be elected as moderator of the United Church of Canada, 1980.

8. **Bertha Williams:** First female Supreme Court Judge, Ottawa, 1982.

9. **Daurene Lewis:** First Black woman in Canada to be elected as a mayor in North America, in 1984, in Annapolis Royal, Nova Scotia. She is also a descendant of Rose Fortune, the first female police officer in Canada.

10. **Jean Sauve:** Canada's first Canadian woman Governor General. She was also one of the three first women members of Parliament to be elected from Quebec, the first woman federal cabinet minister from Quebec, and the first woman Speaker of the House of Commons.

11. **Sharon Wood:** First woman from North America to scale Mount Everest, 1986.

12. **Audrey McLaughlin:** First Canadian federal party leader. She was elected leader of the federal New Democratic Party in 1989.

13. **Rita Johnson:** First Canadian woman Premier, 1991. She spent most of her career as a municipal councillor in Surrey, British Columbia, but her foray into provincial politics landed her several cabinet minister posts and a short stint as Premier of British Columbia.

14. **Roberta Bondar:** First Canadian Woman in Space, 1992. A neurology researcher, she was one of the six original Canadian astronauts selected in 1984 to train at NASA. Eight years later she became the first Canadian woman and the second Canadian astronaut to go into space.

15. **Manon Rheaume:** First woman to play in the National Hockey League. Played goal for the Tampa Bay Lightning in a pre-season game, 1992.

16. **Micheline A. Rawlins:** First Black woman to become a judge for the Ontario Provincial Court, 1992.

17. **Kim Campbell:** First Canadian woman prime minister.

18. **Jean Augustine:** First Black woman elected as a federal Member of Parliament, in 1993.

19. **Adrienne Clarkson:** First Chinese-Canadian (and second woman) to hold the position of Governor General of Canada from 1999–2005.

20. **Chief Justice Beverley McLachlin:** First Canadian woman to head the Supreme Court of Canada.

# 🍁 CANADIAN WOMEN IN BUSINESS

## ▦ Elizabeth Arden (Elizabeth Arden Inc. Cosmetics)

"I want to keep people well, and young and beautiful," Florence Nightingale Graham declared when she dropped out of school while living near Woodbridge, Ontario.

When keeping people healthy by following the path of her famous English nurse namesake didn't work, she turned her attention to keeping them beautiful. After moving to New York City and changing her name to Elizabeth Arden, the diminutive, blue-eyed Canadian became an innovator of renown in the world of beauty and one of America's wealthiest businesswomen as owner of the world-famous Elizabeth Arden cosmetics empire.

Early in life Graham made it known that celebrity status was on her radar screen. As a child growing up near Toronto in the late 1800s, Graham used to tell friends and family that her goal was to be "the richest little girl in the world."

One of five children of Susan and William Graham, she was raised on a rented tenant farm where she helped her father tend horses and sell produce at local markets. After a career in nursing fizzled, largely because the indignity of illness offended her, a brief working relationship with a hospital chemist who was experimenting with skin-healing creams led her to begin cooking up beautifying potions in the family kitchen.

When her father urged her to get a paying job, Graham worked as a clerk, stenographer, and dental assistant in Toronto, before moving to New York in 1908. She landed a job as a bookkeeper with the E.R. Squibb Pharmaceutical Company but soon moved to the laboratory where she spent long hours learning about skin care. Eventually, she left Squibb for a position with a beauty parlour where she learned how to gently rub creams into the sagging skin of many a wealthy New York woman. Before long clients were asking for "that nice Canadian girl." Soon after, she went into business with Elizabeth Hubbard, who had developed skin creams, tonics, and oils.

The pair opened a salon on Fifth Avenue but the partnership soured and Graham went solo. After borrowing $6,000 from her brother to pay the rent, she changed her name to Elizabeth Arden, keeping her former partner's first name and choosing Arden from Tennyson's famous poem "Enoch Arden." She also called herself "Mrs." to gain respectability and came up with the idea of the brilliant red door which became the Elizabeth Arden signature.

As manager of a salon, the aggressive and confident Arden concocted a series of rouges and tinted powders that reflected her genius for shades of colour and enhanced her growing reputation with an ever-increasing number of clients, including wealthy socialites who dubbed her "the little Canadian woman with the magic hands."

Following a trip to Paris during which she met Thomas Lewis, a banker whom she would marry in 1915, Arden and a chemical company developed Venetian Cream Amoretta, her signature product. They also introduced a lotion to go with it, known as Ardena Skin Tonic. Throughout the 1920s and 1930s, Arden competed furiously with competitors such as Helena Rubenstein and Dorothy Gray by opening salons in Rome, Cannes, and Berlin, and marketing her wares worldwide. In 1944, it was reported that Arden was marketing about one thousand different products, although some accounts put the number at three hundred.

Over the years, she became known as a woman who couldn't accept criticism and railed against anyone who infringed on her right to run her own show. Her stiff backbone probably led to the failure of her first marriage after 19 years, and the demise of her marriage to a Russian Crown Prince after just 13 months.

For three decades, the little girl from Woodbridge lived on Fifth Avenue in a 10-room apartment decorated almost entirely in pink, her favourite colour. In her eighties, she continued to approve advertisements, check every new product, and visit salons unannounced.

Never one to look her age, the five-foot-two impeccably coiffed and attired Arden was on the leading edge of the cosmetics industry throughout her career. She inspired new ideas and breakthroughs such as full service salons, exercise classes, and makeup to match skin colour. She was also an active supporter of many charities.

In 1954, she was honoured by the Canadian Women's Press Club of Toronto, and in the same year, attended the opening ceremonies of Dalziel Pioneer Park (now Black Creek Pioneer Village) where she planted a tree on the land where she was born, lived, and played.

Arden died of a heart attack in 1966, at age eighty-two, although some observers pegged her age at 84 and others at 89. At the time, her company's annual sales were $60 million and the fortune she left behind was estimated at between $30 million and $40 million.

**Biz BITE!**

In the late 1920s, Arden renewed her love of horses and began raising thoroughbreds on a farm in Lakeside, Maine. In 1946, when her stable won more races than any other in the United States, she made the cover of Time magazine. A year later, she became the first woman owner in history to win the Kentucky Derby with her thoroughbred Jet Pilot.

## Charlotte and Benjamin Bowring (Bowring Stores)

Watch- and clockmaker Benjamin Bowring was full of hope and enthusiasm when he set up shop in the booming frontier port of St. John's, Newfoundland, in 1811. But a year later he abandoned his enterprise.

Happily for the native of Exeter, England, his business closed because of the success of a dry goods outlet operated next door by his wife, Charlotte. Instead of working on timepieces, Bowring decided to help her develop a retail and importing business that dealt in soaps, fabrics, china, and a host of other goods the townspeople had taken a shine to.

For Bowring, who was in his thirties at the time, the decision to focus on a single enterprise proved to be astute. With the community's retail trade thriving, the shop evolved into a prosperous family-operated general department store business. Nearly two centuries later, Bowring is a successful chain of upscale gift stores with more than sixty locations across Canada. The company also runs a smaller chain of home furnishings outlets.

Despite uncertain economic conditions in St. John's in the early 1800s, Bowring managed to establish the company because of his family's business connections in England, which came in handy when he bought dry goods and manufactured goods. He was also known as an adventurous merchant who was willing to take risks. He and his wife were helped by their five sons who were employed in the business; over the years, five generations of Bowrings built the enterprise into a vast global empire.

In 1823, Benjamin purchased two schooners to transport goods from England, and over the next half-century the company acquired a fleet of ships that travelled around the globe. After rebuilding following a fire in 1833, Bowring gave control of the firm to his son Charles and returned to England with the rest of his family to set up a trading company.

From 1885 to 1940, Bowring family companies were known for their oil tankers, cargo fleet, Red Cross trans-Atlantic passenger line, marine insurance, coastal mail service down the east coast of North America, seal fishing, and shipping dried salt cod fish to Europe and South America.

After Benjamin died in Liverpool, England, on June 1, 1846, the company expanded its insurance business and obtained substantial interests in metals, coffee, fertilizers, foodstuffs, petroleum products, chemicals, and many other commodities.

Two world wars wiped out a large share of the Bowring shipping fleet, and following the Second World War the main activity of the Newfoundland company was retailing. The business operated its landmark department store on Water Street in St John's, which was later expanded into a chain of smaller shops that became the basis for the current national chain of Bowring stores in Canada.

**Biz BITE!**

The company logo is the Terra Nova, a Bowring ship chartered by the British Navy for Admiral Robert Scott's famous journey to the Antarctic in 1911.

In 1984, the original Canadian arm of the global company was sold to outside interests. Though no longer connected to the founding family, Bowring remains a privately held, family owned and operated Canadian company. Its product line includes tableware, crystal and glass stemware, table linens, vases, patio accessories, lighting, garden accessories, soaps, bathroom accessories, decorative accents, furniture, music CDs, and art.

## Susannah Oland (Oland Breweries)

In the 1870s, female commercial brewers were unheard of in Canada.

So, when Susannah Oland began building her brewing business in 1877, she called her company S. Oland Sons and Company to downplay the fact that a woman owned the business.

As the lifeblood of the operation, Oland built the company into the dominant brewer in the Maritimes. In doing so, she reclaimed a role held by women centuries earlier, when virtually all brewmasters were females.

"For thousands of years, female brewers were priestesses, healers, and respected members of their communities," the Brewers Association of Canada wrote in the November 2000 edition of *Way Beyond Beer, The Many Contributions of Canada's Brewers.*

Although Susannah is known as the founder of Oland Breweries, the company's roots date back to 1867 when the original company, known as Army and Navy Brewery, was founded as a partnership between British army officer Francis DeWinton and Susannah's husband John. The Olands and their six children had immigrated to Canada from England in the early 1860s.

The original brewery — which used Susannah's recipe for beer — was located on a twelve-acre property at Turtle's Cove in Dartmouth, on the east side of Halifax harbour. Soon after, however, John Oland died in a riding accident and DeWinton sold his shares in the company to Susannah before leaving Canada for military service.

Susannah was known as a capable businesswoman, and under her leadership, with the able help of sons John, Conrad, and George, S. Oland Sons and Co. prospered, despite a major fire that gutted the brewery. Gradually, the sons, all of whom had become accomplished brewmasters, began running the operation. In 1886, Susannah died at age 68 while wintering in Richmond, Virginia.

**Biz BITE!**

The image on the Canadian dime is the Bluenose II sailing ship, a replica of the original Bluenose, which was built in 1921 to win the International Fisherman's Trophy from the Americans. The Bluenose II was commissioned in 1963 by Oland & Son Breweries as a tribute to the original vessel.

**The Bluenose was destroyed near Haiti.**
Photo courtesy of Library and Archives Canada, PA-30803.

Near the end of the century, the Oland brewery was sold to a large syndicate.

In the 20th century, first under George and later under his son Sidney and other members of the family, the Oland name would resurface when other regional breweries in Nova Scotia and New Brunswick were purchased or launched. These companies purchased the Alexander Keith Brewery in Halifax and a brewery in New Brunswick which became Moosehead Breweries Ltd.

In May 1971, Oland and Son Limited's breweries in Halifax and Oland's Brewery in St. John, New Brunswick were purchased for $12 million by John Labatt Limited and renamed

Oland's Breweries (1971) Limited. Eight years later, Oland's Nova Scotia and New Brunswick breweries were amalgamated to form Oland Breweries Limited.

Oland Breweries Limited brews Schooner, Oland Export, Keith's India Pale Ale, Keith's Light, Blue, Blue Light, Wild Cat, Maximum Ice, and, under license, Bud and Bud Light.

## Vickie Kerr (Miss Vickie's Potato Chips)

Like most moms, Vickie Kerr wanted her young children to steer clear of junk food. And like most young farm couples, she and her husband Bill were often challenged to make ends meet.

So, in 1986, Kerr began making her own potato chips in the kitchen at the family's 165-acre potato farm near New Lowell, Ontario, northwest of Toronto.

After experimenting for more than a year with potatoes hand-picked on their farm, the couple came up with their own brand of homemade chips. Made with thick-sliced potatoes with the skins left on, cooked and stirred by hand in kettles of peanut oil, and lightly salted with sea salt, her chips were crisp and free of cholesterol and preservatives. They also contained plenty of the vitamin A and potassium that are lost when chips are commercially produced.

Miss Vickie's chips were a hit with her children, her neighbours, and, within a few months, several retail outlets in the New Lowell area.

"We had come up with a healthy snack food for the kids," says Kerr, a Montreal native who had worked as a hotel receptionist, pre-school teacher, and co-owner of a tavern before deep-frying her first potato chip. "But we also had the potential for a business, which is something I wanted from the start. Potato growing was a cutthroat business … one farmer would think nothing of cutting another out of the business. Financially, we were always on the edge, so Miss Vickie's was a godsend."

After taking a third mortgage on their property, the Kerrs went into the potato chip business in earnest in 1989 on the farm they'd purchased nine years earlier, near the land on which her husband's family had grown potatoes for several generations. Ironically, potato chip maker Humpty Dumpty was among the buyers of the Kerrs's early crops.

After importing a cooking kettle from New Hampshire, Kerr developed a business plan, increased production, and took aim at the health food market. As she canvassed local retail outlets in her pickup truck, her first question to product buyers was always the same: "Are you willing to pay more for a snack food that is healthy and tastes better?" Because money was needed to cover expenses, her second question was usually, "Are you willing to pay cash?"

On both counts, the answer was often "yes."

Kerr's first customer was a gas station/variety store in New Lowell, which purchased seventy-two bags of her chips. Within weeks, Miss Vickie's chips were being stocked by grocery stores, drug stores, and other businesses in the immediate area. She often received calls at home from retailers wondering how they could get her product, which sold to customers for more than $2 for a 180-gram bag, about double the price of other brands.

"We never had trouble keeping up with the demand," she says.

Soon, the operation had expanded from one kettle to six and the Kerrs had converted a potato storage building into a processing facility. Two dozen trucks were on the road, and within 12 months her chips were being sold in the Toronto area.

First-year sales were about $1 million and by the second year, when her products were being sold throughout southern and central Ontario and as far east as Montreal and Ottawa, sales had risen by 200 percent. The product line consisted of salted and non-salted varieties. Eventually, barbecue-flavoured chips were added under the name Mr. Vickie's, as a way of recognizing the work of husband Bill, who was the small company's production expert, while Vickie handled promotion, marketing, and quality control. In 1992, Miss Vickie's Salsa and Corn Chips were added.

By then, their chips — still hand-stirred in kettles and using peanut oil — were being made in plants in Coquitlam, British Columbia and Pointe Claire, Quebec, as well as on their farm.

A year later, as the couple was developing a salt and vinegar-flavoured chip and seeking a better distribution channel, they sold the company to Hostess Frito-Lay for an undisclosed sum. With daily production of 85,000 bags of chips, the company held a little more than 1 percent of the Canadian potato chip market.

"The company was our baby, so selling out was tough," said Vickie, noting that the couple was putting in eighty-hour weeks and vacations were rare. "We had planned on keeping the company for a long time as a place where the kids would work. But we wanted a change, we wanted to slow down and spend more time with our growing family."

After visiting Phoenix, Arizona, for several years because Bill wanted drier weather, the family moved there full-time in the mid-1990s. Bill died in a car accident in 1997, and Vickie was working for a criminal attorney in Phoenix.

In 2002, Miss Vickie's chips were being made in Canada in plants in Taber, Alberta and Pointe Claire, Quebec. Several new flavours have been added since Kerr ran the company.

**Biz BITE!**

Victoria's was the initial name for Vickie Kerr's chips but that was later changed to Miss Vickie's. "After returning from a food convention in the U.S., Bill just seemed to think it sounded better," says Vickie.

# Laura Secord (Laura Secord)

Generations of Canadians have associated her name with candies and chocolates, but Laura Secord was much more than just a name on a pretty box of treats.

Secord, as many know, was a heroine during the War of 1812 who warned British troops of an American surprise attack and thus prevented a potentially devastating defeat for Upper Canada. This is especially interesting when you consider that she was born in the United States and that her father had supported the rebels during the American Revolution. Her husband, James Secord, however, was a Loyalist.

Secord was born Laura Ingersoll on September 13, 1775 in Great Barrington, Massachusetts. Though her father sided with rebel forces to gain independence from the British, he found business tough in post-Revolutionary times. When he heard of land being offered to settlers willing to relocate to Upper Canada, he moved his family to Queenston. Laura was 18 when the Ingersolls arrived there.

Here she met a Loyalist named James Secord, and they married around 1798. Secord did well as a merchant, but in 1812 the Americans declared war on the British and made several attacks on what is now Canadian soil. In June 1813, it's believed that some American troops billeted in the Secord house began talking about a plan to surprise the British at nearby Beaver Dams. Laura supposedly overheard them, and because her husband had a bad leg, she decided to make a thirty-kilometre trek behind enemy lines to warn Lieutenant James FitzGibbon of the impending attack.

Secord travelled through bush, swamp, and rough terrain and managed to get word to FitzGibbon, allowing him to capture the Americans and thwart their plan. Fear of future reprisal from Americans led the Secords to remain silent about Laura's role in the encounter. For many years, she received little or no recognition for her bravery, but thanks to others, including FitzGibbon, Secord's trek soon became public knowledge, and in 1860 she received £100 from the Prince of Wales who heard about her story. Secord died in 1868.

So what does this have to do with chocolate? In 1913, a century after Laura's heroic walk, Frank P. O'Connor opened a candy shop on Yonge Street in Toronto and named it after Secord. In addition to that year being the one hundredth anniversary of Secord's heroism, it's thought that O'Connor chose her name for the enterprise because it represented courage, loyalty, and devotion to Canadians.

O'Connor began making his own products on site and when demand grew he opened more shops in Ontario and Quebec. By the 1930s, there was a Laura Secord office in Winnipeg, but rationing during the Second World War meant shops could only stay open for four hours daily. Laura Secord shops boomed in the 1950s, and there were operations coast to coast by 1969. The company has been owned by several firms since then, and in 1999 became part of the Archibald Candy Corporation, an American firm with headquarters in Chicago. There are approximately 140 Laura Secord shops across Canada selling chocolates, ice cream, and other candies.

## Worth Knowing!

Laura Secord's father wasn't the only supporter of rebels in the family. Her great-nephew, Dr. Soloman Secord, left his home in Kincardine, Ontario to enlist in the Twentieth Georgia Infantry as a surgeon during the U.S. Civil War. He fought for the South, even though he opposed slavery, possibly because he had friends in Georgia. When he died in 1910 in Kincardine, a monument was erected in his memory, perhaps the only such tribute in Canada to a Confederate officer.

# CHAPTER 4
# Can Con Culture: Literature and the Arts

 ## THE BUSINESS OF BOOKS

 ## McClelland & Stewart Ltd.

A teetotalling Irishman and a Bible salesman meet up in Toronto.

It sounds like the start of a joke, but the partnership they formed was no laughing matter; the pair launched what became Canada's best-known and arguably most prestigious publishing house.

John McClelland, an Irishman born in Glasgow, Scotland came to Toronto in 1882 as a young boy. He was a fervent Orangeman who went to work as a teen to help out with his family's financial difficulties. He landed a job at the Methodist Book and Publishing House (later called Ryerson Press after its founder Egerton Ryerson). According to *Jack: A Life with Writers: The Story of Jack McClelland* by James King, John McClelland eventually became manager of the library department and evaluated manuscripts. He was instrumental in having Robert Service's *Songs of a Sourdough* published by the firm.

In the spring of 1906, at age 29, McClelland and another Methodist Book employee, Frederick Goodchild, formed their own publishing company, called McClelland & Goodchild. Among their successes was *The Watchman and Other Poems* by the Canadian author Lucy Maud Montgomery.

In 1913, George Stewart, who had a reputation of being the best bible salesman in the country, left his job at Oxford University Press to come on board and helped create McClelland, Goodchild & Stewart. When Goodchild left in 1918 (rumour had it that McClelland had discovered him cavorting with nude women), the company became McClelland & Stewart.

The publishers initially thrived by acting as distributors for British and American publishing houses, but they also realized the need to establish Canadian authors as well. Between the two World Wars, McClelland & Stewart published such Canadian writers as Bliss Carman, Stephen Leacock, Frederick Philip Grove, and L.M. Montgomery. The company struggled through the Depression, selling only $196,000 worth of books in 1936 (compared to more than twice that in 1919), but McClelland & Stewart was able to survive.

McClelland, a teetotaller and strict non-smoker, worked long hours, hustled business, and along with Stewart, who was more affable and fun-loving, managed to make the company prosperous. McClelland's son Jack was not initially interested in joining the firm and, in fact, the company had an agreement that no partner's child could take charge. But the agreement only lasted a year, and with Jack eventually deciding that publishing was what he wanted as a career and Stewart's only child, a daughter, not interested, the stage was set to pass the company to a new generation.

John McClelland stayed in charge until 1952, but would remain an advisor and sometimes thorn in the business side of his son for many years after. He died in May 1968. Stewart had died in 1955, and shortly afterward Jack bought 49 percent of the founding partner's shares from his widow for $65,000. Jack McClelland had begun working at the firm in 1946 and would eventually become the most famous publisher in the country, championing many Canadian writers and publishing some of the most successful books in this country's history.

Avie Bennett bought the firm in 1986 (McClelland retired in 1987), acquired some other publishing houses over the next several years, and in June 2000, announced that he was making a gift of the company to the University of Toronto. As Bennett said at the time, "What better way can there be to safeguard a great Canadian institution, a vital part of Canada's cultural heritage, than by giving it to the careful stewardship of another great Canadian institution."

## Book BITE!

The list of authors over the years published by McClelland & Stewart is a virtual who's who of Canadian literature: among the company's many authors are Margaret Atwood, Mavis Gallant, Alistair MacLeod, Alice Munro, Michael Ondaatje, and Leonard Cohen.

## Coles: The Book People

If a maverick is defined as an unorthodox or independent-minded person, then Jack Cole probably fit that definition better than anyone in the bookstore business.

He and his older brother Carl not only created one of the most renowned bookstore chains in the country, they did it with a style that often rattled their fellow entrepreneurs as well as some in the publishing business.

Carl and Jack, whose real last name was Colofsky, were both born in Detroit, the sons of a Russian immigrant. They later moved to Toronto and had difficult and poor childhoods. In 1935, when Carl was 22 and Jack was 15, they opened their first bookstore in Toronto, not for any real love of books but because they saw a good opportunity, Jack's son David told us in an interview. The Book Exchange near the corner of Bloor and Spadina was a second hand bookstore that helped Carl to pay his way through university. They changed the store's name to Coles in 1938.

Their second bookstore opened in 1939 at the corner of Yonge and Charles streets, and it did well enough that by 1956, the brothers opened another store at Yonge and Dundas. Other stores in the Toronto area followed before the company expanded, first to Richmond Hill and then to St. Catharines. The stores were not typical of what existed in Canada at the time. They had bright lights, lots of signs, specials, and remainder bins full of books at incredibly low prices.

According to David Cole, Jack was the one who ran the business while Carl handled the financing. "My dad was a real innovator," he says. "My dad was fond of books, but was he a book lover? No. He was a retailer."

**They Said It!**

"I have to spend so much time explaining to Americans that I am not English and to Englishmen that I am not American that I have little time left to be Canadian – on second thought, I am a true cosmopolitan – unhappy anywhere."

– Laurence Peter, author of The Peter Principle

That might explain why Coles also sold sporting goods in the 1950s and 1960s in the same stores that carried books. That's why Coles stores of all places were the first in Canada to sell the Hula Hoop, the Slinky, and the Mechano set, according to David. The brothers, however, abandoned sporting goods by the late 1960s.

Jack Cole was often at odds with publishers because he didn't think they catered to public tastes and raised their ire by trying such marketing stunts as selling books by the pound. He was once described as "a schlock merchant, a hard-nosed hustler in a genteel world."

**They Said It!**

"Canada is so far away it hardly exists."

– Argentine writer Jorge Luis Borges, 1974, when asked what he thought of Canada.

Cole also didn't endear himself to teachers with the introduction of Coles Notes in 1948. To the delight of many Canadian students and later those in more than 70 countries, Coles Notes offered a quick reference guide to a variety of subjects from English literature to math and chemistry. He sold the American rights to the guides, where they became the popular Cliff's Notes found south of the border.

Coles also opened stores in the United States in the early 1970s, but they proved unsuccessful and the idea was later abandoned. On June 7, 1972, Coles was the first bookseller to go public, but Jack and Carl still retained control of the company, which by now had more than 200 stores. They sold their interest to Southam Inc. in 1978 for $34 million. Shortly thereafter, in 1980, the company opened one of the original book superstores, the 67,000-square-foot World's Biggest Bookstore, in downtown Toronto.

"They were proud of what they built," David said. "My father was always a step ahead when it came to merchandising."

David remembers Jack as a great family man who coached hockey and took his children fishing. He was an avid stamp collector and doted on his 16 grandchildren until his death in January 1997. Carl Cole, who tended to shun the limelight, had died in 1994.

In 1994, Southam sold Coles to Pathfinder Capital and in April 1995, Coles and SmithBooks merged to form Chapters Inc. About six years later, Chapters had merged with Indigo Books to dominate the bookstore industry in Canada. Larry Stevenson, former CEO of Chapters, once said Jack Cole "was a guy who was always willing to try innovative things and often go against the grain."

**Book BITE!**

The first Coles Notes, written in 1948, was for the French novella *Colomba* by Prosper Mérimée. The notes for *Merchant of Venice* followed shortly thereafter.

## *Maclean's* Magazine/ Maclean Hunter

The man who launched one of the most successful magazine empires in Canada might never have done so if he'd had better marks in English.

John Bayne Maclean was tapped to become a principal at a high school in Port Hope, Ontario, but his low English marks prevented him from taking the post. Instead he turned to journalism. Within a few years, he began publishing his own trade magazines and would eventually found one of Canada's most notable periodicals, *Maclean's* magazine.

Maclean was born in Crieff, Ontario, on September 26, 1862, the son of a minister, Andrew Maclean, and Christine Mclean, née Cameron. He attended school in Owen Sound before heading to Toronto to complete his education. When a career in education didn't pan out, Maclean got a reporting job in 1882 at the *Toronto World* newspaper for the grand salary of five dollars a week.

Toronto was a thriving city of 86,000 then, with busy city streets full of bicycles and horse-drawn streetcars, the kind of place where a hard-working young man could succeed. Though Maclean was supplementing his income with some freelance pieces, he moved over to the *Toronto Daily Mail* within a couple of months at almost twice the salary. He soon became an editor handling business news, and despite his busy schedule, took up fencing and became the national junior champion.

Maclean, who would also spell his name McLean and MacLean at times, saved his money, and in 1887 started his own publication, the *Canadian Grocer*. In an era when few magazines thrived, Maclean was able to establish it on a firm foundation — so firm, in fact, that the magazine still exists today. The first issue was 16 pages and carried a subscription price of two dollars a year.

The success of *Canadian Grocer* led Maclean to create other trade publications, such as *Hardware and Metal*, *The Dry Goods Review*, and *Druggist's Weekly*. If that wasn't enough, Maclean, a longtime admirer of Canada's first prime minister, Sir John A. Macdonald, also edited the financial pages of the *Empire*, a Toronto newspaper with a definite Conservative party slant.

Maclean's success also gave him a taste for the cosmopolitan life, and in the 1890s he moved to Montreal. With the help of his brother Hugh, he still managed the trade papers in Toronto but also pursued his lifelong interest in the militia. He would eventually carry the rank of colonel.

The editor/publisher liked moving in wealthy circles in both Canada and the U.S. On October 31, 1900 he married Anna Denison Slade, who had grown up well-to-do in Boston. The couple settled in Toronto and their son Hector Andrew was born in 1903. That same year Maclean hired Horace Talmadge Hunter as an ad salesman, and the young man immediately worked well with Maclean and eventually ran the day-to-day activities of the publishing company. Several years later, when he was made a full partner, the company name was changed to Maclean-Hunter.

Maclean continued to launch and acquire new magazines, notably *The Business Man's* magazine. He changed its title to *Busy Man's* magazine and then re-named it *Maclean's* in 1911. It was an era when several other magazines such as *McCall's* and *Collier's* bore the name of their publishers. He also started *The Financial Post* in January 1907 and *Chatelaine* in 1928.

**They Said It!**

"It's going to be a great country when they finish unpacking it."

– *Andrew H. Malcolm*, New York Times *journalist and author, speaking about Canada in 1989*

Despite all this success, Maclean's life wasn't without tragedy, according to his biography, *A Gentleman of the Press* by Floyd Chalmers. Maclean's wife was struck with polio early in their marriage and their son Hector died in 1919. A perfectionist, frugal, and often hard-working man, Maclean nevertheless enjoyed riding and travelling. When he died on September 25, 1950, he left an estate of just over $1 million and his company was publishing more than 30 magazines.

Maclean-Hunter, now owned by Rogers Communications, continues to publish a wealth of trade magazines as well as the ever-popular *Maclean's* and *Chatelaine*.

# 🍁 BOOK BITES

- Leslie McFarlane of Haileybury, Ontario, wrote the first 20 books in the famous Hardy Boys series under the pen name Franklin W. Dixon. They were among the best-selling boys' books of their time, but McFarlane received no royalties.

**Book BITE!**

Though trade magazines helped Maclean amass his fortune, their titles were not the most gripping. Among the magazines he owned during his lifetime were *The Sanitary Engineer, Men's Wear Review,* and *Bookseller and Stationer.*

- *Anne of Green Gables*, the story of the little red-haired orphan from Prince Edward Island, written by Lucy Maud Montgomery, was first published in 1908 and is considered the best-selling Canadian book of all time.

  Though Lucy Maud Montgomery is best known for her *Anne of Green Gables* books, the prolific author also published some 450 poems and 500 short stories during her illustrious career.

- Irving Layton is considered one of Canada's greatest poets, but based on what he studied at university you wouldn't think rhyming couplets would have been his career. He holds a Bachelor of Science in agriculture and he did graduate work in political science.

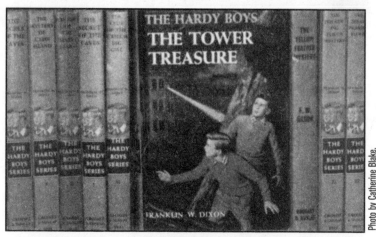

Photo by Catherine Blake.

The Hardy Boys were popular with many young Canadian readers.

- Saul Bellow won the Nobel Prize for literature in 1976. Though born in Lachine, Quebec, in 1915, he had lived in the United States since he was nine and was an American citizen when he won the award.

# ♦ HAVE YOU READ THESE?

## The First 10 Winners of the Governor General's Literary Award for Fiction

1. **1936:** *Think of the Earth* by Bertram Brooker.
2. **1937:** *The Dark Weaver* by Laura G. Salverson.
3. **1938:** *Swiss Sonata* by Gwethalyn Graham.
4. **1939:** *The Champlain Road* by Franklin Davey McDowell.
5. **1940**: *Thirty Acres* by Ringuet (Philippe Panneton).
6. **1941:** *Three Came to Ville Marie* by Alan Sullivan.
7. **1942:** *Little Man* by G. Herbert Sallans.
8. **1943:** *The Pied Piper of Dipper* by Thomas Raddall.
9. **1944:** *Earth and High Heaven* by Gwethalyn Graham.
10. **1945:** *Two Solitudes* by Hugh MacLennan.

## Book BITE!

The Fall of a Titan, which won a Governor General's Award in 1954, was written by Igor Gouzenko, once a cipher clerk for the Soviet Embassy to Canada in Ottawa. He defected in 1945 with 109 documents that detailed Soviet espionage activities in the West, including plans by Joseph Stalin to steal nuclear secrets. It is thought that his defection and the subsequent exposure of these facts was one of the significant events that triggered the Cold War. Gouzenko often appeared on television promoting his books with a hood over his head.

## LITERARY QUIZ 1

1. This famous poet once appeared in a film with John Wayne and Marlene Dietrich. Was it?

   a) Irving Layton
   b) Raymond Souster
   c) Robert W. Service
   d) Earle Birney

2. Which of the following authors have not won three or more Governor-General's Literary Awards?

   a) Pierre Berton
   b) Margaret Atwood
   c) High MacLennan
   d) Michael Ondaatje

3. Robertson Davies' Deptford trilogy is made up of *Fifth Business*, *World of Wonders*, and what other book?

   a) *Leaven of Malice*
   b) *The Manticore*
   c) *The Rebel Angels*
   d) *Tempest-Tost*

### They Said It!

"Men who are attractive to most women are rarities, in this country at any rate. I think that it is because a man, to be attractive, must be free to give his whole time to it, and the Canadian male is so hounded by taxes and the rigours of our climate, that he is lucky to be alive, without being irresistible as well."

– Robertson Davies,
Canadian author

4. *This Side Jordan*, published in 1960 and set in Ghana, was which Canadian author's first novel.

5. What is the name of the town that is in several Margaret Laurence novels, including *The Stone Angel* and *A Jest of God*.

a)  Maniwaki
b)  Manawaka
c)  Minaki
d)  Moonstone

6.  Poet and children's author Dennis Lee once co-wrote songs for which TV program?

   a)  *Sesame Street*
   b)  *Fraggle Rock*
   c)  *Mr. Rogers' Neighborhood*
   d)  *Mr. Dressup*

7.  Only three Canadian English writers have won the Governor General's Award in both the fiction and poetry category. Name at least one.

8.  This acclaimed Canadian short story writer has spent most of her adult life in Paris, France. Name her.

9.  Mordecai Richler's first novel was

   a) *Cocksure*
   b) *The Apprenticeship of Duddy Kravitz*
   c) *The Acrobats*
   d) *St. Urbain's Horseman*

10. How many Governor General's awards did the late Ontario-born poet/playwright James Reaney win?

   a)  none
   b)  one
   c)  two
   d)  three
   e)  five

11. Which of the following authors have written for *Maclean's* magazine?

    a) Pierre Berton
    b) Hugh Garner
    c) Peter Newman
    d) Mordecai Richler
    e) all of the above

12. The late Milton Acorn, a native of Charlottetown, was a renowned Canadian poet. What trade was he skilled at?

    a) masonry
    b) plumbing
    c) carpentry
    d) house painting

➡ **Answers on page 341**

# 🍁 READ ALL ABOUT IT

- *Heavy reading.* A 100-page Canadian newspaper contains an average of more than 300,000 words of reading material, equivalent to three full-length novels.

Words, words, and more words.

- Canada's oldest newspaper is the *Halifax Gazette*, first published on March 23, 1752. Since September 2002, a copy of the first edition of the paper has been part of the National Library's rare books collection in Ottawa. The one sheet copy of the paper was purchased for $40,000 from the Massachusetts Historical Society.

#  Superman Artwork: Missing in "Action"

Canadians may be familiar with their country's connection to Superman, the most famous comic book hero of the twentieth century. Although the caped crime fighter had a reputation for fighting for truth, justice, and the American way, he was the co-creation of a Canadian.

Joseph Shuster was born in 1914 in Toronto, Ontario, and at age nine moved with his family to Cleveland, Ohio. There, Shuster met future collaborator Jerry Siegel, and Shuster began making a name for himself as an artist writing an array of cartoons. In the mid-1930s the two began to provide DC Comics with such features as *Dr. Occult*, *Slam Bradley*, and *Radio Squad* before selling their most famous creation: Superman. The powerful superhero first appeared in DC's *Action Comics* #1 in 1938.

Shuster drew Superman through 1947, but eventually bad eyesight cut short his career. He died in 1992 of heart failure, but both he and Siegel had established their place in popular culture.

Copies of the *Action Comics* #1 are rare and reportedly worth up to almost $500,000 in mint condition. But what about Shuster's original artwork for Superman? Is it still around? We contacted several comic book experts and all doubted the drawing still existed.

A spokesperson at DC Comics says the policy there was always to return the artwork to the artist, and no record exists in its archives of the company having these drawings.

"My guess is that it is long lost," adds R.C. Harvey, a comic book expert. "I think the first published story was a cut-and-paste job: Shuster cut up daily comic strips and re-configured them into page format. The resulting messy appearance wouldn't have seemed precious to anyone seeing it at the print shop. And of course they tossed out stuff like that all the time."

Comic books weren't thought of as having value back then, he says. And while that attitude may have changed soon afterward, "I doubt, even then, that the artwork was considered valuable."

The original Man of Steel artwork from 1938 seems to have disappeared.

An interview with Shuster and Siegel by historian Tom Andrae printed in *NEMO, the classics comic library*, in 1983, does provide some insight into the two men behind Superman. In the interview, Shuster mentions the rough drafts were usually done in pencil and he noted that the first *Action* comic came about "very fast":

> They made the decision to publish it and said to us, "Just go out and turn out thirteen pages based on your strip." It was a rush job, and one of the things I like least to do is to rush my artwork. I'm too much of a perfectionist to do anything which is mediocre. The only solution Jerry and I could come up with was to cut up the strips into panels and paste the panels on a sheet the size of the page. If some panels were too long, we would shorten them — cut them off — if they were too short, we would extend them.

Shuster also mentions an earlier prototype drawing of Superman done in 1933, which was reprinted in *NEMO* along with the interview showing the comic book hero without a cape and wearing a strongman's outfit. The story that went along with it was presumably destroyed.

While the artwork for the *Action Comics #1* may no longer exist, Superman certainly lives on for comic book lovers everywhere. The summer 2006 release of *Superman Returns* starring Brandon Routh confirmed the superhero's longevity with fans (a sequel is in the works for release in 2011). And in addition to the popular 1950s TV series based on the comic book and the 1970s movies that starred the late Christopher Reeve, the 1990s saw a comic book on the "death" of Superman and his subsequent return and marriage to long-time flame Lois Lane. Both Canada Post and the U.S. Postal Service have issued a Superman stamp — in 1995 in Canada and in 1998 south of the border. The U.S. Postal Service then announced in 2006 the issuance of commemorative DC Comics superhero stamps, including two of Superman.

# CHAPTER 5
# Celebrating, Canadian Style

## LABOUR DAY QUIZ

Canadians have officially been celebrating Labour Day since 1894 but in modern times the last statutory holiday of the summer is often associated with festivals, fairs, and season-ending visits to the cottage or a favourite campground.

Whatever your reason for celebrating, the holiday remains rooted in workers' struggles in the 19th century to improve conditions for all employees which ultimately led to such perks as paid holidays, safe work places, employment insurance, even the time off on weekends we now take for granted.

As a tip of our cap to workers past and present, we've devised a quiz that we hope won't make you work overtime.

1.  In 1901, the first annual report of the federal Bureau of Labour criticized the continued employment of children under what age?

    a) 8
    b) 12
    c) 16
    d) 18

2.  The first labour parade in Canada took place in 1872 in what city?

    a) Montreal
    b) St. Catharines
    c) Toronto
    d) Winnipeg
    e) Ottawa

3. Match these working songs with the artist who had the hit.

a) "Working for the Weekend"  i) Jim Croce
b) "Working in the Coal Mine"  ii) Johnny Paycheck
c) "Workin' at the Car Wash Blues"  iii) Loverboy
d) "Take this Job and Shove It"  iv) Leo Dorsey

4. True or false? One of the fallouts from the 1919 Winnipeg General Strike was a government motion to disband the RCMP for its bad handling of the affair.

**They Said It!**

"When I'm looking at an issue like the economy, or globalization, or plant closures, I always think of what will happen to families."

– *former union leader Bob White on why workers were his main focus*

5. The New Democratic Party has historically been linked with labour since the party's founding. In what year was the NDP founded?

a) 1959
b) 1961
c) 1963
d) 1965

6. Unscramble the letters below to spell words that signify a form of union security whereby employers deduct a portion of the salaries of all employees within a bargaining unit, union members or not, to go to the union as union dues.

udmhatelrroafn

7. NUPGE is short form for which Canadian union?

a) National Union of Provincial Government Employees
b) Native Union of Provincial Gamefarm Employees
c) Northern Union of Parking Garage Employees
d) National Union of Public and General Employees

8. In which Canadian city did former Canadian Auto Workers leader Bob White join his first trade union?

a) Woodstock, New Brunswick
b) Oshawa, Ontario
c) Woodstock, Ontario
d) Lethbridge, Alberta

→ **Answers on pages 342–343**

## VICTORIA DAY QUIZ

Victoria Day was originally celebrated to honour the famous British queen of the 19th century, but these days it has the added significance for many Canadians of being the official start to summer.

That can mean cracking open a cold beer or two, a trip to the cottage, planting gardens, or watching fireworks and parades. Most of all, it means an enjoyable long weekend.

To add to your enjoyment, we've come up with 12 terrific trivia puzzlers about Victoria – the name, the queen, and the holiday itself.

1. Given that many Canadians refer to Victoria Day as the May 2-4 holiday, it's appropriate that a famous Canadian brewer is said to be responsible for introducing the idea of celebrating it as a national holiday. Was it

   a) John Molson
   b) Thomas Carling
   c) John Labatt
   d) Alexander Keith

2. According to organizers, the annual Island Farms Victoria Day parade in Victoria, British Columbia, with more than 155 entries and 35 American marching bands is the largest annual parade in Canada. Which city boasts the second largest?

a) Calgary, the Calgary Stampede
b) Toronto, the Santa Claus Parade
c) Ottawa, the Gay Pride parade
d) The city hosting the annual Grey Cup

3. Queen Victoria was not only Empress of the British Empire but was queen of her household too. How many children did she have?

a) four
b) nine
c) six
d) 10

4. What British rock band had a Top 10 hit in Canada in 1970 with the song "Victoria?"

a) The Rolling Stones
b) The Who
c) The Moody Blues
d) The Kinks

5. When she was a girl, what was Queen Victoria's nickname?

a) Drina
b) Tory
c) Vicky
d) Princess

6. True or false? Thomas Ricketts, the youngest soldier to ever receive the Victoria Cross, the British Empire's highest military honour, also happened to be from Victoria.

7. Whom did Queen Victoria succeed when she came to the throne?

a) George III
b) William IV

c) Edward VI

d) Anne I

8. When Queen Victoria died in January 1901, who was prime minister of Canada?

a) Robert Borden

b) Charles Tupper

c) Wilfrid Laurier

d) Mackenzie Bowell

9. For much of the 20th century, Victoria Day was celebrated on May 24, regardless of what day it fell on, unless it was a Sunday. An amendment to the Statutes of Canada stated that the holiday would always be on the Monday before May 25. In which of the following years was the amendment introduced?

a) 1945

b) 1952

c) 1960

d) 1967

➥ **Answers on pages 343–344**

## RIDEAU CANAL SKATING QUIZ

You haven't had a true taste of Ottawa's annual Winterlude festival until you've skated on the Rideau Canal, touted by the National Capital Commission as the world's largest skating rink.

Before you strap on the blades for a leisurely skate along the 7.8-kilometre ice surface, try your luck at this Rideau Canal Skateway trivia quiz. If you get eight or more right, treat yourself to a Beaver Tail, a tasty treat served at kiosks along the frozen waterway. Enjoy. And stay warm!

1.  Which came first, skating on the Rideau Canal or Winterlude?

2.  Which of the following celebrities have skated on the canal over the years?

    a) Hilary Clinton
    b) Mitsou
    c) Jean Charest
    d) Brian Orser
    e) all of them

3.  How deep is the water beneath the canal ice surface?

    a) 15.25 centimetres
    b) 2.5 metres
    c) 50 centimetres
    d) from one to four metres

4.  Clearing the canal for skating was the brainchild of Douglas Fullerton. What was Mr. Fullerton's position when he dreamed up his scheme in the early 1970s?

    a) mayor of Ottawa
    b) Chairman of the Regional Municipality of Ottawa-Carleton
    c) Chairman of the National Capital Commission
    d) president of the Ottawa District Minor Hockey Association.

5.  How thick must the ice be before the canal is opened to skaters?

    a) 12 centimetres
    b) 35 centimetres
    c) 45 centimetres
    d) 25 centimetres

6. On February 14, 2004, the Ottawa Senators Alumni played a game of shinny on the canal against alumni from another National Hockey League team. Was it the Montreal Canadiens or the Toronto Maple Leafs?

7. Only once it its 27-year history has the Rideau Canal's entire 7.8-kilometre ice surface been temporarily closed to the public for reasons other than poor ice conditions. What was the reason?

   a) A major hockey festival took place on the canal
   b) The canal was closed for security reasons when former United States president Bill Clinton visited Ottawa
   c) Ottawa police were conducting a murder investigation
   d) The canal was closed because of an earthquake warning

8. The canal's skating surface is comparable to how many Olympic-sized hockey rinks?

   a) 50
   b) 80
   c) 90
   d) 175

9. While taking a leisurely skate along the canal you will pass Lansdowne Park, home of the Central Canada Exhibition and once the home of the Ottawa Renegades and Rough Riders football teams. Who or what is the park named for?

10. Unscramble the letters below to find four common sights found on or around the canal during Winterlude.

    a) veabrelaist
    b) cieoghs
    c) souqet
    d) etsepksadse

➥ **Answers on pages 344–345**

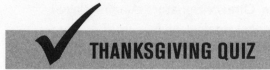

## THANKSGIVING QUIZ

Turkey and pumpkin pie, family get-togethers, and the chance to celebrate and be thankful for Canada's bounty are among the high points of Thanksgiving.

But there's much more to this favourite holiday, which was first celebrated in North America more than 400 years ago. While the turkey's in the oven and the potatoes are simmering on the stove, carve into our Thanksgiving quiz to get a better taste for this special day.

No fowl play, please!

1. From 1921 to 1930, Thanksgiving in Canada was observed on the same date as another day of significance. Was it:

   a) Armistice Day
   b) Labour Day
   c) Yom Kippur
   d) Halloween

2. I am an explorer who celebrated the first Thanksgiving in North America, more than 40 years before the Pilgrims in Massachusetts. Who am I?

   a) Samuel de Champlain
   b) John Cabot
   c) Martin Frobisher
   d) Jacques Cartier
   e) Hernando Cortez

3. The first Thanksgiving Day in Canada after Confederation in 1867 was observed on what date?

   a) October 12, 1867

b) April 15, 1872
c) October 19, 1867
d) November 11, 1868

4. Canadians celebrate Thanksgiving on a Monday. On what day of the week do Americans celebrate their Thanksgiving?

5. During North American Thanksgiving celebrations in the early 1600s, why was the potato not part of the meal?

    a) potatoes did not grow in North America at the time
    b) blights eradicated much of the potato crop
    c) the newly discovered potato was considered by many Europeans to be poisonous
    d) the potato was considered to be a "dirty" food because it is was grown beneath the soil

6. The Horn of Plenty, or Cornucopia, which symbolizes abundance and is one of the most recognizable symbols of Thanksgiving, originated in what country?

    a) Holland
    b) Greece
    c) The United States
    d) Canada
    e) Norway

7. True or false? Fresh cranberries are composed of almost 90 percent water.

8. What are Beltsville Small Whites, Slates, White Hollands, and Bourbon Reds?

9. Since 1931, Canadian Thanksgiving has been celebrated on the second Monday of October, with the exception of 1935, when it was moved to Thursday, October 24. Why was the date changed that year?

a) A general election was held on the second Monday of October
b) Canada's stock of turkeys was depleted by disease
c) At the height of the Depression no one wanted to give thanks
d) King George V had died in early October

10. Who was prime minister on January 31, 1957, when Canada's Parliament issued a proclamation that permanently fixed the second Monday in October as Thanksgiving?

11. In Canada, Thanksgiving and Christmas account for what percentage of whole turkey sales?

    a) 98 percent
    b) 93 percent
    c) 86 percent
    d) 64 percent

12. What are the origins of the word *pumpkin*?

    a) from the Greek word *pepon*, which means large melon
    b) from the French, who used the term "pompon"
    c) from *pumpion* as it was referred to by the English
    d) all of the above

➥ **Answers on pages 345–346**

# CHAPTER 6
# Colourful Canucks: The Famous and the Infamous

##  INFAMOUS CANADIANS OF THE PAST CENTURY
(in no particular order)

1. **Brian Mulroney:** No prime minister has altered the political landscape as much as Mulroney, whose government negotiated a free trade agreement with the United States, implemented the Goods and Services Tax, and, according to some, revived support for the Parti Québécois. For his efforts, not to mention years of scandals and party patronage, the boy from Baie-Comeau has been called the most loathed Canadian politician of the 20th century.

2. **Alan Eagleson:** In 1998, the former hockey lawyer and player agent pleaded guilty to fraud and theft charges, was fined $1 million, and was thrown in jail for swindling players and stealing disability insurance money and Canada Cup money that was intended for the players' pension fund. He was later stripped of his Order of Canada medal, disbarred by the Law Society of Upper Canada, and booted out of Canada's Sports Hall of Fame. He also resigned from the Hockey Hall of Fame.

3. **Ernst Zundel:** The Holocaust denier and advocate of Jewish conspiracies was repeatedly accused, over a period of more than 20 years, of violating Canada's hate laws and, in the process, incurred the wrath of many Canadians. He left Canada for the United States in 2000 but was detained and deported back to Canada in 2003. Here he was detained for a further two years before being deported to Germany, where he was tried in the state court of Mannheim on charges of incitement for Holocaust denial dating back to the 1990s. He was convicted in 2007 and sentenced to a maximum term of five years in prison.

4. **Harold Ballard:** People, especially long-suffering Toronto Maple Leaf fans, were never happy with the direction Ballard took the team in the 1970s and 1980s. "Pal Hal," as he was known, added insult to injury in 1972 when he was convicted on 47 charges of fraud and theft involving $205,000 in Maple Leaf Gardens' funds.

5. **Ben Johnson:** Canadians were elated after Johnson won the gold medal for the 100 metres in the 1988 Olympics. But the cheers faded quickly after drug screening showed the Toronto athlete had tested positive for steroids. He was stripped of the gold and his actions led to an inquiry into drugs and sport in Canada that has had world-wide ramifications. He is most recently remembered for making light of his indiscretion by appearing in an ad campaign for Cheetah energy drink, stating in it, "I cheetah all the time!"

6. **Conrad Black:** The media mogul was convicted in July 2007 for defrauding shareholders of his Hollinger International newspaper empire out of millions of dollars. He was sentenced to six and a half years in prison in December 2007 for his conviction on three counts of fraud and one count of obstruction of justice (Associated Press, December 10, 2007).

# ♦ CANADIAN'S MOST NOTORIOUS MURDERERS

1. **Ronald Turpin:** The last prisoner to die by hanging in Canada. Turpin robbed a Toronto restaurant in February, 1962. When he was pulled over by police officer Frederick Nash for a broken taillight, Turpin pulled out a .32 calibre handgun and shot Nash in the chest. He tried to escape in Nash's cruiser but was quickly apprehended. He was tried and convicted of murder and sentenced to die by hanging. At 12:02 a.m. on December 11, 1962, Turpin was hanged along with another prisoner, Arthur Lucas, at Toronto's Don Jail. When he heard that he and Lucas would likely be the last prisoners hanged in Canada, Turpin apparently said, "Some consolation."

2. **Richard Blass:** An infamous Canadian gangster and a multiple murderer. Born in Montreal, he was nicknamed *Le Chat*, French for "The Cat", so nicknamed because of his luck in evading death after surviving at least three assassination attempts, a police shootout, and escaping from custody twice.

3. **Evelyn Dick:** The murder trials of Evelyn Dick remain the most sensationalized events in Canadian crime history. Dick was born in Beamsville, Ontario. She was arrested for murder after local children in Hamilton, Ontario, found the torso of her missing estranged husband, John Dick. His head and limbs had been sawed from his body and evidence that they had been burned in the furnace of her home later surfaced.

    A well known school yard song at the time went as follows:

*You cut off his legs...*
*You cut off his arms...*
*You cut off his head...*
*How could you Mrs. Dick?*
*How could you Mrs. Dick?*

4. **Clifford Olson:** Canadians were outraged by the sex slayings of at least 11 Vancouver area children, for which he was charged in 1981, and many felt his life sentence on several counts of first degree murder wasn't sufficient punishment. His conviction once again raised the issue among Canadians of reinstituting the death penalty. He has come up for parole twice, once in 1997 and again in 2006. Both times he was denied.

**Crime BITE!**

1880: In one of the most notorious murders in Canadian history, five members of the Donnelly family were massacred in Biddulph Township, near Lucan, Ontario. No one was convicted.

5 & 6. **Paul Bernardo and Karla Homolka:** The duo responsible for the murders of Leslie Mahaffy, Kristen French, and Karla's sister, Tammy, between 1990 and 1992 were tried in one of the most notorious murder cases in Canadian history. Even the books written about the case and a movie depicting the murders have come under attack for being sensationalistic and not sensitive enough to the victims' plight. Bernardo was sentenced to life imprisonment while Homolka received two 12-year sentences to run concurrently. She became eligible for parole in 2001. To many people's horror, she was released from prison on July 4, 2005. In 2007 she gave birth to a baby boy, and in 2008 reportedly left Canada for the Antilles in the West Indies so her child could lead a "more normal life." Bernardo remains in prison and, although he will become eligible for parole in 2010 under the "faint hope" clause, it is unlikely that he will be released as he has been declared a dangerous offender.

7. **Robert William "Willie" Pickton:** This pig farmer and serial killer from Port Coquitlam, British Columbia, was convicted in 2007 on six counts of second-degree murder in the deaths of six women. He was also charged in the deaths of an additional 20 women, many of them prostitutes and drug users from Vancouver's Downtown Eastside. As of December 11, 2007, he was sentenced to life in prison, with the possibility of parole after 25 years — the longest sentence available under Canadian law.

During the trial's first day, January 22, 2007, the Crown stated he confessed to 49 murders to an undercover police officer posing as a cell mate. The Crown reported that Pickton told the officer that he wanted to kill another woman to make it an even 50, and that he was caught because he was "sloppy."

8. **Marc Lépine:** Born Gamil Gharbi, Lépine was a 25-year-old man from Montreal, Quebec, who murdered 14 women and wounded 10 other women and four men at the École Polytechnique, an engineering school affiliated with the Université de Montréal, in what is known as "the Montreal Massacre." He then turned the gun on himself.

9. **David Shearing:** The 23-year-old murdered a family of six while they were camping in Wells Gray Park in a remote area of British Columbia in August of 1982 — Bob and Jackie Johnson and their two girls, aged 11 and 13, along with Jackie's retired parents, George and Edith Bentley.

   Shearing pleaded guilty to six counts of murder and was sentenced to six concurrent terms of life imprisonment with no possibility of parole for 25 years. He came up for parole in 2007 and was denied release.

10. **James Roszco:** Shot four members of the Royal Canadian Mounted Police dead at his farm in Mayerthorpe, Alberta, northwest of Edmonton, on March 3, 2005. Roszko shot and killed RCMP constables Peter Schiemann, Anthony Gordon, Lionide Johnston, and Brock Myrol as the officers were executing a property seizure on his farm. It was the worst tragedy to befall the Mounties in nearly 100 years.

11. **Roch "Moses" Thériault:** The charismatic Quebecer established a commune near Burnt River, Ontario, in 1987. Between 1977 and 1989 he held sway over as many as 12 adults and 26 children. He used all of the nine women as concubines, and probably fathered most of the children in the group. He was arrested for assault in 1989, and convicted of murder in 1993. During his reign, Thériault mutilated several members. He once used a meat cleaver to chop off the hand and part of the arm of one of his concubines. He also removed eight of her teeth. Thériault was accused of castrating a two-year-old boy, as well as one adult man. His major crime was to kill Solange Boilard, his legal wife, by disembowelment while trying to perform surgery on her. He is serving a life sentence and was denied parole in 2002.

# 🍁 TOP 10 GREATEST CANADIANS

On April 5, 2004, the polls opened for Canadians to nominate their choice for the man or woman they felt was the best Canadian in history. They were asked to vote again when the top 10 were revealed. Here are the results of that poll in order of votes received:

1. Tommy Douglas (father of Medicare, premier of Saskatchewan)
2. Terry Fox (athlete, activist, humanitarian)
3. Pierre Trudeau (prime minister)
4. Sir Frederick Banting (medical scientist, co-discoverer of insulin)
5. David Suzuki (geneticist, environmentalist, broadcaster, activist)
6. Lester Bowles Pearson (prime minister, former United Nations General Assembly president, Nobel Peace Prize laureate)
7. Don Cherry (hockey coach, commentator)
8. Sir John A. Macdonald (first post-Confederation prime minister)
9. Alexander Graham Bell (Scottish-born scientist, inventor, founder of the Bell Telephone and Telegraph Company)
10. Wayne Gretzky (hockey player)

## Terry Fox

On April 12, 1980, Terry Fox left St. John's, Newfoundland, and began running along the Trans-Canada Highway en route to Canada's west coast. The Winnipeg native's goal was to raise money to fight the cancer that had taken his right leg.

Along the way, he captivated the imaginations of thousands of Canadians before learning on December 22, 1980, that terminal cancer had returned. Fox died on June 28, 1981. By the time his run was cancelled, he had covered 5,373 kilometres or the equivalent of 143 marathons.

Across Canada, Terry Fox Runs held every September keep the memories of Fox alive as does millions of dollars raised by The Terry Fox Foundation to fight the killer disease.

Other bits of memorabilia also keep Terry's legacy in the minds of Canadians, says his brother Darrell, who was involved in the run and is national director of the foundation.

The artificial leg, the tattered white sock he wore on that leg, a pair of his running shorts and one of the 26 pairs of shoes he wore during the run, as well as many gifts he received along the way are on display at the Terry Fox Library in Port Coquitlam, British Columbia, Terry's hometown.

Most of the memorabilia that Terry received while on the road or that was forwarded to his father Rolly and mother Betty, is on display or in storage at the British Columbia Sports Hall of Fame in Vancouver. His parents have other more personal belongings, such as Terry's journal.

The home at 3337 Morrill Street in Port Coquitlam where Terry spent his formative years was sold. The van used to accompany Terry on his run, its whereabouts unknown for 28 years, has now resurfaced and, on May 22, 2008, was unveiled at a ceremony in the lobby at Ford of Canada in Oakville. The 1980 Ford Ecoline van had been painstakingly restored to the condition it was in when it served as Terry's home and support vehicle during his brave journey.

On May 25, 2008, the van started out from St. John's, Newfoundland, for a cross-Canadian tour to raise funds for cancer research. It was to end in Victoria on September 14, to coincide with the start of the annual Terry Fox Run.

Since its inception the Terry Fox Foundation has raised more than $400 million for cancer research.

## Roger Woodward: Falls Survivor

In the summer of 1960, Roger Woodward was at the centre of what the history books have recorded as the "Niagara Falls miracle."

On the afternoon of July 9, the seven-year-old Niagara Falls, New York youngster and his 17-year-old sister Deanne were enjoying their first-ever boat ride in an aluminum fishing boat piloted on the Niagara River by family friend Jim Honeycutt.

While cruising above Canada's Horseshoe Falls the 12-foot craft's 7.5-horsepower outboard motor hit a rock, sheared its cotter pin, and lost power. As it was swept toward the falls, it capsized, tossing Honeycutt and the Woodward children into the frothing waters.

Roger was wearing nothing but a swimsuit and a lifejacket as he floated toward the brink of the falls, which drop 162 feet into a pile of rocks. His sister managed to slip into a life jacket before the boat flipped.

John Hayes and John Quattrochi, both tourists, pulled Deanne out of the water 20 feet from the top of the of Canadian falls but Roger was not so lucky. He went over the edge into an area strewn with boulders.

Miraculously, he escaped with nothing more than minor cuts and bruises, suffered when he landed at the bottom, and a concussion, which happened before he went over the brink.

Woodward has vivid memories of his experience.

"One minute I was looking over the gorge, then I was floating in a cloud, I couldn't see anything. I could not discern up or down or where I was," he told us in an interview several years ago. "What I remember next is a severe throbbing in my head, likely from the concussion, which happened in the rapids or when I fell out of the boat...I had surrendered to the fact that I was going to die; then through the mist I saw the *Maid of the Mist*."

Why did he not perish like others who have gone over the falls?

"There were not a whole lot of places to land but by the grace of God, I landed in a pool of water. Had I even grazed one rock on the way down it would have shattered every bone in my body."

The 55-pound boy was pulled from the river by the crew of a *Maid of the Mist* tour boat, which luckily was cruising nearby with a load of tourists who were snapping photographs of the falls. Roger immediately asked about the whereabouts of his sister, and then requested a glass of water.

"I had probably drank half the Niagara River, but I was pretty thirsty," he said.

Back on shore, he was taken to the Greater Niagara General Hospital in Niagara Falls, Ontario, where he remained for three days for treatment of his injuries.

Deanne, with only a cut hand, was treated at a hospital in Niagara Falls, New York, where she learned of her brother's fate. The body of Honeycutt, who also went over the falls, was found in the river four days later. He was not wearing a life jacket.

When the world learned that Woodward had become the first person to go over the falls unprotected, the media descended on the boy and his family. Newspapers took his picture. Movie producers wanted his story.

"The story became famous," he recalled. "It was a time when the daredevil thing and going over the falls was pretty amazing and here you had two kids from a blue collar family who ended up in a horrific accident and a man was killed...the fact that we lived when many others had died going over the falls was quite amazing."

In 1962, the Woodward family moved to Florida, in part to escape the prying eyes of the media. The parents never talked about the incident with Roger and Deanne. In Florida, Roger met and married his high school sweetheart, Susan. After college he joined the Navy and later worked for a business and office products company in Atlanta for 13 years before a career change took the family to Michigan where he worked in the telecom industry for 17 years.

In 1996, the Woodwards and their three sons moved to Huntsville, Alabama, a city of 350,000 people 90 minutes southwest of Atlanta where Roger was working in real estate. In 2006, Deanne was living in Lakeland, Florida.

Roger Woodward has returned to Niagara Falls, Ontario several times since the accident.

On the 25th anniversary in 1985 he and all of those involved in the mishap, including Deanne, were given a key to the city and a portrait of the falls.

Five years later, he spoke to the congregation at Glengate Alliance Church in Niagara Falls, Ontario. The audience was silent as Woodward, 37-years-old at the time, told how Honeycutt's boat was caught in the fast flowing current and dragged toward the edge of the falls.

In 1994 Woodward and Deanne returned to the city to retell their story on a half-hour Canadian television special. Joining Roger and his sister were the two men, in their eighties at the time, who rescued Deanne before she went over the falls.

## Colourful Fact!

The incident at the Horseshoe Falls was not Roger Woodward's only brush with death. In his junior year of high school in 1970, a tractor-trailer ran a red light and broadsided his motorcycle. He landed on a set of railroad tracks, escaping with only a broken finger on his left hand. In the fall of 1994, while on a nighttime boat trip across Lake Huron with his 9-year-old son, Jonathan, the pair became disoriented in a fog bank. Their boat was narrowly missed by a freighter. The boating incident "was the single most frightening experience since Niagara Falls," said Woodward.

# REST IN PEACE – BUT WHERE?

Not all the subjects lend themselves to an easy interview, and since we don't have psychic powers we had no way of reaching the many famous Canadians who have died. But we were curious as to where their last resting place is, and we thought you would be too.

**Pierre Berton**, who died in 2004, was one of Canada's best known and beloved writers. In addition to his many books on Canada, Berton was also a one time managing editor of *Maclean's* magazine, a TV host, and a regular panellist on CBC's *Front Page Challenge*. Berton was cremated and his ashes scattered in Kleinburg, Ontario, where he had lived for many years.

**Charles Best**, the co-discoverer of insulin was born in West Pembroke, Maine, of Canadian parents. While studying medicine at the University of Toronto, he came to meet and become the assistant to **Sir Frederick Banting** in 1921, who was working on ways to extract insulin. Their work in finding a treatment for diabetes was possibly the most famous Canadian scientific discovery in this country's history. Banting shared half of the credit and monies from his Nobel Prize in physiology and medicine with Best, who died in 1978. He's buried, as is Banting, in Mount Pleasant Cemetery in Toronto.

Best known for the title roles in television's *Perry Mason* and *Ironside*, **Raymond Burr**, a British Columbia native, also acted in more than 80 movies. A long-time Hollywood icon, Burr died in 1993 and is buried in Fraserview Cemetery, New Westminster, British Columbia.

Known as the father of Medicare and most recently chosen the greatest Canadian, **Tommy Douglas** died in 1986. Originally from Scotland, Douglas came to Canada in 1910 and settled with his family in Saskatchewan. He helped found the Co-operative Commonwealth Federation (CCF), which later evolved into the NDP. Douglas is buried in Beechwood Cemetery in Ottawa.

**Glenn Gould**, whose piano playing brilliance brought him acclaim from around the world, was born in 1932. He made his professional debut just 14 years later and went on to delight audiences in the United States, Europe, and the U.S.S.R. He left performing to focus on studio recordings. He died in 1982 and is buried in Mount Pleasant Cemetery in Toronto.

**Tim Horton** is probably better known today for the doughnut chain that bears his name than for his prowess as a stellar NHL defenceman from 1950 to 1974 when he died in a car crash. But the launch of his famous doughnut business is perhaps his greatest legacy. Horton is buried in York Cemetery in Toronto.

His 1957 hit "Swinging Shepherd Blues" brought jazz musician **Moe Koffman** his greatest fame, but he was a fixture in jazz circles for decades recording a range of styles. Koffman died in 2001 and is buried in Pardes Shalom Cemetery in Richmond Hill, Ontario.

Considered one of the greatest Canadian novelists of all time, **Margaret Laurence** was born in Neepawa, Manitoba in 1926. She studied English in Winnipeg and went on to pen several books that made her reputation including *The Stone Angel* and *The Diviners*. She died in 1987 and is buried in Riverside Cemetery in her home town of Neepawa.

**Marshall McLuhan**, influential thinker, professor, and philosopher gained acclaim in the 1960s with his "the medium is the message" tome. Born in 1911, this influential figure wrote several books and received several awards for his work. He died in 1980 and is buried in Holy Cross Catholic Cemetery in Thornhill, Ontario.

**Lester B. Pearson** gained fame not only as prime minister of Canada from 1963 to 1967 but also received the 1957 Nobel Peace Prize for helping to resolve the Suez Crisis. He died in 1972 and is buried in McClaren Cemetery in Wakefield, Quebec.

**Mary Pickford**, silent film star and "America's Sweetheart," was born Gladys Smith in 1892 in Toronto. Pickford started acting as a child and began her film career in 1909. She became the best known and well-loved star of the silent era, but also made sound films, winning an Academy Award as Best Actress in 1929. She was also a founding member of United Artists, along with her then-husband Douglas Fairbanks. She died in 1979 and is buried in Forest Lawn Memorial Park in Glendale, California.

The man who inspired the formation of the Group of Seven is still revered today for his landscape paintings. **Tom Thomson** is arguably one of Canada's most famous and revered artists. He drowned while canoeing in northern Ontario in 1917, a death still regarded as suspicious by many. Thomson is buried in Leith United Church Cemetery in Leith, Ontario.

**Johnny Wayne and Frank Shuster** were long Canada's most beloved television comedians. The duo performed together for some 50 years, most notably on their

Photo courtesy of National Archives of Canada PA-125406.

Mystery surrounds the death of Tom Thomson. He died while on a canoe trip in Algonquin Park.

many CBC specials and in dozens of appearances on *The Ed Sullivan Show*. Wayne died in 1990 while Shuster passed on in 2002. Both are buried in Holy Blossom Cemetery in Toronto.

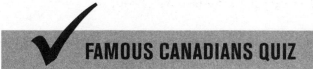

## FAMOUS CANADIANS QUIZ

Test your knowledge of some exceptional Canucks.

1. Name the Ottawa photographer who gained worldwide fame with his portraits of such well-known figures as Winston Churchill, Ernest Hemingway, and Albert Einstein.

2. Of these three explorers, who first reached what is now Canada – Samuel de Champlain, John Cabot, or Jacques Cartier?

3. True or false? A Canadian invented the Wonderbra in 1964.

4. What was Terry Fox's run across Canada in 1980 better known as?

5. What is Winnie Roach Leuszler's claim to fame?

    a) first Canadian woman pilot
    b) first Canadian world champion in her sport
    c) first Canadian woman to swim the English Channel
    d) first Canadian woman to scale Mount Everest

6. For what did Thomas Wilby and F.V. Haney gained fame in 1912?

    a) first Canadians to appear on radio
    b) first to drive across Canada
    c) first to fly in a helicopter
    d) first two members of Parliament to receive a government pension

7. In May 1877, this great Sioux chief crossed into Canada with hundreds of his people and thousands of horses seeking a safe haven from the Americans after the Battle of the Little Bighorn. Name him.

8. What was Marshall McLuhan's first name?

    a) Joseph
    b) Herbert
    c) Marshall
    d) Peter

9. About 125 libraries were built in Canada from 1901 to 1923 because of grants from a wealthy American. Who was it?

    a) Henry Ford
    b) Andrew Carnegie
    c) J. P. Morgan
    d) John Rockefeller

10. True or false? Canadian cartoonist Lynn Johnston, known for her strip *For Better or Worse*, began her career illustrating medical journals.

➦ **Answers on page 347**

# CHAPTER 7
# Eureka! Canadian Contributions to Science and Medicine

 ## TEN SIGNIFICANT SCIENTIFIC DISCOVERIES INVOLVING CANADIANS

1.  **Discovery of insulin** for the treatment of diabetes. Toronto, in 1922 by Frederick Banting and Charles Best: Banting shared his Nobel Prize, Medicine, winnings with Best in 1923. Banting was born in Alliston, Ontario, while Best was the son of a Canadian-born physician but was born in Maine.

2.  **Mapping the visual cortex of the brain**, enabling medical practitioners to determine where different vision processing tasks take place, such as lines, brightness, and colour: Work done at Harvard University by David Hubel of Montreal in the 1960s and 1970s. Hubel shared the Nobel Prize, Medicine, in 1981 with Torsten Wiesel, who was Swedish.

3.  **Development of site-based mutagenesis**, a new way of creating mutations in living organisms to produce improved plants and animals: The discovery was made in the early 1980s in Vancouver by Michael Smith, who moved to Canada from England in 1956. Smith won the Nobel Prize, Chemistry, in 1993.

4.  **Characterization of free radicals**, which are crucial to understanding the mechanism in countless chemical reactions: The discovery was made in Ottawa in 1959 by Gerhard Herzberg, who came to Canada in 1935 from Hamburg, Germany. He won the Nobel Prize, Chemistry, in 1971.

5.  **Invention of CCD chip** for camcorders and telescopes, which takes light and converts it into digital data that can be manipulated by computers and electronics to form images in camcorders and TV cameras: Willard Boyle of Amherst, Nova Scotia, was co-inventor of the chip in 1969 at Bell Laboratories in New Jersey.

6. **Development of computerized weather forecasting systems** now used worldwide: The theories were developed in Montreal and Boulder, Colorado, between the 1970s and 1990s by Roger Daley, who was born in London, England, but grew up in West Vancouver.

7. **Development of Ricker curve** used worldwide to determine sustainable fisheries catches: The theories were developed at the Fisheries Research Board of Canada in Ottawa and Nanaimo in the 1950s and 1960s by William Ricker, a native of Waterdown, Ontario.

8. **Theory of plate tectonics**, the notion that the Earth's crust is made up of a series of floating plates: Developed during the 1970s in Toronto by Ottawa native John Tuzo Wilson.

9. **Discovery of the t-cell receptor**, a key to the understanding of the human immune system: Discovered in 1983 in Toronto by Tak Wah Mak, who came to Canada from China in the early 1970s.

10. **Ellucidation of the geometry of higher dimensions**, such as the fourth dimension, which can be very useful to comprehend cosmological concepts such as space-time and computer networks: Developed by H.S.M. Coxeter, who came to Toronto in 1937 from London, England.

*List prepared by Barry Shell, Research Communications Manager, Simon Fraser University, and author of* Sensational Scientists.

# BLAST OFF: 12 NOTEWORTHY CANADIAN EVENTS IN SPACE

1. **September 29, 1962:** Canada launches the Alouette I satellite to study the ionosphere. Although Alouette had to be sent into space from California, it was still the first satellite built entirely by a country other than the United States or the U.S.S.R.

2. **July 20, 1969:** U.S. spacecraft Apollo 11 lands on the moon with Canadian-built landing gear.

3. **November 9, 1972:** Launch of Anik A-1, the first of a series of Canadian satellites. Canada becomes the first country with a domestic communications satellite system in geostationary orbit (moving so as to remain above the same point on the Earth's surface).

4. **November 13, 1981:** Launch of Canadarm aboard Space Shuttle *Columbia*. This remote manipulator system was mounted on the shuttle and successfully moved payloads in and out of the shuttle bay.

5. **October 5, 1984:** Marc Garneau becomes the first Canadian in space aboard Space Shuttle *Challenger*.

6. **September 29, 1988:** Canada signs an intergovernmental agreement/memorandum of understanding to participate in the international space station project.

7. **March 1, 1989:** Creation of the Canadian Space Agency to promote the peaceful use and development of space and ensure space science and technology provide social and economic benefits to Canada.

8. **September 12, 1991:** Canada's Wind Imaging Interferometer (WINDII) is launched aboard NASA's Upper Atmospheric Research Satellite (UARS) to provide new measurements of the physical and chemical processes taking place at altitudes 10 to 300 kilometres above the Earth's surface.

9. **January 22, 1992:** Roberta Bondar becomes the second Canadian and first Canadian woman in space aboard Space Shuttle *Discovery*.

10. **November 4, 1995:** RADARSAT is launched. It is Canada's first Earth observation satellite and first non-communications satellite since 1971. It can provide images of the Earth's surface day and night, in any climate condition, to clients all over the world.

11. **April 19, 2001:** First space walk by a Canadian: Astronaut Chris Hadfield performed an Extravehicular Activity (EVA) and was the lead spacewalker who helped to install Canadarm2 on the International Space Station. The new arm acted like a construction crane and helped build and later maintain the station.

**Science BITE!**

Canadians wanting to get up close and personal with the Canadarms that have travelled into space are out of luck but full-size inoperable models of the Canadarm are on display at the Canada Science and Technology Museum in Ottawa and the Ontario Science Centre in Toronto.

**12. Mid-March, 2008:** Dextre is sent into space: The sophisticated two-armed robot is part of Canada's contribution to the International Space Station. Canadarm2, a moveable work platform called the mobile base, and Dextre form the Mobile Servicing System. These three robotic elements can work together or independently. The sophisticated, two-armed robot Dextre is designed to perform exterior construction, and service tasks on the International Space Station. It is part of the Mobile Servicing System contributed by Canada. On this mission, Dextre will be assembled in orbit and the crew will put it through a series of tests. Dextre is to carry out a lot of the fine manipulation work for maintenance outside the space station, reducing the number of spacewalks required.

*Numbers one to 10 prepared by Mac Evans, former president, Canadian Space Agency.*

 # MAJOR MEDICAL BREAKTHROUGHS BY CANADIAN PHYSICIANS

1. **Dr. Roberta Bondar:** Conducted back pain experiments aboard the 1992 Space Shuttle *Discovery* to determine how the body changes in space.

2. **Dr. Bruce Chown and Dr. Jack Bowman:** Developed methods for diagnosis, treatment, and prevention of RH disease in pregnant women. (RH disease occurs during pregnancy when there is an incompatibility between the blood types of the mother and baby.)

3. **Dr. Jean Dussault:** Discovered a blood test to identify newborns with thyroid deficiency and subsequently prevent severe mental retardation in these infants.

4. **Dr. Oleh Homykiewicz and Dr. Andre Barbeau:** Discovered the use of levodopa, a synthetic compound, for the treatment of Parkinson's disease.

5. **Dr. Robert Korneluk:** In collaboration with an international team of scientists, located the defective gene responsible for myotonic dystrophy, a rare, slowly progressive hereditary disease involving the muscles.

**Science BITE!**

Winnipeg native John Hopps invented the heart pacemaker in a National Research Council laboratory in 1950 to keep the weak of heart alive and kicking.

6. **Dr. Lap-Chee Tsui:** Identified the defective gene responsible for cystic fibrosis.

7. **Dr. Claude De Montigny:** Initiated the use of Librium in treatment of depression.

8. **Dr. William Mustard:** Devised an operation to correct the "blue baby" heart defect.

9. **Dr. Robert Noble:** Discovered an effective anti-cancer drug, vinblastine sulphate, which helps control the growth of cancers.

## Science BITE!

Daniel David Palmer of Port Perry, Ontario, is considered to be the world's first chiropractor. While working in Iowa in 1865, Palmer supposedly cured a man of hearing loss by straightening his spine. He began to study how manipulation of the spine solves health problems and later taught his techniques to others.

10. **Dr. Hans Selye:** A world-famous pioneer and popularizer of research on biological stress in humans, he theorized that stress plays some role in the development of every disease. He founded the International Institute of Stress in 1977, through which he increased the understanding of stress.

11. **Dr. Arthur Vineberg:** A cardiovascular surgeon who developed a surgical procedure for the relief of angina.

12. **Dr. Ronald Worton:** Identified the defective gene responsible for Duchenne muscular dystrophy.

## Science BITE!

In 1987, the first aortic valve replacement in the world was performed using the Toronto Heart Valve, which is now used worldwide.

 Q AND A

*Q. Where were the first dinosaur remains found in Canada? How old are they and where are they now?*

**A.** Many Canadians think the only dinosaur bones unearthed in Canada were found in Alberta and Saskatchewan but that's not the case.

Richard Day, spokesman for the Canadian Museum of Nature in Ottawa, says the oldest dinosaur remains in Canada are actually from sediments along the Bay of Fundy in Nova Scotia's Minas Basin and are approximately 200 million years old. Evidence of dinosaurs, both foot imprints and isolated bones between 65 and 150 million years old, has also been found in British Columbia; in the northern Yukon Territory; the McKenzie Mountains of the Northwest Territories, and on Bylot Island in the Arctic.

But let's not take any credit away from Saskatchewan and Alberta: Day says the dinosaur faunas in the two provinces are some of the richest in the world for the Upper Cretaceous period (65 to 75 million years ago), especially in the badlands along the Red Deer River at Dinosaur Provincial Park in Alberta.

The first evidence of dinosaur bones in Canada was found in southern Saskatchewan, when isolated bones of duck-billed dinosaurs, known as hadrosaurs, were discovered in 1874 by Geological Survey of Canada geologist George M. Dawson in the Frenchman Formation exposures near Wood Mountain (in southern Saskatchewan.) These bones are believed to be about 65 million years old. Later in the same year, Dawson and his geological mapping party found more evidence, on the Milk River in Alberta, of the duck-billed dinos which are about 75 million years old.

Other dinosaur remains, generally pieces of leg bones and the vertebral column of hadrosaurs, were found between 1874 and 1884 when J.B. Tyrrell — namesake of the Royal Tyrrell Museum in Drumheller, Alberta — was mapping the area around the Red Deer River near Drumheller for its geological resource potential. Tyrrell found the first dinosaur skull in Canada, from a small tyrannosaurid that was subsequently named Albertosaurus. This 70-million-year-old specimen, discovered at Kneehill Creek, was the first example of the genus found anywhere in the world and is held in the Canadian Museum of Nature collection. It is not on display.

The first fairly complete dinosaur specimen mounted in a Canadian museum was that of a 70-million-year-old hadrosaurian dinosaur, Edmontosaurus, which was collected in 1912 by the first professional dinosaur hunters in Canada, Charles Hazelius Sternberg and his three sons, Charles M., Levi, and George, of Kansas. The Edmontosaurus has been on display since 1913 at the Canadian Museum of Nature.

Other dinosaurs can be seen at the Royal Tyrrell Museum, which, with thirty-five complete skeletons on display, has the largest number assembled under one roof in the world. The Royal Ontario Museum in Toronto and the Royal Saskatchewan Museum in Regina also exhibit dinosaur skeletons.

# CHAPTER 8
# Flora and Fauna

Canada is a country known for it's bounty of natural wonders. Here are some facts about the forests and wildlife that is such an integral part of our identity. From our rolling forests to the creatures that have become synonymous with Canada — the loon, the beaver, and the mighty moose.

- After Russia, Canada has the largest continuous forested area on Earth. Covering nearly half the nation's land mass and constituting 10 percent of the globe's forest cover, Canada's forests shelter 200,000 plant and animal species and provide one of every 17 Canadian jobs.

Forests continue to be an important part of Canada's economy.

- The Douglas fir takes its name from David Douglas, a Scotsman who came to Canada in the early 1800s and introduced some 250 plants to Europe from North America, more than any other person.

### Flora BITE!

On average, forest fires in Canada destroy twice the number of trees harvested by the country's forest industry.

- The arbutus, Canada's only evergreen hardwood, is found only on the west coast. Its distinctive features are red bark and glossy green, oval-shaped leaves.

- The Chapleau Game Preserve and Wildlife Sanctuary in Northern Ontario, which encompasses about 800,000 hectares (about 1.9 million acres), is the largest game preserve in the world. Creatures seen there include wolves, various birds of prey, otters, mink, fox, moose, and black bears.

# 🍁 CANUCK CRITTERS

- In 1910, when beavers were beginning to overrun Ontario's Algonquin Park, live trapping of these and other species became a lucrative project to meet the demand for zoo animals from all over North America.

- One of the claims to fame of Exeter, Ontario, is that it is home to a rare type of white squirrel. Though they are a genetic anomaly, these squirrels are not albinos.

- The beaver attained official status as an emblem of Canada when an "act to provide for the recognition of the beaver (*castor canadensis*) as a symbol of the sovereignty of Canada" received royal assent on March 24, 1975.

- There are no rats in Alberta thanks to a program created in the mid-1950s by the Alberta Department of Agriculture. The program, using traps and poison, was concentrated along the Saskatchewan border to keep rats from entering the province.

- Before the cardinal was named after its red-robed counterparts in the Roman Catholic Church, this popular backyard bird was called simply the "redbird" by early settlers to North America. Though cardinals are a common sight in Canadian backyards, the colourful birds are not native to this country. They moved here from the U.S. in the early 1900s.

- The bison, or North American buffalo, is the largest native land animal in Canada. A mature male can be 3.8 metres long, 1.8 metres tall at the shoulder, and weigh up to 720 kilograms.

Photo by Ella Wright.

Canada's largest native land mammal.

- Atlantic salmon are found in about three hundred rivers in Labrador, Quebec, and the Maritimes. They were also commonly found in Lake Ontario until the late 19th century.

- There are approximately 1,000 species of bees in Canada; some can even be found north of the Arctic Circle. Among the species that live here are bumblebees, honeybees, cuckoo, sweat, and mining bees.

- In 1950, there were one million Canada geese in North America. Today, the Canadian Wildlife service estimates there are five million, crediting the increased numbers to restrictions on hunting and the establishment of new colonies.

- Atlantic sturgeon, the largest fish in the St. Lawrence River, have been known to live for up to 60 years, reach 4.5 metres in length, and weigh up to 360 kilograms.

Canada geese thrive in the country that gave them their name.

## 🍁 ONLY IN CANADA, YOU SAY? FIVE FOUR-LEGGED FRIENDS UNIQUE TO THIS COUNTRY

- **The Tahltan Bear Dog:** This small dog with white and black patches and a distinctive tail that ends in a wide brush is extinct in this country. It was kept by the Tahltan Indians of northwestern British Columbia for use mainly as hunters of bear and lynx and was once recorded by the *Guinness Book of Records* as the world's rarest breed.

- **Nova Scotia Duck Tolling Retriever:** Foxlike in colour and intermediate in size, the tolling retriever's roots trace back to Yarmouth County, Nova Scotia, where the breed was developed in the late 19th century. Several breeds and crosses were key to its evolution, including the Irish setter, which gave the breed its colour, and the yellow farm collie, the source of its bushy tail. Among the Toller's most unique attributes is its ability to mimic the behaviour of a fox to draw waterfowl within the firing range of hunters.

The duck tolling retriever.

- **Canadian Eskimo Dog:** Used mainly as a sled and backpack dog, this is the only breed of dog associated with the Aboriginal peoples of the Arctic. The history of this powerfully built canine dates back between 1,100 and 2,000 years when it was taken to the North American Arctic by the Thule Eskimos and gradually spread to Greenland.

The Canadian Eskimo Dog is intermediate in speed and strength and in all seasons is a hunting companion with a nose keen enough to locate seal breathing holes in the ice and brave enough to hold large game at bay until the hunter comes in for the kill.

- **Newfoundland:** According to Newfoundland folklore, the breed's progenitor was the Tibetan Mastiff, which had migrated across the Canadian north to Newfoundland and into Viking settlements before being crossed with the Viking bear dog in AD1001. Known as the "gentle giant" of Canadian breeds, the heavy, long-coated dogs are excellent swimmers and are renowned as family companions and guardians with strong life-saving instincts.

- **Labrador Retriever:** The Labrador, whose ancestors were discovered in Newfoundland and Labrador by 18th-century colonists, is thought to have descended from dogs abandoned in the region by European fishermen. In the early 1800s, specimens were taken to Britain where they were crossed with other retrievers to become the most valued game dog in the country. Skilful hunters known for their intelligence and gentle, affectionate natures, the Labrador is one of the best gundogs in existence and is used extensively as a "seeing eye" dog. Most are black but some are yellow, chocolate, and cream.

# 🍁 MORE CANADIAN CREATURES

- The loon, featured on Canadian stamps and the dollar coin, is related to the penguin. They have large webbed feet that allow them to swim at great speeds but on land, loons are awkward and can barely stand upright.

- The moose is not native to Newfoundland but was introduced there on two different occasions. In 1878, a bull and a cow were brought from Nova Scotia and released at Gander Bay and in 1904 two bulls and two cows from New Brunswick were released near Howley. Today there are approximately 120,000 moose on the island of Newfoundland.

- Jumbo, the famous circus elephant of the 19th century, was killed in St. Thomas, Ontario, after colliding with a locomotive. Jumbo was being led along the tracks on September 15, 1885, when an unscheduled train appeared out of the fog and collided with him. One hundred years after his death, a life-size statue of the elephant was erected in St. Thomas.

- Since the 1980s, a wide array of unusual creatures has been found on Canadian farms, including elks, emus, ostriches, wild boars, and llamas. In fact, farmers

Photo by Mark Kearney.

Jumbo's statue greets visitors in St. Thomas, Ontario, where the famous elephant was killed.

across Canada are tending more than 100 species of exotic creatures, mainly because of changes in consumer preferences.

- Slippery, a famous sea lion from London, Ontario, made international headlines in 1958 by escaping from the city's Storybook Gardens and swimming down the Thames River. He was later captured in Lake Erie near Sandusky, Ohio, and brought home. His exploits were later turned into a documentary and stage play.

- The waters of the Pacific Ocean off the coast of British Columbia are home to the world's largest species of octopus, octopus dofleini. This eight-armed creature can grow up to nine metres wide and weigh more than 100 kilograms.

- The peregrine falcon, which makes its home in Canada's Yukon Territory, is among the fastest creatures on Earth, capable of flying 200 kilometres per hour.

- Nova Scotia was the first province to choose an official bird. It is the osprey, a fish-eating species with long, sharp talons. There are some 250 active osprey nests in the province.

- Canada fed 3.5 million cattle in 2007. Producing 3.5 billion pounds of beef in 2007, the cattle industry remains the largest single source of farm receipts in Canada.

# CHAPTER 9
# Geographically Speaking

## 🍁 FROM SEA TO SEA (TO SEA)

- Canada has a land mass of 9,970,610 square kilometres, making it the second-largest country in the world, after Russia. From east to west, Canada encompasses six time zones. Should Quebec ever separate, we'd drop to number five because China, the United States, and Brazil would leap over us.

- Queen Victoria Park in Niagara Falls, Ontario, was created in 1887, becoming Canada's first provincial park. It was designed to save the area from hucksters and promoters.

- Pingos are ice-cored hills unique to permafrost areas in Canada's north. They form when underground ice expands and pushes upward on the ground to form a mound as high as 50 metres and up to 300 metres in diameter. With some 1,400 pingos, the Tuktoyaktuk Peninsula in the Northwest Territories has the world's largest concentration of the hills. Before the arrival of freezers the Inuit used them to preserve food.

- The Dempster Highway is the only Canadian highway that crosses

**Geo BITE!**

From sea to sea … to sea? Canada's motto, "From sea to sea," is geographically inaccurate. In addition to its coastlines on the Atlantic and Pacific, Canada has a third sea coast on the Arctic Ocean, giving it the longest coastline of any country.

**Geo BITE!**

Sandbanks Provincial Park on Lake Ontario has the world's largest freshwater sand bar and dune system.

**Geo BITE!**

Canada occupies half of North America and nearly 7 percent of the total surface of the Earth.

Photo courtesy of RWED, GNWT.

Pingos: ice-cored hills in Canada's north.

the Arctic Circle. It runs for 741 kilometres just east of Dawson to Inuvik, but the most northerly leg is only accessible in winter when the Mackenzie River is frozen. Because it's a gravel road with few services, travellers need to carry spare tires, extra fuel, and other supplies.

• The constellations Ursa Major and Ursa Minor (Latin for "great bear" and "little bear") permanently dominate the firmament of Canada's Far North. Because of their constant presence, the region that lies within the boreal polar circle is called the Arctic, from *arktos*, the Greek word for "bear."

• Permafrost, which is ground that remains at or below 0° C continuously for at least two years, underlies 40 to 45 percent of Canada and is beneath about 25 percent of the Earth's surface. It may be composed of cold, dry earth; cold, wet earth; ice-cemented rock; or frozen subsurface and surface water.

**They Said It!**

"Very little is known of the Canadian country since it is rarely visited by anyone but the Queen and illiterate sport fishermen."
– American humourist P.J. O'Rourke

• Due to erosion, the falls at Niagara are about 11 kilometres from their place of origin at the present-day community of Queenston. The falls erode the soft shale and limestone they spill over by 1.2 metres every year.

• Prince Edward Island began as three islands. When glaciers of the last ice age melted, the water level in the Atlantic Ocean rose and only one island remained, likely about 3,000 years ago.

• Toronto Island is actually an archipelago of 15 islands in Lake Ontario. The eight largest islands are Centre, Muggs, Donut (the one with the hole in the middle), Forestry, Olympic, South, Snake, and Algonquin.

Photo by Randy Ray.

The Falls lose ground every year.

- Saskatchewan has more than one-third of all the farmland in Canada, with more than a quarter-million square kilometres. With only 335 square kilometres, Newfoundland, also known as The Rock, has the least amount of farmland of any province, including Prince Edward Island. In PEI, about 5,660 square kilometres of land are used for farming.

- The terrain stretching from northern Africa to Scandinavia bears a striking resemblance to the Atlantic shores of the Maritimes and Newfoundland because they were once part of the same land mass. The continents split apart 200 million years ago.

**Geo BITE!**

When it comes to water volume, Canada's side of Niagara Falls is the clear winner. The Horseshoe Falls has a flow of 155 million litres per minute, compared to 14 million litres per minute on the American side.

 Canada's 10 Largest Islands

| 1. | Baffin Island | 507,451 sq. km |
|---|---|---|
| 2. | Victoria Island | 217,291 |

| 3. | Ellesmere Island | 196,236 |
|---|---|---|
| 4. | Newfoundland Island | 108,860 |
| 5. | Banks Island | 70,028 |
| 6. | Devon Island | 55,247 |
| 7. | Axel Heiberg Island | 43,178 |
| 8. | Melville Island | 42,149 |
| 9. | Southampton Island | 41,214 |
| 10. | Prince of Wales Island | 33,339 |

 ## Canada's 10 Highest Mountains

| 1. | Mount Logan | 5,959 metres |
|---|---|---|
| 2. | Mount St. Elias | 5,489 |
| 3. | Mount Lucania | 5,226 |
| 4. | King Peak | 5,173 |
| 5. | Mount Steele | 5,067 |
| 6. | Mount Wood | 4,838 |
| 7. | Mount Vancouver | 4,785 |
| 8. | Mount Fairweather | 4,663 |
| 9. | Mount Macaulay | 4,663 |
| 10. | Mount Slaggard | 4,663 |

## Canada's 10 Largest Lakes
(in area and completely in Canada)

| 1. | Great Bear Lake | 31,328 square kilometres* |
|---|---|---|
| 2. | Great Slave Lake | 28,568 |
| 3. | Lake Winnipeg | 24,400 |
| 4. | Athabasca Lake | 7,935 |
| 5. | Reindeer Lake | 6,650 |
| 6. | Lake Nettilling | 5,542 |
| 7. | Lake Winnipegosis | 5,370 |
| 8. | Lake Nipigon | 4,848 |
| 9. | Lake Manitoba | 4,630 |
| 10. | Dubawnt | 3,833 |

* total lake area, including islands

## ON THE ROAD AGAIN: 10 MOST SCENIC DRIVES

(in no particular order)

1. **British Columbia via the Sunshine Coast and Inside Passage to Prince Rupert:** From Horseshoe Bay, Vancouver, take the ferry to Langdale, then drive the spectacular "Sunshine Coast" to Powell River. Cross by ferry to Comox on Vancouver Island, and then continue northward to Port Hardy. Ride the ferry from Port Hardy up the Inside Passage to Prince Rupert for more spectacular scenery.

**Geo BITE!**

Described as Canada's Loch Ness Monster, Ogopogo is a legendary creature of the deep that is said to live in Okanagan Lake in British Columbia. Sightings have been reported since the 1930s of a prehistoric creature with a small head and a long neck. It was first captured on film in 1968 in a movie that showed serpent-like movements across the surface of the lake. Fact or fiction? You decide.

2. **Newfoundland's Viking Trail and Labrador coast:** Make sure to take in Gros Morne National Park, as well as historic Viking and Basque settlements.

3. **The Icefields Parkway between Banff and Jasper:** Drive in either direction through Banff and Jasper national parks for some truly majestic mountain scenery. Stop off at the Athabasca Glacier.

**They Said It!**

"I've never been any place before where they have four seasons in one day. I'm wearing out my body changing clothes."

*– comedian Bob Hope during a spring visit to Toronto in the 1960s*

4. **Yukon Gold Seekers' Trail:** Starting in Skagway, Alaska, trace the prospectors' trail over the Chilkoot Pass, through Whitehorse and down the Yukon River to Dawson City. Then, for good measure, loop through a small slice of Alaska and skirt magnificent Kluane National Park before returning to Whitehorse.

5. **Cape Breton's Cabot Trail:** Enjoy some of Nova Scotia's finest scenery.

6. **Shore of Lake Ontario:** The lakeshore route from the Quebec border to Toronto's eastern suburbs via the Thousand Islands and Kingston.

7. **Toronto to Ottawa via Algonquin Park:** Drive through Ontario's "Cottage Country" and Algonquin Park to the Ottawa River and on to Canada's capital city.

8. **The Fundy Coast:** From Amherst, Nova Scotia, to New Brunswick's Fundy National Park and on to Saint John and St. Andrews.

9. **PEI's Blue Heron Drive:** Take the famed P.E.I. National Park as well as the south shore.

10. **Nova Scotia's south shore and Annapolis Valley:** From Halifax around the Nova Scotia peninsula's south shore.

 Q AND A

### Q. Has Niagara Falls ever run dry?

**A.** To many it's unthinkable, but yes, it has happened on several occasions at the hands of Mother Nature and once when man intervened.

The first and only time both the American Falls and the Horseshoe Falls on the Canadian side fell silent was on the night of March 29, 1848, when an ice jam formed on Lake Erie near Buffalo, blocking the water that flows along the Niagara River and over the falls, says Dave Phillips of Environment Canada.

By the next morning a throng of up to 5,000 sightseers had converged on the area to find the American Falls had slowed to a dribble and the thundering Canadian falls were stilled, Phillips wrote in a book entitled *The Day Niagara Falls Ran Dry, Canadian Weather Facts and Trivia*. Some daredevils explored cavities at the bottom of the dry river where they picked up bayonets, muskets, swords, gun barrels, tomahawks, and other relics of the War of 1812. Others crossed the river above and below the falls on foot, horseback or by horse and buggy — a historic opportunity, to be sure.

But the waterless river course wasn't seen as an opportunity by everyone: Superstitious people became fearful and anxious and many went to special church services. The falls wouldn't stay silent for long, though. On the night of March 31 — 30 hours after Mother Nature turned off the tap — balmy weather and shifting winds dislodged the ice and a sudden wall of water surged down the river bed and over the falls, restoring the ever-present Niagara spray and rumble and boom of the falls.

The American falls were also shut off on six other recorded occasions including in 1909, 1936, and 1947, each time when they froze over completely. And in 1969 the American side was silent again — this time at the hands of humans. For seven months the U.S. falls were turned off when the United States Army Corps of Engineers diverted the river to permit repairs to the eroding face of the American Falls.

According to Phillips, Canada's Horseshoe Falls aren't likely to be blocked by ice again. Since 1964 a boom has been positioned at the head of the Niagara River every winter to prevent the formation of ice blockages and to safeguard hydroelectric installations.

### Q. How long does it take for water to pass through the Great Lakes to the Atlantic Ocean?

**A.** If a drop of water could talk, what a story it would tell.

On average, a drop of water which finds its way into Lake Superior from runoff or rainfall takes more than two centuries to travel through the Great Lakes system and along the St. Lawrence River to the ocean, says Environment Canada's Ontario region office in Burlington, Ontario. To be precise, water which entered Superior in 1794 — the year the reign of terror came to an end in France following the French revolution — didn't make it to the Atlantic until 1998.

The travelling time is based on retention times, or how long, on average, it takes for each of the lakes to replace its water with new water. To get a grip on this theory, think of each of the lakes as a 10-gallon bathtub with the drain slightly open and the tap running slowly. If one gallon of water flows in and another out every minute, after 10 minutes you will have emptied 10 gallons and added 10 new gallons. One drop might come in through the tap and go out the drain in only a few seconds, while another drop might stay in the tub for an hour or more, but the average length of stay is 10 minutes.

In Lake Superior, the tap is rain and runoff and the drain is the St. Marys River, which flows into Lake Huron. After 173 years, much of the water in Superior has flowed out of the lake and been replaced with new water. In Lake Huron replacement averages 21 years; Lake Erie, 2.7 years; and Lake Ontario, 7.5 years. Add the numbers together and you will see that drops of water which fell into Lake Superior in 1794 worked their way to the Atlantic slightly more than 204 years later.

The time span is much less for lakes closer to the Atlantic. Water you were swimming in at the beaches of Grand Bend on Lake Huron in 1967, when Canadians were celebrating Canada's 100th birthday, arrived at the Atlantic in 1998, while water which poured into Lake Erie in 1988, when the Canada-U.S. Free Trade Agreement was signed, also made it to the ocean in 1998. If your son or daughter is seven and a half years old, water now streaming into the Atlantic was in Lake Ontario about the same time he or she was born.

It should be noted that all of the water in each of the Great Lakes is never completely replaced. For instance, 37 percent of the water that was in Lake Superior 173 years ago is still there, says Environment Canada.

## They Said It!

*"If some countries have too much history, we have too much geography"*
— former prime minister William Lyon Mackenzie King

 # CANADA'S WATERWAYS

- The Grand Banks have been called the "wheat fields" of Newfoundland. The shallow continental shelf extends 400 kilometres off the east coast, where the mixing of ocean currents has created one of the richest fishing grounds in the world. Once thought to contain a virtually inexhaustible supply of fish, the banks are now a vulnerable resource that must be wisely managed.

- There are about two million lakes in Canada, covering about 7.6 percent of the country's land mass. The main lakes, in order of the amount of surface area located in Canada, are Huron, Great Bear, Superior, Great Slave, Winnipeg, Erie, and Ontario. The largest lake situated entirely in Canada is Great Bear Lake, 31,326 square kilometres, located in the Northwest Territories.

- Most people know that the Mackenzie and St. Lawrence rivers are the two longest in Canada, but did you know that the third longest is the Nelson River in Manitoba, which is 2,575 kilometres long and flows into Hudson Bay? The Yukon River is actually longer, but only 1,149 kilometres are within Canada.

- The Canadian falls at Niagara are spectacular, but they are far from the highest in Canada. There are 12 other waterfalls in the country with higher vertical drops, led by Della Falls at Della Lake, British Columbia, at 440 metres and Takakkaw Falls at Daly Glacier, also in B.C., at 244 metres. Canada's Horseshoe Falls in Niagara sends water plummeting 57 metres.

## Geo BITE!

The largest lake within a lake in Canada is Lake Manitou, covering 106.42 square kilometres and found on Manitoulin Island in Lake Huron.

- Lake Superior is the deepest of the Great Lakes, with a maximum depth of 406 metres. The shallowest of the five lakes is Lake Erie, which is 64 metres deep. Lake Huron is 229 metres deep, Lake Ontario is 243 metres deep, and Lake Michigan is 282 metres deep.

- Hydrologically speaking, lakes Michigan and Huron are actually one lake, separated by the Straits of Mackinaw. The Mackinac Bridge, nicknamed the "Mighty Mac," spans the straits, connecting Michigan's upper and lower peninsulas.

**Geo BITE!**

Lake Superior is big enough to contain the other four Great Lakes plus three additional lakes the size of Lake Erie.

- The Great Lakes are the largest bodies of fresh water in the world. They are said to hold enough water to cover all the land in Canada to a depth of three metres and drain an area larger than Great Britain and France combined.

- Though you wouldn't know it to look at it today, in the late 1700s, Toronto's Don River had an excellent salmon fishery, which made the river a selling feature for properties in the area.

**Geo BITE!**

In 1632, French explorer Samuel de Champlain called Lake Ontario "Lake St. Louis"; Lake Huron, "Mer Douce"; and Lake Michigan, the "Grand Lac."

# THE NAME'S FAMILIAR: HOW THE PROVINCES AND TERRITORIES WERE NAMED

**Newfoundland:** Because John Cabot was considered to have found this "new isle," it was first called "Terra Nova" before the English "Newfoundland" became more popular.

**Prince Edward Island:** Its original British name was the Island of Saint John, but in 1799 it was changed to its present name to honour a son of King George III, who was stationed with the British army in Halifax at the time.

**Nova Scotia:** From the Latin for "New Scotland," it was officially named when King James I, a Scot, was on the throne of England.

The wide, sandy beaches of Prince Edward Island.

**New Brunswick:** It was named in 1784 after the German duchy of Brunswick-Lunenburg, which was also ruled at that time by King George III of England.

**Quebec:** First applied to the city only and then later to the province, it comes from an Algonquian word meaning "where the river narrows."

**Ontario:** Possibly derived from the Iroquois word *kanadario*, meaning sparkling or beautiful water. May also mean "beautiful lake" or "large body of water," given that the name was given to the Great Lake first and later to the land near it.

**Manitoba:** A word that means "where the spirit lives" in the languages of the province's Aboriginal people.

**Saskatchewan:** Derived from the Plains Indian word *kisiskatchewan*, which means "swiftly flowing river." Saskatchewan is also the name of the major river system in the province.

## Geo BITE!

According to Native legend, the Thirty Thousand Islands in Ontario's Georgian Bay were created when Kitchi-Kiwana, the last of a race of giants, fell with a mountain in his arms, which shattered into 30,000 pieces.

**Alberta:** Named after Princess Louise Caroline Alberta, fourth daughter of Queen Victoria.

**British Columbia:** Stems from the province's intense "Britishness" in its early years and originated with Queen Victoria. The name was officially proclaimed in 1858.

**Yukon:** From the Loucheux Native name *Yu-kun-tah* for the "great river" (Yukon River) that drains most of its area.

**Northwest Territories:** Describes the territory acquired in 1870 from the Hudson's Bay Company and Great Britain, Rupert's Land, and the North-Western Territory, which was located northwest of Central Canada.

**Nunavut:** Means "our land" in Inuktitut, the Inuit language. It officially became a territory on April 1, 1999.

# CHAPTER 10
# Great White North

 WACKY WEATHER FACTS

- Canada's most disastrous tornado struck Regina, Saskatchewan, on June 30, 1912, when the Regina "Cyclone" left at least 28 dead and hundreds injured.

- On October 15, 1954, Hurricane Hazel swept across Toronto, dumping 178 millimetres of rain, killing 83 people, and destroying entire streets in the west part of the city. Hazel remains Canada's worst inland storm.

- The highest humidex reading in Canada in recent history occurred in Carman, Manitoba, on July 25, 2007, when it hit 53.0°, surpassing the previous record of June 20, 1953, when it hit 52.1° C in Windsor, Ontario. Canada is the only country whose meteorologists use the humidex scale to reflect the combined heat of temperature and humidity.

- Though Hurricane Hazel is the best-known storm to hit Canada, others have been deadlier. A cyclone in August 1873 in the Maritimes destroyed 1,200 boats and 900 homes, while another that struck Newfoundland in September 1775 led to the drowning of several thousand British sailors.

- Landslides and snow avalanches have resulted in more than 600 deaths in Canada since 1850 and have caused billions of dollars of direct and indirect damage to Canada's economic infrastructure.

### Geo BITE!

In the summer, an average of one tornado every five days is reported in Canada, compared to five tornadoes every day in the United States.

### They Said It!

"I am told that the Inuit have some sixty words for snow … for different kinds of snow. That doesn't surprise me; they see a lot of it. I live considerably south of the treeline, but even I have 17 words for snow — none of them usable in public."

– Arthur Black, author and humourist

- The sunshine capital of Canada is Medicine Hat, Alberta, with the greatest number of hours of sunshine per year: 2,512.9 hours, based on an 82-city survey by Environment Canada weather expert David Phillips.

- The driest place in Canada is Whitehorse in the Yukon Territory, where annual precipitation is 267.40 millimetres per year.

- St. John's, Newfoundland, is the foggiest city in Canada with 119 days every year with fog. It is also the windiest city, with an average annual wind speed of 23.8 kilometres per hour.

- Quebec is the coldest province in Canada with an average annual temperature of -2.57° C. Nova Scotia is the warmest, at 6.20° C.

### They Said It!

"With the thermometer at thirty degrees below zero and the wind behind him, a man walking on Main Street, Winnipeg, knows which side of him is which."

– *Stephen B. Leacock, Canadian humourist*

The most expensive disaster in Canadian history.

- The most expensive natural disaster in Canada was the 1998 ice storm. For six days in January of that year, freezing rain coated Ontario, Quebec, and New Brunswick with up to 11 centimetres of ice. Trees and hydro wires fell and utility poles and transmission towers came down causing massive power outages, some for as long as a month. According to Environment Canada, the storm directly affected more people than any other previous weather event in Canadian history.

#  TEN MAJOR CANADIAN EARTHQUAKES

(in order of magnitude)

1. **1949:** Magnitude 8.1 on the Richter Scale. The epicentre was off the Queen Charlotte Islands in British Columbia. It was Canada's largest earthquake in the 20th century. The shaking was so severe on the islands that cows were knocked off their feet and people could not stand, but the value of the damage was not high because of the sparse population. The quake was felt over a wide area of western North America. There were no reported fatalities.

> **Weather BITE!**
>
> **Damage Caused by the 1998 Ice Storm**
>
> - 945 people injured
> - 28 people killed, most from hypothermia
> - 600,000 people had to leave their homes
> - 4 million people left without power, some for up to a month
> - Estimated cost of the storm was $5,410,184,000.00

2. **1970:** Magnitude 7.4. Offshore, south of the Queen Charlotte islands. The quake was widely felt but there was no damage reported.

3. **1933:** Magnitude 7.3. Baffin Bay. Largest earthquake known to have occurred north of the Arctic Circle.

4. **1946:** Magnitude 7.3. Central Vancouver Island. Canada's largest on-land earthquake in the 20th century. Extensive property damage along the east coast of Vancouver Island; 75 percent of the chimneys were knocked down in the closest communities of Courtenay, Cumberland, and Union Bay. One person was drowned and one died of a heart attack. The earthquake was felt from Oregon to Alaska and east to the Rocky Mountains.

5. **1929:** Magnitude 7.2. Atlantic Ocean, south of Newfoundland. Most serious loss of life in any recorded Canadian earthquake. Felt over a wide area of eastern North America, the earthquake caused a large underwater landslide which broke 12 trans-Atlantic telegraph cables and generated a tsunami (tidal wave). Twenty-seven people were drowned and much damage was caused by the five-metre-high wave along the Burin Peninsula. A two-storey house was swept out to sea in southern Newfoundland.

**They Said It!**

"I don't trust any country that looks around a continent and says, 'Hey, I'll take the frozen part.'"

*– Jon Stewart, TV star and satirist*

6. **1918:** Magnitude 7. Near the west coast of Vancouver Island. The earthquake occurred just after midnight on December 6 and awakened people all over Vancouver Island and in the greater Vancouver area. Damage was light due to the very sparse population in the epicentral area. Estevan lighthouse and a wharf in Ucluelet were damaged.

7. **1985:** Magnitude 6.9. Nahanni region, Northwest Territories. Widely felt in the Northwest Territories, Alberta, and British Columbia. A smaller event (magnitude 6.60 that occurred in the same area two months earlier triggered an immense rock avalanche containing five to seven million cubic metres of rock.

8. **1925:** Magnitude 6.2. Charlevoix-Kamouraska region, Quebec. Felt over most of Quebec, the Maritimes, southern Ontario, and parts of the United States. There was considerable damage in the epicentral region, and on both shores of the St. Lawrence River, with churches in Saint Urbain and Rivière-Ouelle severely damaged. Buildings were damaged in the lower-town area of Quebec City and also in Shawinigan, about 250 kilometres from the epicentre.

9. **1988:** Magnitude 5.9. Saguenay region, Quebec. Felt to a 1,000-kilometre radius from the epicentre. The earthquake occurred in the Laurentian Fauna Reserve some 40 kilometres south of Chicoutimi. It caused several tens of millions of dollars damage, with damage reported as far away as the city hall in Montreal, about 350 kilometres from the epicentre.

10. **1944:** Magnitude 5.8. Eastern Ontario-New York border. Widely felt. Although the earthquake was of relatively low magnitude, it caused considerable damage in Cornwall, Ontario and Massena, New York. Damage totalled $2 million.

*List prepared by the National Earthquake Hazards Program, Geological Survey of Canada, National Resources Canada.*

# ❧ TEN OF CANADA'S WORST DISASTERS

1. On October 23, 1958, North America's deepest coalmine collapsed at Springhill, Nova Scotia, trapping 174 miners. Seventy-five died.

2. Canada's first recorded marine disaster took place on August 29, 1583, when the *Delight* was wrecked off Sable Island, about 300 kilometres southeast of Halifax. Eighty-five lives were lost.

3. Fifty-five people died on May 26, 1896, when the Point Ellice Bridge between Victoria, British Columbia, and Esquimault collapsed, sending riders and pedestrians into the water below. It was the worst accident in Canadian transit history.

4. The worst avalanche in Canada took place in British Columbia in 1910 at Rogers Pass, derailing a train and killing 66 people.

5. A dust explosion at a coal mine in Hillcrest, Alberta, on June 19, 1914, killed 189 miners.

6. On December 6, 1917, the French munitions ship *Mont Blanc* collided with the Belgian relief ship *Imo* in Halifax Harbour, causing an explosion that killed more than 1,600 people and seriously injured 9,000 more. Six thousand people were left homeless, and damage was estimated at $50 million.

7. Between 1918 and 1925, an outbreak of Spanish Influenza affected all regions of the country, killing more than 50,000 Canadians.

8. A Mississauga, Ontario, train derailment in October 1979 forced the evacuation of 220,000 people after poisonous chemicals were spilled just west of Toronto. Fortunately, no one was killed.

9. A crash of an Arrow airplane on December 12, 1985, at Gander, Newfoundland, is the worst aviation disaster in Canadian airspace. The crash killed 256 people.

10. The Swissair Flight 111 crash near Peggy's Cove, Nova Scotia, on September 2, 1998, was the second worst aviation tragedy, killing 229. The Swissair crash took more than lives. Also lost were a painting by Pablo Picasso, a kilogram of diamonds, and 50 kilograms of banknotes.

##  The Titanic's Ties to Canada

One hundred and fifty *Titanic* victims are buried in Halifax. Of the 328 bodies recovered by Canadian vessels, 116 were buried at sea, usually because they were damaged or decomposed beyond preservation. It has been suggested that given the class attitudes of the times, most of these were third class passengers and crewmembers. Two hundred and nine were brought back to Halifax; 59 were claimed by relatives and shipped to their home communities. The remaining 150 victims are buried in three cemeteries: Fairview Lawn, Mount Olivet, and Baron de Hirsch, each open to the public.

Additional *Titanic* artifacts in Canada can be found at the Maritime Museum of the Atlantic which has a large number of items in its *Titanic* Exhibit, most donated and some loaned by descendants of Nova Scotians who were involved in recovering *Titanic* bodies. These include:

- A pair of small, brown, leather shoes, worn by an unknown child, thought to be about two years old, who died in the disaster. The shoes are displayed next to the gloves of railway tycoon Charles Hays, which were also recovered after *Titanic* sunk.

  "The shoes of a third class infant will sit beside the gloves of a millionaire … a reminder of the cross-section of humanity which perished in this shipwreck," said Dan Conlin, curator of the Maritime Museum of the Atlantic.

  The little boy's body was brought home on the *Mackay-Bennett* and buried in Fairview Lawn Cemetery, where his gravestone has become one of Halifax's most famous memorials.

- A deck chair that bears a carved five-pointed star, the emblem of the White Star Line. Made of mahogany and unidentified hardwood, it is one of the only intact chairs in the world that matches those seen in *Titanic* photographs.

- Lounge panelling that contains musical instruments and scroll in the Louis XV style used in the room. It comes from the arch over the forward entrance to the first-class lounge, the area where the *Titanic* broke in half just before plunging to the bottom.

- A newel post face from newel posts of either the forward or aft first-class staircase.

- Oak trim with a vegetable, fruit, and flower design. Made of quarter-cut English white oak, its image is easily spotted in photographs, paintings, and movie recreations of the *Titanic*'s grand first-class staircase.

- Ornamental oak from the sides of the balustrade of the forward first-class staircase. The S-shaped twist indicates it was from the portion of the staircase leading to the first-class reception room on D-Deck, where passengers gathered for meals in the nearby dining room.

- A cribbage board made by *Minia*'s ship's carpenter, William Parker, from a piece of oak taken from the water after *Titanic* sunk. It is typical of the crib boards, picture frames, and other practical knick-knacks made of *Titanic* wood by *Minia* crew members.

The Newfoundland Museum in St. John's is caretaker of the lifejacket James McGrady was wearing, which has been a popular artifact since the release of James Cameron's epic movie *Titanic*.

For more information, visit the Newfoundland Museum (www.therooms.ca/museum) and the Maritime Museum of the Atlantic (www.museum.gov.ns.ca).

## SUMMER QUIZ

Summer's the season when Canadians love to revel in the warm weather, take up residence in a comfortable lawn chair, and sip a cool beverage next to a favourite lake.

If you're a summer lover, try your luck at the questions below to test your knowledge of the season Canadians wait all year for. And best of all, you don't even have to get out of that chair. Enjoy!

1.  Where is the world's longest freshwater beach?

    a) Thunder Bay
    b) Lake Winnipeg
    c) Belleville, Ontario
    d) Wasaga Beach

2. Strawberries, a tasty summer treat grown on farms across Canada, are a member of the rose family. True or false?

3. Name the 1970s Canadian group that had a hit with the song "Sunny Days."

4. True or false? No one has ever successfully swum across Lake Erie.

5. Which province was the site of the highest recorded temperature ever in Canada at 45 degrees Celsius?

   a) British Columbia
   b) Ontario
   c) Saskatchewan
   d) Quebec

6. The Great Lakes are a popular summer playground for campers and cottagers. Name the lakes in order of size from biggest to smallest.

7. Name the province that joined Confederation on July 1, 1873.

8. The first ever Canada Summer Games were held in which city?

   a) Quebec City
   b) Halifax-Dartmouth
   c) Ottawa
   d) Saskatoon

9. True or False? Ontario is home to more than 50 types of mosquitoes.

10. In the summer of 1973, I fell from the sky at Cedoux, Saskatchewan, setting a record that has yet to be beaten. Unscramble the word below to figure out what I am.

    iheltsoan

11. If you operate a vehicle during your summer vacation with one tire under-inflated by eight pounds per square inch (56 kPa) how many kilometres will you shave off the life of that tire?

   a) 4,000 kilometres
   b) 10,000 kilometres
   c) 15,000 kilometres
   d) 25,000 kilometres

➥ **Answers on pages 348–349**

## SIX TO SAVOUR QUIZ

1. True or false? There are fewer than 20 species of ferns found in Canada.

2. Before it was renamed Lake Louise in 1882, what was this beautiful body of water in Alberta called?

   a) Shining Lake
   b) Lake Wilson
   c) Banff Lake
   d) Emerald Lake

3. Which of the following bridges does not connect the Niagara Falls, Ontario, area to the United States?

   a) Ivy Lea Bridge
   b) Rainbow Bridge
   c) Whirlpool Bridge
   d) Queenston-Lewiston Bridge

4. "Rock doctor" is a Canadian slang term for which profession?

    a) disk jockey
    b) geologist
    c) jeweller
    d) highway construction worker

5. Unscramble the following words to come up with animals found in Canada.

    a) obraciu
    b) darbeg
    c) toyeco
    d) lewayle

6. I'm a period of six or more hours with winds above 40 kilometres per hour, visibility reduced below one kilometre by blowing or drifting snow, and temperatures below -12° C. What am I?

 **Answers on page 349**

## COAST TO COAST QUIZ

1. True or false? The 10 highest mountains in Canada are all located in the Yukon.

2. Who owns the North Pole?

    a) Canada
    b) The United States
    c) The United Nations
    d) no one

3. Name the only two Canadian provinces that do not have a coast on salt water.

4. Why is the historic Chateau Montebello hotel on the Ottawa River between Montreal and Ottawa referred to as "a seventh wonder of the world"?

      a) It was built using 10,000 logs from British Columbia.
      b) It was built on a swamp.
      c) It is the largest hotel in the world.
      d) It was built in two months.

5. Which is longer, the St. Lawrence or the Mackenzie River?

➥ **Answers on pages 349–350**

# CHAPTER 11
# Hollywood North

## Jack Warner (Warner Brothers)

Some might think it a bit of a stretch to claim the renowned Hollywood film company and its famous movie mogul Jack Warner as Canadian. The famous producer of Warner Brothers fame was born in London, Ontario in 1892, but only lived here for the first two years of his life before his family moved to Youngstown, Ohio.

Still, in 1960, Warner received the Order of the British Empire and in a 1973 interview talked about being from Canada along with so many others from Hollywood's earliest days.

Jack Warner was the only one of the famous brothers born in Canada. His father Ben had emigrated from Poland in 1890 and settled in Baltimore, Maryland. He got a job as a cobbler and sent for the rest of his family. Eventually Ben changed trades and became a peddler, a job that brought him eventually to London. Jack apparently had no birth certificate, but later chose August 4 as his birth date. Ben's business didn't thrive in the southwestern Ontario community, so the family pulled up stakes and moved.

### They Said It!

"You in Canada should not be dependent either on the United States or on Great Britain. You should have your own films and exchange them with those of other countries. You can make them just as well in Toronto as in New York City."

*– pioneering silent film director D.W. Griffiths in a 1925 speech to the Canadian Club in Toronto.*

Warner and his brothers got their start when they opened a theatre in Pennsylvania to show films. One account says they had to borrow chairs for the theatre from an undertaker, which meant patrons had to stand if a funeral was taking place while a film was showing. The Warners's first Hollywood effort was in 1917–18, but they would produce thousands of films over the next five decades, including the popular Bugs Bunny cartoons and several award-winning movies.

Known as a gambler and a "no-good sonofabitch" who often clashed with famous stars, Warner nevertheless won Oscars for such films as *Casablanca*, *The Life of Emile Zola*, and *My Fair Lady*. He was apparently proudest of *The Jazz Singer*, the 1927 film that helped usher in the sound era, and for which he later received a special Academy Award. In his retirement years before he died of inflammation of the heart in 1978, Warner said "you're nothing if you don't have a studio. Now I'm just another millionaire, and there are a lot of 'em around."

Warner Brothers is still one of the best-known studios in the business, having merged with the Time Inc. in 1990 and then becoming AOL Time Warner in 2001. It is one of the biggest media/entertainment conglomerates in the world, producing such films as *The Matrix* and *Harry Potter* and TV shows such as *ER*, *Friends*, and *The West Wing*.

## Louis B. Mayer (MGM)

Many Canadians besides Jack Warner have been involved in Hollywood's movie industry from its early days. Another one in the spotlight was Louis B. Mayer, one of the *M*'s in MGM studios.

Mayer was born in Minsk, Russia in 1885, but came to Canada with his family when he was three, settling in Saint John, New Brunswick. Mayer's father was involved in the scrap metal industry, a business young Louis entered when he quit school. At 19, he moved to Boston, eventually bought into some nickelodeons (early movie theatres), and began producing films. He moved to California in 1918, co-founding Metro-Goldwyn-Mayer (MGM) in 1924.

**Film BITE!**

British Columbia is the third-largest film and television production centre in North America, after New York and Los Angeles. Early in this century, an average of more than 200 movies and TV shows were shot in the province annually, injecting about one billion dollars into the provincial economy.

In addition to producing a wealth of movies during his long career and overseeing the careers of hundreds of Hollywood stars, Mayer was also a key figure in creating the Academy Awards. He devised the scheme partly as a way to keep labour unrest in the movie business from getting out of hand.

Mayer was a major force in motion pictures until the 1950s and died in 1957. Though Canadian-raised, Mayer not only became an American citizen but falsely claimed he was born on the Fourth of July, American Independence Day. Mayer received a special Academy Award in 1950.

# THE ENVELOPE PLEASE

## Canadian Actresses Nominated for Academy Awards
(in chronological order)

1.  **Mary Pickford:** Winner in 1929 for Best Actress in *Coquette*. The Toronto-born actress also received an honorary award in 1975.

2.  **Norma Shearer:** Won in 1930 for Best Actress in *The Divorcée*. The Montreal native was also nominated in the same category that same year for *Their Own Desire*, in 1931 for *A Free Soul*, in 1934 for *The Barretts of Wimpole Street*, in 1936 for *Romeo and Juliet*, and in 1938 for *Marie Antoinette*.

3.  **Marie Dressler:** The Cobourg, Ontario, star won in 1931 for Best Actress in *Min and Bill*. She was nominated in the same category the following year for her role in *Emma*.

4.  **Deanna Durbin:** The Winnipeg-born actress was one of the best-known young stars in the 30s and 40s, and was awarded a miniature Oscar in 1938 for "bringing to the screen the spirit and personification of youth." Her films included *Three Smart Girls* and *One Hundred Men and a Girl*.

5.  **Genevieve Bujold:** The Montreal performer was nominated in 1969 for Best Actress in *Anne of a Thousand Days*.

6.  **Meg Tilly:** Raised in Victoria, British Columbia, she was nominated for Best Supporting Actress in 1985 for *Agnes of God*.

7.  **Kate Nelligan:** The London, Ontario, native was nominated in 1991 for Best Supporting Actress in *The Prince of Tides*.

8.  **Anna Paquin:** Born July 24, 1982, in Winnipeg, Manitoba, she won the Best Supporting Actress award for *The Piano*.

9. **Jennifer Tilly:** The Vancouver actress matched her sister Meg with a nomination for Best Supporting Actress for her role in *Bullets over Broadway* in 1995.

10. **Ellen Page:** At just 20 years of age, this talented young actress who hails from Halifax, Nova Scotia, was nominated in 2008 in the Best Actress category for her starring role in *Juno*, a small-budget Canadian film that also garnered nominations for Best Picture, Best Director (Canadian Jason Reitman), and Best Original Screenplay (by first-time screenwriter Diablo Cody, who was the only one to pick up an Oscar that night).

## Canadian Actors Nominated for Academy Awards
(in chronological order)

1. **Walter Houston:** The Toronto-born actor was first nominated in 1936 for Best Actor in *Dodsworth*. He was nominated in the same category in 1941 for *All That Money Can Buy*. He got the nomination for Best Supporting Actor in 1942 in *Yankee Doodle Dandy*, and won in that category in 1948 for *Treasure of the Sierra Madre*.

2. **Gene Lockhart:** The London, Ontario, native was nominated for Best Supporting Actor in 1938 for *Algiers*.

3. **Raymond Massey:** The Toronto actor received a Best Actor nomination in 1940 for *Abe Lincoln in Illinois*.

4. **Walter Pidgeon:** From Saint John, New Brunswick, Pidgeon was nominated for Best Actor in 1942 for *Mrs. Miniver* and in the same category the following year for *Madame Curie*.

5. **Alexander Knox:** The Strathroy, Ontario, native was nominated in 1944 as Best Actor in *Wilson*.

6. **Hume Cronyn:** From London, Ontario, Cronyn was nominated in 1944 for Best Supporting Actor in *The Seventh Cross*.

7. **Harold Russell:** The Sydney, Nova Scotia, native was nominated and won in 1946 for Best Supporting Actor in *The Best Years of Our Lives*. A war amputee (Russell was missing both arms), he also received a special Oscar that year for "bringing hope and courage to his fellow veterans" with his appearance in the film.

8. **John Ireland:** The actor from Vernon, British Columbia, was nominated for Best Supporting Actor in 1949 for *All the King's Men*.

9. **Chief Dan George:** Hailing from the Burrard Indian Reserve in North Vancouver, George was nominated in 1970 for Best Supporting Actor in *Little Big Man*.

10. **Dan Aykroyd:** The Ottawa-born comedian was nominated in 1989 for Best Supporting Actor for his role in the Best Picture winner *Driving Miss Daisy*.

11. **Graham Greene:** Born at the Six Nations Reserve near Brampton, Ontario, Greene received a Best Supporting Actor nomination in 1990 for *Dances with Wolves*.

> **They Said It!**
>
> "The heart never knows the colour of the skin"
>
> – *Chief Dan George (1899-1981)*

## ✔ ACADEMY AWARDS QUIZ

Test your movie awards knowledge in this Oscar quiz, and you just may be worthy of giving your own acceptance speech.

1. In what Canadian province was the Oscar-nominated movie *Capote* filmed?

2. Toronto-born actor Walter Huston won a Best Supporting Actor award in 1948 for *The Treasure of the Sierra Madre*. Name his famous actress granddaughter.

3. In what year did the National Film Board win its first Academy Award?

   a) 1936
   b) 1941

   c) 1962
   d) 1977

4.   True or false. Canada has never won the Academy Award for Best Foreign Language Film at the Oscars?

5.   What Ontario-born director was behind the camera for the multi-Oscar-winning film *Titanic*?

   a) David Cronenberg
   b) Norman Jewison
   c) Ivan Reitman
   d) James Cameron

6.   What 1999 film was the Academy Award-nominated song "Blame Canada" from?

7.   Which of the following Canadian films was not nominated for an Oscar for Best Foreign Language Film?

   a) *Water*
   b) *The Decline of the American Empire*
   c) *Mon oncle Antoine*
   d) *Jesus of Montreal*
   e) *The Barbarian Invasions*

8.   Canadian writer and director Paul Haggis is the only screenwriter to have two of his films win back-to-back Oscars for Best Picture, in 2004 and 2005. Name the two films.

➥ **Answers on page 351**

# ❦ THE SMALL SCREEN

- Canada's first colour television set was set up in an operating theatre at the Royal Victoria Hospital in Montreal on June 21, 1951. It allowed Dr. Gavin Miller to give a running commentary of an abdominal operation.

- The Viewer Chip, or V-Chip, used by parents to block violent or offensive television shows from coming into their homes, was invented by Tim Collins, a professor at the Technical University of British Columbia in Surrey, British Columbia.

- The comedy team Wayne and Shuster, who were legends in the history of Canadian entertainment, appeared a record 67 times on the *Ed Sullivan Show*, which was broadcast on Sunday nights on CBS television from 1948 to 1971.

- Game show host Alex Trebek may be Canada's most famous quizmaster today, but another Canadian, Roy Ward Dickson, gets credit for inventing the genre. His radio program *Professor Dick and his Question Box* debuted in Toronto on May 15, 1935.

- The Canadian TV show *Hammy Hamster*, which debuted in 1959, is still seen in more than 20 countries around the world.

*Courtesy of the National Archives of Canada, PA-152117.*

Johnny Wayne and Frank Shuster were stalwarts on *The Ed Sullivan Show*.

- Long before he gained renown as Pa Cartwright on the TV series *Bonanza*, Canadian-born actor Lorne Greene made a name for himself as a radio broadcaster. During the Second World War he was known to CBC listeners as the "Voice of Doom."

- Actor Matthew Perry, one of the stars of the *Friends* TV sitcom, first performed before an audience while studying at Ashbury College in Ottawa, where he played the fastest gun in the West in a play called *The Life and Death of Sneaky Fitch*. He lived in Ottawa until he was 15; his mother, Suzanne Perry, was former prime minister Pierre Trudeau's press secretary.

- In the 1950s, CBC ran a Canadian version of the popular American show *Howdy Doody*. Instead of using American host Buffalo Bob, the CBC came up with Timber Tom, a forest ranger, who was played in a few episodes by future *Star Trek* star William Shatner. Interestingly, the role of Timber Tom had been first offered to James Doohan, who would later play Scotty on *Star Trek*.

## ❤ QUOTABLE QUOTES BY FAMOUS ENTERTAINERS

"Wherever you go in the world, you just have to say
you're a Canadian and people laugh."
— *the late John Candy, Canadian comedian and actor*

"In my proudest moments, I think I had a real hand in the creative force
of making *Star Trek*. But most of the time, I don't think about it."
— *Canadian-born actor William Shatner, on the famous 1960s TV series*

"We've got a stuttering newscaster. We've got the black, we've got the
Asian, we've got the woman. I could be a lesbian,
folk-dancing, black woman stutterer."
— *Avery Haines, Canadian TV announcer,
in an inadvertent on-air comment that led to her being fired*

"When I'm in Canada, I feel like this is what the world should be like."
— *Actress Jane Fonda, quoted from a 1987 interview*

"Canada is the essence of not being. Not English, not American,
it is the mathematic of not being. And a subtle flavour —
we're more like celery as a flavour."
— *Canadian comedian Mike Myers*

"The U.S. is our trading partner, our neighbour, our ally and our friend
… and sometimes we'd like to give them such a smack!"
— *Canadian comedian Rick Mercer*

# ❦ WHERE ARE THEY NOW?

## 📺 Steve Smith (aka Red Green)

Steve Smith has left his mark in several corners of Canada's entertainment industry but he's probably best known for the Red Green character he portrayed for 15 seasons on the television show of the same name.

Smith grew up in Toronto and after working at several jobs, including as a teacher and musician, he launched his television career with *Smith & Smith*, a sketch comedy series starring Steve and his partner and wife, Morag. During this period he created his

Photo courtesy of Space Media.

Gemini winner Steve Smith.

most popular alter ego, gravel-voiced homespun TV handyman Red Green, the president of the Possum Lodge, a fictional men's club in the small northwestern Ontario town of Possum Lake, near the also-fictional town of Port Asbestos.

He and his fellow lodge members had their own TV show in which they give humorous lessons and demonstrations in repair work and outdoor activities and advice for men on relating to women, among other things.

Smith starred in the show and also produced and co-wrote it. It eventually evolved into Christmas specials and a movie. The series finale aired in April 2006.

Smith also wrote and produced 26 episodes of *Me & Max* and 60 episodes of *Comedy Mill*, which won a Canadian Gemini Award. In his spare time he was head writer of a 13-episode series called *Laughing Matters* for the Global network and wrote a pilot called "Out Of Our Minds," starring David Steinberg for Tribune Entertainment.

Smith and fellow *Red Green Show* actor Pat McKenna won the 1998 Gemini Award (Canada's equivalent of the Emmy Awards) for Best Performance in a Comedy Program or Series. In 2005, he was a recipient of the Order of Canada.

The father of two boys' most recent project is the biographical book *We're All in This Together*, co-written with Mag Ruffman, a television producer and writer, actress, and building contractor.

Photo courtesy of Roy Timms.

Smith as Red Green.

Steve is the author or co-author of three other books: *Red Green Talks Cars: A Love Story*; *The Red Green Book: Wit and Wisdom of Possum Lodge*; and *Red Green's Duct Tape is Not Enough*.

Smith and his wife live in Hamilton and spend winters near Fort Myers, Florida. He plays golf three times a week, spends plenty of time on his houseboat and he and his wife are members of The Fabulous Miromars, a musical trio that performs 1960s tunes mixed with comedy, mostly in Florida. Smith turned 63 on December 24, 2008.

# CHAPTER 12
# How We Get Around

 TEN TRANSPORTATION TIDBITS

- The Peterborough Lift Lock on the Trent-Severn Waterway at Peterborough, Ontario, is the highest hydraulic lift in the world. Work began in 1896, and when the job was completed in 1904 it enabled boaters to overcome a difference in elevation of more than 19 metres between Little Lake and Nassau Mills.

- Canada has more than 900,000 kilometres of roads and highways and a national highway system that is more than 24,000 kilometres in length.

- The idea of having white lines down the middle of highways is thought to have originated near the Ontario-Quebec border in 1930. J.D. Millar is credited with introducing the lines; his boss at the Ministry of Transportation thought the innovation was foolish.

Hundreds of highways criss-cross Canada for thousands of kilometres.

- The first train tunnel in British North America was built in Brockville, Ontario, between 1854 and 1860. The Brockville Railway Tunnel enabled Grand Trunk Railway trains to travel through a wedge of rock to the nearby waterfront. Victoria Hall, Brockville's city hall, was constructed on top of the tunnel in the early 1860s.

- The first airmail flight in Canada took place in 1918. A military aircraft took off in Montreal in the morning with 120 letters, refuelled in Kingston, Ontario, and made its delivery in Toronto late that afternoon.

- The first electric streetcar system in Canada was installed in Windsor, Ontario, in 1886,

Photo courtesy of the Brockville Museum.

The Brockville Railway Tunnel.

whereas Toronto's wasn't in place until 1892. By the First World War, 48 Canadian cities and towns had streetcar systems.

• At the time of Confederation, the Grand Trunk Railway, which ran from Montreal through parts of southern Ontario and included links to the U.S., was the largest railway system in the world.

• When the Canadian Pacific Railway introduced the streamlined, all stainless steel transcontinental train *The Canadian* on April 24, 1955, the rail trip between Montreal and Vancouver was reduced to 71 hours and 10 minutes. That's 16 hours less than previous trains took to make the trek.

• The first steam locomotive manufactured in Canada was built in 1853 by James Good of Toronto. It was named *Toronto* and was part of the great flurry of industrial activity that marked the country's first great railway boom in the 1850s.

• Toronto's Yonge subway was the first subway line built in Canada. It was constructed between 1949 and 1954 and officially opened on March 30, 1954. It initially ran from Eglinton to Union Station, a trip that took about 12 minutes.

 BREAKING NEW GROUND

 First Train Across Canada: Chugging into History

On June 28, 1886, nearly eight months after the last spike was driven at Craigellachie, British Columbia, the first transcontinental Canadian Pacific Railways train left Montreal for the Pacific Ocean.

At noon hour on July 4, 1886, Train No. 1, the Pacific Express, with 150 passengers on board, rolled into Port Moody, B.C. It was an occasion one history book described as "the most significant event in the history of Port Moody." The 2,892.6-mile trip across four time zones took 139 hours.

Whatever happened to the train that made the first trip across Canada on the brand new east–west rail line?

For starters, only two of the 10 cars that made up the train as it left Montreal — the *Honolulu*, a sleeper car and Car 319, carrying mail, express, and baggage — made the entire westward journey. Other cars were picked up and dropped off along the way; as the train made its way across Canada, its locomotives were changed more than two dozen times.

Locomotive 371, which was placed on the train at North Bend, B.C., just east of Port Moody, was

## Trivia BITE!

Lord Strathcona drove the last spike in a ceremony at Craigellachie, British Columbia, thus completing the Canadian Pacific Railway. The spike was made of iron, not silver or gold as some have thought.

Photo courtesy of Library and Archives Canada, C-003693

Bring the hammer down … let the trains roll.

the engine chosen to pull the first transcontinental train into the terminal at Port Moody, where Vancouver-bound passengers were transferred to a stage coach for the final 12-mile leg of the trip.

According to the Canadian Pacific Archives, Locomotive No. 371, which was built in Montreal in 1886, was scrapped in October 1915. The baggage, mail/express car, which was built in 1884 by the CPR at its Hochelaga shops, was renumbered several times before being scrapped in 1937 at Montreal. The *Honolulu*, built in 1886 by Barney & Smith, was renamed *Pembroke* in 1918, renumbered 1705 in 1926, then scrapped in 1930 at Montreal.

The first engine and rail cars to arrive on the west coast may be long gone, but another engine of significance is still intact and honoured for its historic role: Locomotive No. 374, which on May 23, 1887, became the first engine to haul a train into Vancouver once tracks were extended from Port Moody, is on display at the Roundhouse Community Arts and Recreation Centre in Vancouver.

The locomotive was extensively rebuilt in October 1915 and remained in service until July 1945, when it was retired and donated to the City of Vancouver, says CP Archives.

In the 1980s, the West Coast Railway Association and the Canadian Railroad Historical Association undertook a round of cosmetic work that restored No. 374 to the way it looked in 1945.

For more information, visit www.roundhouse.ca or www.seevancouverheritage.com/eng374/eng374.htm.

## ✈ Casey Baldwin's Airplane: First in Flight

Frederick "Casey" Baldwin gained fame on March 12, 1908, when he flew about 97 metres (319 feet) in a biplane over icy Keuka Lake in Hammondsport, New York. By doing so, Baldwin became the first Canadian to fly an airplane.

Though he wasn't the first to fly on Canadian soil — that would happen the following year when John McCurdy piloted the *Silver Dart* in Nova Scotia — Baldwin earned his place as one of the key pioneers in aviation history. His flight, watched by several spectators, is considered the first *public* heavier-than-air airplane flight in U.S. history. The Wright brothers' flight in 1903 was very much a private affair.

According to accounts, Baldwin got to fly the plane, named the *Red Wing*, because on the frigid day he was the only one of the aviation team who wasn't wearing ice skates. Since he was slipping on the ice, the others decided he would be most useful sitting in the cockpit. The flight had been more than a year in the making since Alexander Graham Bell established the Aerial Experiment Association (AEA), whose purpose was to build a practical airplane for $20,000.

The *Red Wing*, designed by American Thomas Selfridge and so named because of the red silk that covered its frame, flew only some five to 10 feet off the ground during Baldwin's sojourn but made a smooth landing. There was a small story about the flight on the front page of the next day's *New York Times*, but Baldwin's name wasn't mentioned. The *Red Wing*'s final flight, five days later on March 17, was not as successful. A stiff breeze caught the plane after about 120 feet in the air and sent it and Baldwin to the ground. Although Baldwin escaped injury, the plane's motor and wing were damaged beyond repair.

Over the next two months, the AEA team built a second plane, the *White Wing*, which had considerable success. Accounts from the time make no mention of what happened to the wreckage of the *Red Wing*, however. Was any of it salvaged and used elsewhere? Or was it simply left to the elements? At any rate, the *Red Wing* remains a key piece of the history of flight, and photographs of it exist to this day

Baldwin would go on to make more flights and sit as a politician in the Nova Scotia legislature before dying in 1948. Selfridge, unfortunately, suffered a cruel fate. In September

1908, during a flight in which he was a passenger, the plane crashed, severely injuring him. He later died in surgery, thus becoming the first airplane fatality in the world.

## Canada's First Automobile: Full Steam Ahead

In 1867, Canada's first self-propelled automobile was demonstrated at the Stanstead Fair in the community of Stanstead Plain, southeast of Montreal.

The vehicle, invented by watchmaker Henry Seth Taylor, was powered by steam, had no brakes, and could reach a top speed of just 15 miles per hour.

Despite Taylor's pioneering efforts, it was the subject of considerable ridicule from townsfolk who considered it a "toy of exaggerated size and power," according to an article published by the Antique Automobile Club of America in 1968.

Nevertheless, a local newspaper called the steam car "the neatest thing of the kind yet invented" and Taylor boasted that his vehicle would challenge "any trotting horse."

The basis of the car, which Taylor started building in 1865, was a high-wheeled carriage with some bracing to support a two-cylinder steam engine mounted under the floor. Steam was generated in a vertical coal-fired boiler mounted at the rear of the vehicle behind the seat. The boiler was connected by rubber hoses to a six-gallon water tank located between the front wheels. Forward and reverse movements were controlled by a lever, and a vertical crank connected to the wheels was used for steering.

The vehicle's lack of brakes proved to be its undoing. After driving it for several years and showing it off at carnivals and parades, Taylor lost control one summer day as he drove down a hill. Before he came to a stop, the car had turned on its side, its wheels shattered.

### Road BITE!

Canada's first concrete highway was built between Toronto and Hamilton in 1912 to accommodate a tremendous increase in traffic. In 1907, there were 2,130 cars on Canada's roads; five years later, when the concrete highway was opened to traffic, 50,000 cars were in use.

Discouraged, Taylor put the remains in a barn near Stanstead Plain, where they sat until the early 1960s when Gertrude Sowden of Stanstead purchased the property. She recognized the value of Taylor's creation, but when she couldn't interest museums in it, she sold the remains to American Richard Stewart of Middlebury, Connecticut, president of Anaconda American Brass.

Eventually new wheels were made, the seat and dashboard were recovered with leather, all wooden parts were scraped, sanded, and repainted, and brakes were added. None of the engine parts needed replacing.

The Taylor steam car was acquired by the Canada Science and Technology Museum in Ottawa in 1984. Although it is on exhibit from time to time, the vehicle spends much of its time in a climate-controlled warehouse adjacent to the museum, where public access can be arranged by appointment.

In the summer of 2005, the vehicle was shown four times, twice to individuals and twice as part of a larger tour of the warehouse.

"Looking at the vehicle, one sees the origins of the automobile, even though it predates the blossoming of the auto industry by 40 years," we were told by Garth Wilson, curator of transportation at the Ottawa museum. "It is absolutely significant in that it is first Canadian made auto and, as such, represents Canada's entry into world of automobiles."

For more information, visit http://www.sciencetech.technomuses.ca or call (613) 991-3044.

## The Merchant Ship *Simcoe*: First into the St. Lawrence Seaway System

There will always be debate over who invented the world's first self-propelled automobile, but one thing is certain: Canada's Henry Seth Taylor is in good company. The French say one of their countrymen, inventor Nicolas-Joseph Cugnot, built the world's first self-propelled mechanical vehicle, "Fardier à vapeur" (steam wagon), in 1769. German Karl Benz, generally thought to be the father of the practical motorcar in Europe, unveiled his first vehicle, a three-wheeled, gas-powered car known as "Benz Patent Motor Car" in 1886. American Henry Ford's initial vehicle was the gasoline-powered Quadracycle, first sold in 1896.

The St. Lawrence Seaway opened for business on the morning of April 25, 1959, when the bulk carrier *Simcoe*, commanded by Captain Norm Donaldson, entered the waterway from the eastern end at the St. Lambert lock on the south shore of Montreal.

*Simcoe*, then owned by Canada Steamship Lines (CSL), was the first commercial vessel to transit the seaway, which had been five years in the making and soon became a vital artery that enabled industries in North America's heartland to compete in export markets.

Among *Simcoe*'s passengers was T.R. McLagan, president of CSL. Prime Minister

John Diefenbaker was aboard Canadian Coast Guard icebreaker *d'Iberville*, which also entered the seaway on opening day.

At the time, the 259-foot-long *Simcoe* was a CSL stalwart entering its 33rd year of service for the company. It and other ships of its size would soon be replaced by much larger lakers designed to maximize the increased size allowances offered by the seaway.

The ship was built in England in 1923 by Swan, Hunter & Wigham Richardson Ltd. and was known as *Glencorrie* under its first two owners, Glen Line Ltd. of Midland, Ontario, and Geo. Hall Coal & Shipping Corp. of Montreal. In 1926, it was purchased by CSL and its name was changed to *Simcoe*.

**Trivia BITE!**

Simcoe was the first merchant ship to enter the St. Lawrence Seaway but was not the first vessel to transit the waterway. That honour goes to the icebreaker *d'Iberville*, which entered the seaway on April 25, 1959, just ahead of Simcoe. Built in 1953 by Davie Shipbuilding & Engineering Co. Ltd. for Transport Canada's Canadian Marine Service (later known as the Canadian Coast Guard), *d'Iberville* spent much of its life in the Arctic, where it activated navigational aids and delivered supplies to outposts. It also escorted ships in the St. Lawrence River and cleared ice jams to prevent flooding. The *d'Iberville* was retired at the end of 1982, put up for sale a year later, and scrapped in Kaohsiung, Taiwan, in 1989.

During the Second World War, the ship was chartered by the Canadian government to transport supplies for the military and was one of a handful of bulk carriers to avoid being sunk by enemy torpedoes.

It was owned by CSL until 1961 before being sold to Simcoe Northern Offshore Drilling Ltd. of Kingston, where it was converted to a drilling barge and renamed *Nordrill*.

In 1977, 18 years after making history as the first bulk carrier to enter the St. Lawrence Seaway, *Simcoe* was scrapped at Port Colborne, Ontario.

## ♿ World's First Motorized Wheelchair

Recognizing the difficulties faced by veterans disabled in the Second World War, Canadian inventor George Johnn Klein invented the world's first electric wheelchair.

The Hamilton inventor, whom the *Canadian Encyclopedia* describes as "possibly the most productive inventor in Canada in the 20th century," was able to overcome challenges faced by others with an innovative 24-volt power system, separate and reversible drive units for each of the two main wheels, and an easy-to-use joystick-style control throttle.

The Canada Science and Technology Museum in Ottawa has called the wheelchair "one of the most significant artifacts in the history of Canadian science, engineering, and invention."

It was developed by Klein at the National Research Council of Canada (NRC) in Ottawa in collaboration with Veterans Affairs Canada and the Canadian Paraplegic Association. But, alas, the chair would be produced in the United States instead of Canada.

In the early 1950s, no Canadian manufacturers were able to mass produce the device, so to promote the technology the electric prototype was presented to the United States Veterans Administration at the U.S. Embassy in Ottawa on October 26, 1955. A year later, a California company began churning out motorized wheelchairs.

The prototype wheelchair has been a coveted possession of the Smithsonian's National Museum of American History since 1979. However, it was "repatriated" and has been on display at the Canada Science and Technology Museum in Ottawa since 2005.

Over the years, countless people in Canada and around the world have benefited by having access to the Klein wheelchair.

"It has all of the elements of a significant invention," says Randall Brooks, assistant director of the Collection and Research Division at the Canada Science and Technology Museum. "It freed the disabled up to be independent because previously, anyone who did not have the use of one or both hands was completely reliant on someone else to get around. It allowed people to get out and work, to make a living and contribute to society."

Described in a June 2004 report in the *Ottawa Citizen* as "a clunky looking thing, a far cry from the sleek and speedy mobile machines used today," Klein's chair attracted international attention with its innovative controls, ease of operation, flexible drive system, and dependability.

Klein has been hailed as one of Canada's most remarkable engineers. He also invented medical suturing devices, Canada's first wind tunnel, and gearing systems for the Canadarm used on several U.S. space shuttle missions. He died in 1992.

For more information, visit the Smithsonian Institution at www.si.edu or the Canada Science and Technology Museum at www.sciencetech.technomuses.ca or call (613) 991-3044.

# THE TRANSPORTATION BUSINESS

## Joseph-Armand Bombardier (Bombardier Inc.)

As a young lad of 14, Joseph-Armand Bombardier had a decision to make: Would he forge ahead with his religious studies and become a priest, or pursue his passionate interest in mechanics?

People whose world is covered with snow most of the time should be glad Bombardier chose mechanics.

In 1922, the boy who for years had amazed his family and friends by building toy tractors and locomotives out of old clocks, sewing machines, motors, and cigar boxes built his first snowmobile.

The prototype, tested with his brother Leopold, consisted of a four-passenger sleigh frame supporting a rear-mounted Model T engine with a spinning wooden propeller sticking out the back. As dogs barked and onlookers demanded they shut it down, the noisy and extremely dangerous contraption made its way along the streets of Valcourt in Quebec's Eastern Townships, where Bombardier had been born on April 16, 1907.

He was only 15, but Armand had begun his lifelong infatuation with the concept of a vehicle that would travel on snow and offer relief for country folks isolated during Quebec's harsh and snowy winters.

Two years later Bombardier dropped out of the St. Charles Baromée seminary in Sherbrooke, Quebec, and started working on engines, eventually moving to Montreal where he registered for evening courses in mechanics and electricity. He soon landed a job in a large auto repair garage as a first-class mechanic.

In 1926, with a wealth of theoretical and practical training under his belt, the 19-year-old Bombardier returned to the Valcourt area, where he opened Garage Bombardier. He was a dealer for Imperial Oil and fixed cars, as well as threshers, ice saws, and pumps. His reputation as a mechanic who could diagnose and resolve most mechanical problems quickly helped the business flourish, so much so that he hired several friends and family members to help out.

His strength was his inventiveness: He built equipment with his own hands, once forging a drill and hydraulic press for producing steel and cast iron cylinders, gas tanks, and heaters. He also built his own dam and turbine to harness energy for his own use, long before the town of Valcourt introduced electricity.

**Trivia BITE!**

In the late 1950s, the list price of a Ski-Doo was about $900. Today's models range in price from $8,000 to $13,000.

After marrying Yvonne in 1929, Bombardier turned to the development of a motorized snow vehicle to replace the horse-drawn sled, which was a slow and inefficient mode of winter travel when snow made roads impassable in Quebec. For years, he wrestled with three key challenges — even distribution of the vehicle's weight to keep it level on snow, a safe and reliable propulsion engine, and suspension that would afford passengers a comfortable ride.

A tragedy in his own family played a role in the invention of his first commercial product. In January 1934, Bombardier's two-year-old son Yvon needed immediate hospital treatment for appendicitis and peritonitis. But with roads blocked by snow, there was no way he could get the boy to the nearest hospital, 50 kilometres away in Sherbrooke, Quebec. The death of his son made Armand all the more determined to create a snow machine that would help Quebecers avoid similar tragedies.

Two years later Bombardier invented the B7, which stood for Bombardier and the seven passengers it could carry. With its lightweight plywood cabin, many said it resembled a futuristic tank on skis. He received a patent in June 1937, for his invention of a sprocket device that made the vehicle travel over snow, and production began under the business name L'Auto-Neige Bombardier Limitée.

The B7 sold for slightly more than $1,000, "about the same price as low-end automobiles of the time," writes Larry MacDonald in his book *The Bombardier Story*.

During the Second World War, a variety of models were built and the company erected new factories and added staff. After the war, production soared to 1,000 units a year. In 1947–48, multiple-passenger vehicles were the company's mainstay and had boosted sales to $2.3 million when two events hit the company hard: The winter of that year was virtually snowless in Quebec, and the provincial government committed to keep all major roads clear of snow every winter. As a result, L'Auto-Neige Bombardier's sales dropped by 40 percent to $1.4 million in 1948–49.

These events convinced Bombardier of the need for smaller snowmobiles for people who travelled alone, such as doctors, trappers, and prospectors. He began working on prototypes and meanwhile, the company diversified into all-terrain vehicles for the mining, oil, and forestry industries, eventually developing the Muskeg Tractor, which was unveiled in 1953 to transport supplies over snow and swamps.

Bombardier's greatest breakthrough came in 1959, when after a long struggle to overcome financing issues and design problems, the company unveiled a small, lightweight snowmobile powered by a reliable two-cycle engine and utilizing a seamless, wide caterpillar track invented by his eldest son Germain. It was an instant hit.

In the February 1963 issue of *Imperial Oil Review* the machine was described as a "kind of scooter mounted on toy tracks and which growls like a runaway dishwasher." Bombardier's invention opened up communities across northern Canada in winter and introduced Canadians to a new winter sport — snowmobiling.

Bombardier died of cancer on February 18, 1964 at the age of 56, but not before being granted more than 40 patents and developing a robust business with sales of $10 million. Today, many of his inventions can be seen in the J. Armand Bombardier Museum in Valcourt, Quebec.

Following his death, the company — now known as Bombardier Inc. — diversified further to become Canada's most important transportation conglomerate under the guidance of Germain Bombardier, and later Laurent Beaudoin, Joseph-Armand Bombardier's son-in-law. By the 1990s, more than two million snowmobiles had been sold and the Montreal-based company was also producing the Sea-Doo recreational watercraft, boats, and all-terrain vehicles. The firm had worldwide manufacturing interests in airplanes, trains, military vehicles, and public transportation systems. In the fiscal year that ended January 31, 2008, they posted revenues of US$17.5 billion.

**Trivia BITE!**

When Armand Bombardier invented the snowmobile in 1959, he called it the Ski-Dog, but when the literature was printed, a typographical error changed the name to Ski-Doo. It stuck, and since that faux pas the company has sold more than two million snowmobiles worldwide.

## Samuel Cunard (Cunard Line)

By the time Samuel Cunard died in London at age 78, he had transformed the way ships navigated the world's oceans.

The Halifax-born son of a master carpenter and timber merchant, Cunard created a shipping line that operated the finest passenger liners in the world and dominated Atlantic shipping in the 19th century. Among its ships were the *Lusitania* and the *Queen Elizabeth*.

The hallmarks of the company were safety over profits, the best ships, officers and crew, and a handful of shipping innovations that contributed to the improvement of international navigation.

As a youngster, Cunard demonstrated remarkable business acumen. At age 17, he began managing his own general store and after joining his father in the timber business, he gradually expanded the family interests into coal, iron, shipping, and whaling. A. Cunard and Son opened for business in July 1813, and a year later its ships were carrying mail between Newfoundland, Bermuda, and Boston. Soon, the fleet numbered 40 ships.

Early in his career, Samuel Cunard recognized the economic disadvantages of ships entirely dependent on wind. He dreamed of a steam-powered "ocean railway" with passengers and cargo arriving by ship as punctually and as regularly as by train.

Although his idea was greeted with scorn, in 1833, the *Royal William* became the first ship to cross the Atlantic Ocean entirely by steam. Cunard was one of the vessel's principal shareholders.

In 1839 Cunard won a contract to undertake regular mail service by steamship from Liverpool to Halifax, Quebec City, and Boston. With associates in Glasgow and Liverpool, he established the British and North American Royal Mail Steam Packet Company, the direct ancestor of the Cunard Line. Four steamships were built, and in July 1840, paddle steamer *Britannia* crossed the Atlantic from Liverpool to Halifax, and steamed on to Boston in 14 days and eight hours, a feat that would lead to the decline and eventual disappearance of transatlantic commercial sailing ships.

Photo courtesy of National Archives of Canada PA 124022.

Founder of the Line
Samuel Cunard

Samuel Cunard.

In addition to an unparalleled safety record, Cunard's company was on the leading edge of shipping innovation, initiating the system of sailing with green lights to starboard, red to port, and white on the masthead, which became the standard for the entire maritime world. Its ships were also the first to enjoy the marvels of electric lights and wireless.

Cunard's enlightened views as an employer were far ahead of his time. It was always his view that if he picked employees well, paid them well, and treated them well, they would return the favour with loyalty and pride — and they did.

In 1859, Cunard was honoured by Queen Victoria with a knighthood. He died in 1865. The Cunard group became a public company in 1878, adopting the name Cunard Steamship Limited, and eventually absorbed Canadian Northern Steamships Limited and its principal competitor, the White Star Line.

The company is now known as the Cunard Line and is operated by Miami-based Cunard Line Limited. Its flagship is the

## Trivia BITE!

Not a single life was lost on a Cunard ship in the first 65 years of the company's history until May 7, 1915, when a German submarine torpedoed the *Lusitania*, killing 1,200 people. The disaster occurred 50 years after Cunard's death. Writer Mark Twain once remarked that "he felt himself rather safer on board a Cunard steamer than he did upon land."

luxury cruise ship *Queen Elizabeth 2*, which the company touts as "the world's most famous ship and the greatest liner of her time."

## ✠ The Popemobile: Designed to Withstand a Commando Attack

They were two Canadian-made vehicles specially adapted for Pope John Paul II's 1984 visit to Canada. Not surprisingly, they were known as "Popemobiles."

They were used during the late pope's September 1984 papal tour of Canada, after an assassination attempt in 1981 prompted the Vatican to demand more protection for the pontiff. One was also used by the Pope when he visited Cuba in 1998.

Both Popemobiles were built by Camions Pierre Thibault, a Pierreville, Quebec, emergency vehicle maker well known for its fire trucks. They're modified GMC Sierra Heavy-Duty V8 trucks with a large transparent dome designed to keep the Pope fully protected and comfortable, yet completely visible.

The dome area is fully air-conditioned, and is upholstered in red velvet imported from France. The $15,000 trucks were donated by GM Canada, and the 3.2-centimetre-thick bulletproof glass is made of a special laminate valued at $42,000 and donated by GE Canada.

The cube area accommodated the Pope and four other people. The trucks were equipped with video cameras, which produced footage that was sold to the media and used for security. Total cost for each vehicle was $130,000.

Originally the property of the Canadian Conference of Catholic Bishops, one Popemobile was donated to the Canada Science and Technology Museum in Ottawa in 1985, where it is occasionally placed on display. While in storage the vehicle can be viewed by appointment only by calling (613) 991-3044. The other Popemobile is at the Vatican in Rome.

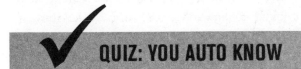

## ✔ QUIZ: YOU AUTO KNOW

A chance to test your knowledge of Canada's highways and byways.

1.  The early 1960s slogan "Put a Tiger in your Tank" was the brainchild of what automobile fuel company?

    a) Supertest
    b) Imperial Oil

      c) Fina

      d) Texaco

2. True or false? In 1903, when Canada's first automobile clubs were founded, there were fewer than 200 cars in the country.

3. In 1900, F.S. Evans set a speed record for the 60-kilometre trip by automobile between Toronto and Hamilton. How long did it take him?

      a) 90 minutes

      b) one hour

      c) two hours and 45 minutes

      d) three hours and 20 minutes

4. What city hosted Canada's first automobile race?

      a) Montreal

      b) Halifax

      c) Winnipeg

      d) Toronto

      e) London

5. What is Canadian driver Earl Ross's claim to fame?

      a) he was once NASCAR's Rookie of the Year

      b) he won the first Can-Am race in the 1960s

      c) he won a race against an airplane in 1917

      d) he was the first Canadian to compete in the Indy 500

6. The Peck was an electric car built in Toronto from 1911 to 1913. What was the company's slogan?

      a) "This car Pecks a punch."

      b) "Keeps pecking."

      c) "A Peck of a smooth ride."

      d) "Drive a Peck today."

7. What is the name of the scenic drive between Banff and Jasper national parks?

8. True or false? Ontario was the first province to establish a Department of Highways.

9. In 1991, Petro-Canada announced one of the following. Was it:

   a) a new consumer-friendly credit card
   b) Canada's first customer rewards program
   c) the sale of its shares to the public
   d) development of a revolutionary touch-free
      car wash system

10. The University of British Columbia's sports teams have the same name as a popular sports car. What is it?

 **Answers on page 352**

# ❧ GET OUT ON THE HIGHWAY

- Canada boasts the longest highway in the world, the Trans-Canada Highway at 7,821 kilometres in length, as well as one of the busiest sections of highway in the world, Highway 401 through the Greater Toronto Area. On a typical day, more than 400,000 vehicles use Highway 401 where it intersects with Highway 400.

- On May 1, 1900, in Winnipeg a horse buggy and a car collided in what was Canada's first recorded auto accident. No word on who got the worst of it.

- In 1903, Ontario became the first province to issue car licences, which took the form of patent leather plaques with aluminum numbers. At the time, other provinces issued individual motorists a number for their vehicle and left it to the owners to make their own plates, usually from wood, metal, or leather.

- At one time in British Columbia, New Brunswick, Prince Edward Island, Newfoundland, and Nova Scotia motorists used to drive on the left side of the road. British Columbia was the first to make the switch to the right side in 1920, followed by Nova Scotia, New Brunswick, and PEI over the next four years. For months after the change, road signs in Nova Scotia warned motorists to stay to the right. Newfoundlanders did not switch to the right side of the road until 1947 in preparation for entering Confederation with Canada in 1949.

- Dr. Perry Doolittle, a native of Elgin County in southwestern Ontario, founded the Canadian Automobile Association in 1913 and was the first physician in Toronto to make his rounds by automobile. He is also the man who bought the first used car in Canada, a one-cylinder Winton, from owner John Moodie of Hamilton. Doolittle was president of the CAA from 1920 to 1933.

# CHAPTER 13
# Innovations and Inventions

 ## NOTED CANADIAN INVENTORS

### ● Peter Lymburner Robertson (Robertson screwdriver)

The Robertson screwdriver is among the tools found at hardware stores and building supply outlets across Canada.

The screwdriver with the square head and the screws used in conjunction with it are the brainchild of P.L. Robertson. At the time he came up with the idea, in 1906 in Milton, Ontario, the slot-head screwdriver was popular but it had a tendency to slip out of the screws as Robertson well knew. The story goes that Robertson once cut his hand using a slotted screwdriver and decided it was time to come up with an improvement. His screwdriver, which he started making in 1908, gripped the square-holed screws better and averted damage to work surfaces and fingers in the process.

One of Robertson's competitors, the Steel Company of Canada, tried to invalidate his patents, and a scathing story about him appeared in a 1910 issue of *Saturday Night* magazine. He responded with a 1,000-word letter to the editor.

Robertson, who was born in 1879, initially had trouble receiving financing to manufacture his invention, but still turned down an offer from Henry Ford. Instead, he founded Recess Screws Ltd. in England and set up a manufacturing plant in Milton, west of Toronto. By the end of the Second World War, he had 500 employees and was a well-known philanthropist. Robertson died in 1951 a millionaire, secure in the knowledge that his screws and screwdrivers were popular worldwide.

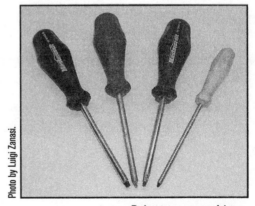

Photo by Luigi Zanasi.

Robertson screwdrivers.

# ℞ William Knapp Buckley (Buckley's Mixture)

For nearly 60 years, William Buckley earned a living by leaving a bad taste in his customers' mouths.

After moving to Toronto in the summer of 1914, the native of Wallace, Nova Scotia, graduated from the Ontario College of Pharmacy in 1915 and landed a job as a pharmacist at the T. Eaton Company's downtown Toronto store. In 1918, he bought his own drugstore, and when a worldwide flu epidemic broke out, "Doc," as he was nicknamed, developed a medicine that suppressed the coughs of his clientele.

The syrup, known as Buckley's Mixture, was mixed in a butter churn and sold for 75 cents a bottle. Its ingredients, including ammonium carbonate, menthol, oil of pine, and extract of Irish moss, tasted awful. But it worked, and Buckley sold 2,000 bottles in the first year. In his words, the mixture tasted "brisk."

Seeing tremendous potential, Buckley in 1920 founded W.K. Buckley Ltd., and converted a nearby house into a manufacturing facility where he made larger quantities of his cough medicine. In 1935, he sold his drug store to concentrate on the production and marketing of Buckley's Mixture.

In the 1930s and 1940s, his elixir was found in medicine cabinets in the United States, the Caribbean, New Zealand, Australia, and Holland. Along the way, Buckley, who had developed a reputation as a born salesman, also developed other products, including Buckley's White Rub and Jack and Jill children's cough syrup.

After Buckley died in January 1978, his son Frank assumed the presidency and became the spokesman in Buckley's "bad taste" ad campaign, which helped increase the company's market share in the cough and cold category by more than 10 percent. In radio, television, and print ads, Frank Buckley declared: "It tastes awful.

## Trivia BITE!

Thanks to his interest in thoroughbreds, William Buckley developed Buckley's Zev, a remedy for respiratory ailments in horses. Named after an early winner of the Kentucky Derby, Zev is found in most Canadian racing stables.

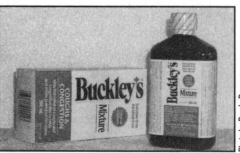

It tastes terrible but it works.

And it works." In other advertisements, he quipped: "I came by my bad taste honestly; I inherited it from my father."

In 1920, the cough syrup people loved to hate rang up $40,000 worth of sales. Novartis, the Swiss-based conglomerate with 2005 sales of $32 billion, purchased ownership of the Buckley's brand and formulas in 2002.

Frank Buckley is often asked why he doesn't improve the taste of the mixture invented by his father. "We can't get rid of the taste," he replies. "If we do, we will be just another 'me too' cough medicine."

## ☎ Alexander Graham Bell and Alexander Melville Bell (Bell Canada)

With the exception of Thomas Edison, there is probably no more famous inventor in the past 150 years than Alexander Graham Bell. Because his last name became synonymous with his primary invention, the telephone, the Bell name has had a familiar ring for decades.

Bell's story is generally well known. The son of Scottish immigrants who came to Canada in 1870, Bell later travelled from his home in Brantford, Ontario, to Boston, Massachusetts, where he taught at a school for the deaf and experimented with his idea of how to send the human voice over a wire. He would discuss his idea at length with his father during visits to Brantford. In 1870, the U.S. Patent Office dropped a requirement that a working model accompany a patent application. Bell filed his patent application for the telephone without having such a model, and fortunately for him, completed it just a few hours before Elisha Gray, another inventor, filed his notice for the same idea. On March 10, 1876, while working in Boston, Bell uttered the famous words to his assistant "Mr. Watson, come here, I want you," that are considered to be the first ever spoken on a telephone.

Bell spent most of his life engaged in scientific research. He worked on the photoelectric cell, the iron lung, and the phonograph. In the early 1900s, he turned his attention to developing aircraft. His wife, Mabel Hubbard, who was deaf, shared his interest in science and philanthropic causes. The telephone made Bell a wealthy man, and his estate near Baddeck, Nova Scotia is one of the most popular tourist spots in the Maritimes. He died there in August 1922.

But an argument could be made that it was his father, Alexander Melville Bell, who gave his name to the Canadian phone company. In fact, he's considered to be the founder of the telephone industry in

### Trivia BITE!

Though most people say "hello" when they pick up the phone, that wasn't the word Bell would have chosen. He suggested telephone users say "ahoy" when answering a call, but the idea never caught on.

Canada. Alexander Graham Bell transferred the Canadian patent rights to his father, who then hired agents to solicit telephone rentals. It was Alexander Melville who established the first telephone networks in this country by leasing telephones in pairs.

Born in Edinburgh, Scotland, in 1819, he became a professor of elocution and invented "visible speech," a written code which indicates how humans make vocal sounds. This was especially beneficial to the deaf.

It's important to remember that while the telephone today is ubiquitous and still a technological marvel, it was initially seen by many as no better a way to communicate than the telegraph. In fact, Bell Sr. tried to sell his patent rights in 1879 for $100,000, and no one bought them. Eventually National Bell of Boston bought the rights from him, and in 1880 Bell Telephone Company of Canada was incorporated. By the end of the first year, there were telephone exchanges in 14 major cities.

Alexander Melville Bell was also a professor at Queen's University in Kingston, Ontario, and moved to Washington, D.C. in 1881. He died there in 1905.

Though Bell is a famous name and company throughout North America, it generally concentrated its efforts in Canada in Ontario, Quebec, and the Eastern Arctic. As for the controversy sometimes raised about whether Canada can lay claim to being the home of the invention of the telephone, we leave it to Alexander Graham Bell himself. In a speech given in 1909 in Ottawa he said: "Of this you may be sure, the telephone was invented in Canada. It was made in the United States."

# 🍁 SOME GREAT CANADIAN INNOVATIONS

- The Jolly Jumper, which has kept youngsters everywhere happy and healthy, was invented in British Columbia in 1959 by Olivia Poole, who is originally from the White Earth Reservation in Minnesota. About one in every five Canadian babies uses the device.

- Dr. James Gosling, who grew up near Calgary, developed Java, a universal computer programming language. Originally known as Oak, it can be used with platforms such as Unix and Windows.

### They Said It!

"The boy who loiters on the way when sent on an errand, too often remains the errand boy throughout life."

– *Thomas Ahearn, Ottawa native, electrical engineer, inventor, and promoter at the height of his career, speaking of his early years.*

- Henry Ruttan of Cobourg, Ontario, introduced air conditioning to train travel in 1858 by channelling a flow of air through a ventilating cap and over a shallow, coldwater tank placed on top of a rail car.

- Sir Sandford Fleming, a civil engineer who immigrated to Canada from Scotland in 1845, is well known for overseeing major surveys when Canada's transcontinental railway was built in the late 1800s. In addition, he designed the "Three-Penny Beaver," Canada's first adhesive postage stamp, and a pair of in-line skates, and proposed the present system of standard time, which in 1884 divided the world into 24 equal time zones.

> **Trivia BITE!**
>
> The first patent issued in Canada after Confederation was registered to William J. Hamilton of Toronto for an invention described as a "machine for measuring liquids." The patent was dated August 18, 1869. Accompanying drawings dated July 30, 1869, and showing a variety of components, including a piston, guide rod, ratchet wheel and cylinder, refer to the device as "Hamilton's Eureka Fluid Meter."

- Chemistry professor Thomas Sterry Hunt of McGill University in Montreal came up with the ink the United States chose to print its money with, beginning in 1862. The special green ink couldn't be reproduced by photography, making it nearly impossible for forgers to produce phony "greenbacks."

- William Leonard Hunt was known in the 1800s as The Great Farini. In addition to his thrilling high-wire acts, the Port Hope, Ontario-born daredevil masterminded the first human cannonball act and invented folding theatre seats and the modern parachute.

- In 1969, when Walter Chell was working at the Westin Hotel in Calgary, he developed the Bloody Caesar. Made with vodka, Clamato juice, Worcestershire sauce, salt and pepper, and garnished with a celery stalk, the drink has become a favourite at bars, brunches, and backyard barbecues.

- Pablum, the vitamin-enriched ready-to-use baby food that came onto the Canadian market in 1931, wasn't the first nutritional breakthrough for Drs. Frederick Tisdall and Theodore Drake, who invented the cereal at the Hospital for Sick Children in Toronto. In early 1930, they developed the Sunwheat "irradiated" biscuit, which contained whole

## Trivia BITE!

The name "Pablum" is derived from the Latin *pabulum* meaning "food." The cereal, which was immediately glommed down by babies when it was introduced in 1931, is a mixture of wheat meal, oatmeal, cornmeal, wheat germ, brewer's yeast, bone meal, and alfalfa. Media reports at the time said the cereal tasted like "boiled Kleenex" and "had the consistency of mucilage and smelled like the inside of an old cardboard box."

wheat, wheat germ, milk, butter, yeast, bone meal, iron, and copper and was high in several vitamins. More than $1 million in royalties from the sale of Pablum and Sunwheat biscuits helped establish the Sick Kids Research Institute, and over the years the money has contributed to key medical breakthroughs such as the discovery of the cystic fibrosis gene and the surgical correction for the heart defect that causes "blue babies."

 Q AND A

*Q: Can the invention of the snowblower be attributed to someone from the Great White North?*

**A:** The snowblower is indeed a Canadian invention. It was created by Arthur Sicard, a Montreal-area farm-boy-turned-entrepreneur, who had tired of having his milk spoil whenever the roads to market were blocked by snow drifts, which happened frequently.

In the late 1800s he experimented with a variety of snow-removal techniques — including scrapers and V-shaped plows attached to automobiles — all to no avail. His idea for a snowblower was sparked by a farm threshing machine, which consisted of revolving metal "worms" and a fan which blew chopped-up straw up a pipe into a strawstack.

Sicard invested his meagre savings in a truck with primitive worms and a blower. It worked on small drifts but broke down on larger ones. When Sicard left farming for the construction business, the idea went on hold until 20 years later when he owned his own company and had enough cash to return to his idea.

With stronger gasoline engines on the market, he sank $40,000 into his first hand-built blower, and it rumbled onto the streets of Montreal in 1924. He patented his invention in the late 1920s and sold his first machine for $13,000 through his own incorporated company. He sold machines to the Quebec Department of Highways, the City of Montreal, and the St. Hubert Airport, and eventually his work force increased to 160 as production jumped to 56 units a year.

Sicard died of a heart attack in 1946, just as his Sicard snowblowers were becoming familiar sights across North America.

**Q: What do condoms and mice have to do with the development of the first anti-gravity suit?**

**A:** Early in the Second World War, researchers led by Canadian medical pioneer Sir Frederick Banting discovered that fighter pilots frequently crashed as they pulled out of steep turns high in the sky.

As their aircraft accelerated, centrifugal force pushed blood into their legs and abdomens and it became too heavy to be pumped by the heart to the eyes and brains, causing pilots to black out or lose consciousness and, in either case, to lose control of their airplanes.

Banting immediately recognized that if pilots could avoid these conditions during dogfights miles up in the sky, Allied crews would have a tremendous tactical advantage.

Enter Dr. Wilbur Rounding Franks, a medical doctor and cancer researcher at the Banting and Best Medical Research Institute at the University of Toronto.

Using condoms fashioned into tiny water-filled G-suits for mice, Dr. Franks and his fellow researchers demonstrated that the rodents could tolerate up to 240 Gs without being harmed.

It was a huge breakthrough, and soon after, Dr. Franks and his team developed overalls made of two layers of rubber with water in between, which laced tight to the pilot's body. The getup was the Franks Flying Suit Mark I, the world's first G-suit used in combat.

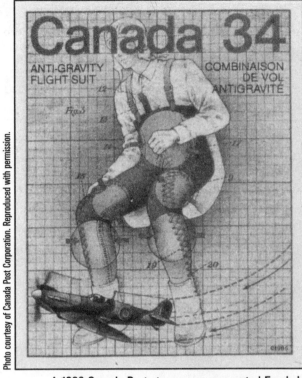

Photo courtesy of Canada Post Corporation. Reproduced with permission.

A 1986 Canada Post stamp commemorated Franks's development of the flying suit.

### Trivia BITE!

Ironically, an air crash took the life of Sir Frederick Banting. In 1941, while on his way to Britain to discuss aviation medicine and demonstrate the Franks Flying Suit Mark II, Banting died when his plane went down in Labrador. In 1921–22, Banting was part of the team that discovered insulin, a lifesaving therapy for diabetes.

The researchers later developed improved versions, including the Franks Flying Suit Mark III, an air inflated, zippered design that squeezed the stomach and legs. The Mark III led directly to the first production model.

Although cumbersome and impractical, the initial design protected pilots from forces of six Gs or more when the downward pressure on the water caused by acceleration created enough force to counteract the downward rush of blood in the body, helping pilots maintain consciousness.

Dr. Wilbur Franks.

Photo courtesy of National Archives of Canada PA 63866.

In May 1940, Franks donned this first rough version of his Franks Flying Suit and climbed into a Fleet Finch trainer aircraft at Camp Borden near Barrie, Ontario, north of Toronto. When he and the pilot were hit with about seven Gs while pulling out of a steep dive, the pilot experienced a temporary blackout but Franks did not.

After the suit was modified to cover only the essential areas of the lower body, it was worn by a Royal Air Force pilot, D'Arcy Greig, who flew a Spitfire at Malton airport in Toronto to become the first pilot to wear a true G-suit in flight. In the spring of 1941, Royal Canadian Air Force Squadron Leader F.E.R. Briggs was the first Canadian pilot to test the suit.

The Franks Flying Suit had its first battle test in 1942, when carrier-based fighter planes from the British Fleet Air Arm swept into Oran in French North Africa. By all accounts it was a success: "Because test pilots no longer blacked out during dangerous maneuvers, they could make observations which led to safer, stronger aircraft," said one report.

Peter Allen, a former commercial airline pilot who wrote a paper on the early years of Canadian aviation medicine for the Canadian Aviation Historical Society's *Journal*, compared Canada's development of early G-suits to the U.S. Apollo space program. Modern G-suits, including those worn by astronauts, use the same physiological principle applied by Dr. Franks.

A 1969 article in *Aerospace Medicine* described the Franks suit as a "rather remarkable World War II achievement of aeromedical research and development." Reporting on a comparison of the combat effectiveness between fighter pilots who used the suit and those who did not, the publication said G-suit-equipped pilots shot down 81 percent more enemy planes per 1,000 sorties and 103 percent more per 10,000 operational hours than those not equipped with the suits.

Between 1940 and 1944 more than 250 modifications were made, and when the suit was manufactured for the British Ministry of Aircraft Production in the early 1940s, it was available in seven standard sizes.

The first anti-G suit, which stretched from high on the neck to toes and fingertips, was secretly sewn together by a tailor on an old sewing machine in Franks's office. A version of the suit is part of the collection at Base Borden Military Museum in Barrie, Ontario. Although it has been on display in recent years, both at the Base Borden museum and off-site, it is not available for public viewing because of its fragility, says retired Lieutenant Colonel Stewart L. Beaton, the museum's director.

"It is made from cotton and rubber, which 65 years ago was not the greatest," says Beaton. "If you picked it up it might fall apart."

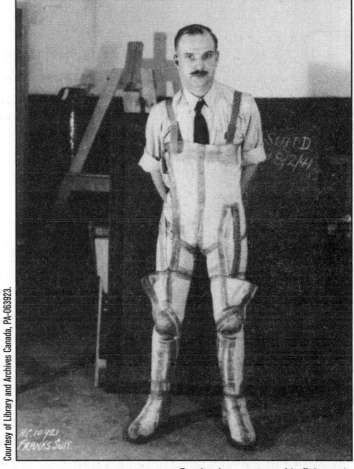

Courtesy of Library and Archives Canada, PA-063923.

Franks demonstrates his flying suit.

Beaton is hopeful that the museum will eventually acquire funds to build a case that would protect the historic suit from the ravages of temperature, humidity, and human hands and allow the public to view it.

Other versions of the Franks Flying Suit have also been preserved. One can be viewed by the public at the Canadian Warplane Heritage Museum in Hamilton, Ontario (www.warplane.com); another is part of the collection of Defence Research and Development Canada in Toronto (www.toronto.drdc-rddc.gc.ca) but is not on public display; and two more are in storage at the Canadian War Museum in Ottawa (www.warmuseum.ca) and are unavailable for viewing.

An exact replica is on display at the Toronto Aerospace Museum (www.torontoaerospacemuseum.com).

# CHAPTER 14
# Moguls and Magnates

 Alfred C. Fuller (Fuller Brush Company)

Alfred Carl Fuller described himself as a bit of a "country bumpkin, unsophisticated and virtually unschooled" when he went into business more than 100 years ago. And given that he grew up on a Nova Scotia farm, could barely read, and was once fired by his brother, the description was apt.

Despite these shortcomings, he managed to build a company that today does millions of dollars in annual sales.

Fuller was born on January 13, 1885, in Welsford, Nova Scotia, in the Annapolis Valley, where the Fullers lived on a 75-acre farm. Alfred, one of 12 children, was called "Uppie" as a child because his friends couldn't pronounce "Alfie" properly. He worked on the farm until he left home at 18, and the only advice from his father was to be thrifty, save money, and live cleanly. He first moved to the Boston area in 1903, where three of his brothers and two sisters lived.

Fuller got a job as a trolley conductor, got fired after he derailed a car, and then held a few other jobs from which he was also fired, including a stint driving an express wagon for his brother Robert. Fuller left packages at wrong addresses and forgot important pickups, and Robert fired him. Alfred then went to work selling household brushes for a company door to door, and after about a year decided he could do better on his own.

Like so many successful businesses of the time, Fuller started his company in a home, in this case in the basement of his sister Annie's house. He had a few ideas for brushes that his previous employer had rejected. Four months later, in April 1906, he moved his operations to Hartford, Connecticut, and decided to call his enterprise the Capitol Brush Company after seeing the state capitol building there.

The company grew as Fuller listened to his customers' needs and then created brushes to solve their cleaning problems. "My customers were my designers," he said. In his first nine months, Fuller grossed $5,000; it was good money for the time, but Fuller dealers would generate that much about every 10 minutes some 50 years later. Fuller began expanding to other states and eventually into Canada. In 1913, he realized he hadn't registered the Capitol company name, so he took the opportunity to rename the firm The Fuller Brush Company. By 1919, the company recorded its first $1 million in annual sales.

## Biz BITE!

Fuller wasn't the first one in his family to own a brush business. His older brother Dwight had been a brush salesman who branched out on his own. But the brush manufacturing process in those days created a lot of dust, and the bad air he breathed is thought to be the reason Dwight died in 1901. No wonder Fuller's parents weren't initially supportive of Alfred's move to the brush-making business.

Fuller's company prospered through the 20th century. The phrase "The Fuller Brush Man" became famous enough to inspire a 1948 movie of that name starring Red Skelton. Two years later Lucille Ball starred in *The Fuller Brush Girl*.

Today, the company's large manufacturing plant in Great Bend, Kansas, offers more than 2,000 different home and personal care products. Fuller, who divorced his first wife in 1930 and remarried in 1932, died in December, 1973.

# Albert Edward LePage
# (Royal LePage Real Estate Ltd.)

Selling real estate was regarded as the lowliest of Canada's professions — until Albert Edward LePage arrived on the scene in the early 1900s.

LePage, who often said "if you failed at everything else, you went into real estate," turned the industry on its ear when he began selling houses in Toronto in 1913.

In an era when real estate agents were viewed as highly unethical and disorganized and who did little selling in the summer and between November and early January, LePage demonstrated a brand of get-up-and-go that polished the tarnished image of his colleagues.

After leaving a job at his father's manufacturing company in Toronto at age 26, the Charlottetown native began selling homes for a friend who had found considerable success on the Toronto real estate scene. Soon after, LePage started A.E. LePage Ltd., where one of his first innovations was the installation of his own office telephone at a time when most sales representatives shared phones. To set himself apart from other agents, he called himself a "bungalow specialist."

LePage, who often arrived for work outfitted in a bow tie and a straw hat, claimed to be the first agent to place descriptive advertisements in newspapers and he was among the first to take clients through the homes he had listed (previously buyers visited properties on their own). In 1929,

Courtesy of Royal LePage Real Estate Services, Ltd.

Albert Edward LePage.

when he was building and selling homes, he accomplished the unbelievable by erecting a five-bedroom bungalow in one day and topped his achievement by selling the place within 24 hours.

At the end of the First World War, his drive to end bad practices in real estate was instrumental in the formation of the Toronto Real Estate Board. He was its president in 1928. By 1940, LePage was subdividing prestigious estates and selling the lots as subdivisions. He is said to be the only real estate agent to have listed Casa Loma in Toronto.

When LePage retired and sold his company in 1953, A.E. LePage Ltd. was a residential real estate company based in Toronto and offering its services within a 20-mile radius of the city. Eventually, it became the largest real estate firm in Canada, engaged in residential sales as well as land assembly. A.E. Lepage Ltd. did much of the appraisal work for the St. Lawrence Seaway and was responsible for assembling land in downtown Toronto where the Toronto-Dominion Centre now stands. LePage died on June 4, 1968.

### Biz BITE!

A.E. LePage's uncle, William Nelson Le Page of Prince Edward Island, founded the LePage glue business in the early 1870s.

In 1984, A.E. LePage and Royal Trust merged their real estate brokerages to become Royal LePage Real Estate Services Ltd.

Today, Royal LePage is Canada's leading provider of franchise services to residential real estate brokerages, with a network of over 14,000 agents and sales representatives in 600 locations across Canada. Royal LePage is managed by Brookfield Real Estate Services, and is part of a brand family that includes Royal LePage, Johnston and Daniel, Realty World, and La Capitale.

#  Jim Pattison (The Jim Pattison Group)

Comedian Bob Hope once described British Columbia as a suburb of Jim Pattison. Over the years, various media reports have concluded that it's virtually impossible to do business in B.C. without dealing with one of the Vancouver billionaire's many enterprises.

In British Columbia, if you purchase or lease cars, buy groceries and magazines, listen to the radio and watch television, Pattison has probably touched your life. If you live east of the Rocky Mountains, he has influenced your life too.

The next time you're out and about — be it in Halifax, Ottawa, Winnipeg, Montreal, or Saskatoon — there's a good chance you'll see Pattison's name on the billboards and advertising signage found along most busy streets.

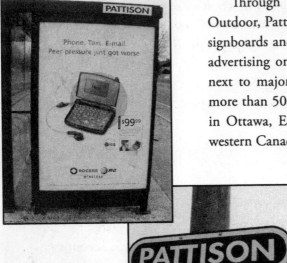

Photos by Randy Ray.

Pattison advertisements can be spotted throughout much of the country.

Through The Jim Pattison Sign Group and Pattison Outdoor, Pattison's name is found on 20,000 large roadside signboards and bus shelters in Canada, and he controls the advertising on hundreds of large neon signs, most located next to major expressways in Toronto and Montreal, and more than 50,000 "poster boards" affixed to transit vehicles in Ottawa, Edmonton, Calgary, and a handful of smaller western Canada cities.

Chances are, you've probably eaten a tin of Gold Seal salmon or visited a Ripley's Believe or Not! museum, theatre, or aquarium. He owns those too.

With his fingers in all kinds of pies and a personal fortune pegged at around $2 billion, Pattison — who's called "Jimmy" by most people — was listed as number 178 on the 2008 *Forbes* Magazine list of the world's richest people and the sixth richest Canadian. His sole proprietorship company boasts assets of $3.1 billion, sales of $5.2 billion, and a workforce of 25,000.

Born in October 1928, in Luseland, Saskatchewan, near Saskatoon, Pattison had his first taste of entrepreneurialism at the age of seven when he began selling vegetable seeds after his family moved to Vancouver. As a University of British Columbia commerce student, he paid for his tuition and other expenses by washing cars at a used car lot and selling vehicles to fellow students.

Although his father, a car salesman, wanted his son to be a lawyer, the car business was soon in the young Pattison's blood. In the late 1950s he ran a Vancouver car lot where he set sales records and convinced the owner to invest in the largest neon sign in North America. In 1961, at age 33, he purchased a General Motors automobile dealership in Vancouver, with a $40,000 loan. Four years later he bought struggling radio station CJOR in Vancouver and was well on his way to fulfilling the vow he made to his wife Mary — that he'd be a millionaire by the age of 40.

Over the years he has gained a reputation as a charming and generous man and a shrewd businessman who has built his company by acquisitions and diversification. He's also been referred to as a hard-boiled softy, ruthless, God-fearing, greedy, and slightly tacky.

On the back of the book *Jimmy: An Autobiography*, the late broadcaster Peter Gzowski calls Pattison "a curious man, part altruist, part egoist, partly private, partly show-off."

The Pattison empire started in the car business, which in 2002 included 12 dealerships in Victoria and the Vancouver area, several of which bear his name, as well as Jim Pattison Lease, a national vehicle leasing company based in Calgary with offices in Vancouver, Victoria, Edmonton, and Toronto.

Companies he's acquired on various buying sprees (and in some cases later sold) include one of the biggest coal ports on the west coast; the Canadian Fish Company, Canada's second-largest producer of Pacific salmon and herring roe; Overwaitea and Save-On-Foods, Canada's largest western-based food store chain; Crush International, which bottles Orange Crush; and airlines, trucking companies, and a manufacturer of mobile homes. The Pattison sign group is the world's largest custom electric outdoor sign company, and he owns 20 radio stations and three TV stations in Alberta and B.C. Also under his control is The Jim Pattison News Group, one of North America's largest wholesale magazine distribution companies, as well as export and financial services companies and packaging firms.

On the way to the top, Pattison has always had three loves — money, cars, and his prairie sweetheart, Mary Hudson. He and Mary were married in 1951 and have a son and two daughters.

Despite his great wealth and success, life in business hasn't always been smooth sailing: In 1969 he almost went bankrupt when one of his holdings, a company called Neonex, attempted to take over Maple Leaf Mills, one of Canada's largest flour mills. Over the years he has battled with the unions that represent his workers, been slammed because one of his companies distributed pornographic magazines, and, according to author Russell Kelly, in his book *Pattison, Portrait of a Capitalist Superstar*, he has raised the ire of employees, shareholders, and business partners over the years for engaging in "blackmail bargaining" and breaking promises.

## Biz BITE!

Pattison is notorious for his personal shopping sprees, which have included the purchase of Frank Sinatra's former home in Palm Springs, California, for US$4.6 million; John Lennon's psychedelic Rolls Royce for US$2.3 million, and a US$1 million collection of Marilyn Monroe memorabilia.

Though he may not be a household name across Canada, Pattison gained a degree of fame during the early 1980s, when Bill Bennett, premier of B.C. at the time, hired him to salvage Expo 86 in Vancouver, which was so far behind schedule it was in danger of being cancelled. Pattison earned a token dollar a year for his stint at Expo and managed to bring the $1.6 billion project in at $32 million under budget.

After that, it was back to business. By the summer of 1998, he owned 148 companies with operations in 12 countries and his empire continued to grow as Pattison reached his mid-70s. In 2002, he owned 54 companies.

During a speech several years ago in his hometown, Pattison attributed the beginnings of his company's success to the values of caring and integrity that he and his parents got from the small prairie community.

With investments in Canada, the United States, Mexico, Europe, Asia, and Australia, The Jim Pattison Group is Canada's third largest privately held company, and was ranked as Canada's 41st largest firm in a *Financial Post* survey. Pattison was appointed to the Order of Canada in 1987 and the Order of British Columbia in 1990. A devout Baptist, Pattison spends most of his time in Vancouver. In December 2008, Pattison was one of 11 prominent Canadians named to an economic advisory council established by federal finance minister Jim Flaherty.

#  Herbert Henry Dow (Dow Chemical Company)

The connection may be tenuous, but Canadians can claim the founder of the world-famous Dow Chemical Company as one of their own.

Herbert Henry Dow wouldn't remember his early life here, but he was born in a brick house at Dundas and Pinnacle streets in Belleville, Ontario, on February 26, 1866, the son of Joseph and Sarah Jane Dow. His father had been living in the eastern Ontario town since 1863, trying to drum up business for Irwin & White, a sewing machine company.

Just six weeks after Herbert was born, Joseph moved his family to Derby, Connecticut, in an effort to find new customers for his company. Unfortunately, the sewing machine enterprise folded soon after.

Joseph had been a born tinkerer, and as a young boy Herbert picked up these skills working alongside his dad trying to solve mechanical problems. Young Herbert invented an incubator for chicken eggs at age 12 and later helped his father develop a steam engine that the U.S. Navy used for many years for torpedo propulsion. The Dows would eventually settle in Cleveland, and it was at the Case School of Applied Science that Herbert Dow would graduate with a science degree in 1888. His interest in chemistry, being taught by some of the great minds of the time, and the ability to tinker and invent new products would help launch the successful company that bears his name.

As a young man, Dow had fallen in love with a schoolteacher named Mabelle Ross, but whether the chemistry wasn't right or she seemed unwilling to move to Midland, Michigan, where Dow was working, he married another teacher, Grace Anna Ball, instead.

Dow is considered by many to be one of the great inventors of the late 19th and early 20th centuries. Dow's development of a new method to extract bromine from the brine trapped underground in Midland was key to establishing his career.

Dow was fired from the Midland Chemical Company in 1893 because he believed in open competition in the marketplace rather than large cartels. He then went off on his own to develop and research more products and techniques, including the production of bleach. He formed the Dow Process Company in 1896, but changed the name to the Dow Chemical Company in May 1897. Ironically, his new firm would absorb Midland Chemical Company three years later.

Dow Chemical would create many products in those first years, including Epsom salts, and during the First World War it produced chemicals for explosives, medicines, dyes, and smokescreens. The early years weren't always easy as Dow had to battle monopolies and international cartels to open up the marketplace. Through the 1920s, Dow concentrated on other products, especially in the automobile industry. His Dowmetal pistons were used in the Indianapolis 500, for example.

Employees remembered Dow as a man full of ideas with a mind constantly at work. He enjoyed jokes and stories, but didn't tell them well himself and seemed to have little sense of play with his children or others. He was a notoriously bad driver, enjoyed travelling, was frugal with his money, and loved solving jigsaw puzzles. He was a great believer in education and his favourite saying was "if we can't do it better than others, why do it?" He held some 90 patents by the time he died on October 15, 1930, of cirrhosis of the liver.

His son Willard took over the company, which continued to blossom through to today. It would return to its Canadian roots when it opened a branch in Sarnia, Ontario, in 1942 to help with the war effort. Though the company has created products that are found in households and industries throughout the world, Dow Chemical has also had its share of controversy over the years. For example, it and other chemical companies' production of Agent Orange, used to defoliate forests in Vietnam, led to a massive lawsuit from veterans of the Vietnam War.

Today, Dow Chemical has annual sales of about $58 billion, more than 100 manufacturing sites in 33 countries, and makes and sells more than 2,000 chemicals and other products worldwide, including Ziploc bags and Styrofoam insulation.

 ## Edward S. Rogers (Rogers Communications Inc.)

Edward Rogers began his march toward broadcast industry stardom long before he started shaving and years before his family name became synonymous with Canadian telecommunications.

Rogers was born in 1900 into a wealthy and highly respected Toronto family descended from Quakers. His parents wanted him to become a business executive, but as a youngster he was enthralled by radio and eventually set up a laboratory in the family garage.

At age 11, he was broadcasting in Morse code from one of Canada's first licensed amateur radios. In 1913, when he was 13, he won a prize for the best amateur-built radio in Ontario and that year was the subject of a feature article in the *Toronto Telegram* newspaper that discussed how he was able to pick up a report of a shipwreck in Ireland on his telegraph set. A year later, he picked up Germany's declaration of war on a homemade radio.

After studying engineering at the University of Toronto for two years, Rogers in 1921 became the first Canadian to transmit a radio signal across the Atlantic Ocean. The signal originated in Newmarket, Ontario, and was sent to a receiving station in Androssan, Scotland, near Glasgow.

Published articles about Rogers' accomplishments referred to him as the "Wireless Wizard." In his early 20s, Ted, as he was known to his friends, launched Canada into the age of electronic information and entertainment when he invented the radio amplifying tube.

The device revolutionized the radio industry by eliminating the need for cumbersome, leak-prone acid batteries, enabling consumers to operate their radios on the alternating current from wall plugs. His invention also drastically cut the cost of radios, making them far more popular. He was well on his way toward achieving his vision of radio as an electric pipeline that would reach into people's homes to entertain, inform, and educate.

In 1925, he began manufacturing the Majestic five-tube batteryless radio, which despite its hefty $260 price tag was an immediate success because it eliminated an annoying hum that plagued battery-operated radios. In 1927, the year he received a patent for his invention, Rogers founded Toronto radio station CFRB, which was Canada's first all-electric radio station and later became one of the country's most influential and successful broadcasting companies. Among the many entertainers the station showcased were Guy Lombardo and his Royal Canadians and orchestra leader Percy Faith.

Rogers was granted the first Canadian television licence in 1931, foreshadowing the dominance in cable television that would be his legacy. Eight years later, while working on the development of radar, Rogers died of a bleeding ulcer. The Rogers estate floundered and CFRB was sold by his wife Velma.

Twenty years later Rogers's son Edward Samuel, also known as Ted, picked up where his father left off. He purchased Toronto radio station CHFI and over the years built a tremendously successful communications empire. Known as Rogers Communications Inc., the Toronto-based company's vast holdings have included radio and television stations, cable TV services and channels, movie theatres, newspapers, magazines and periodicals, Internet service on

**Biz BITE!**

The call letters for Toronto radio station CFRB stand for Canada's First Rogers Batteryless. When Rogers founded the station, it was originally known as 9RB.

cable, wireless communications, and football and baseball teams, including the Toronto Blue Jays.

Rogers died in December, 2008. His key legacy, Rogers Communications, is a leading provider of Wireless, Cable TV, High Speed Internet, and Home Phone services to consumer residences and businesses in Canada. Its annual revenue is approximately $11 billion and it employs about 29,000 Canadians.

##  Daniel Massey (Massey-Harris Company Ltd./Massey-Ferguson Ltd.)

In the years leading up to Confederation, farmer Daniel Massey was distressed by the long hours and backbreaking work involved in tilling fields and raising crops. So he took matters into his own hands.

"The tools on farms all over the world are the same as those used in the days of the Pharaohs," he wrote in an 1840 letter to a newspaper in Cobourg, Ontario, near where he lived and farmed. "There has been a small metal share added to the plough and some smart Scot has put a long handle on the sickle a few years ago ... but the backbreaking chores of sowing, reaping, threshing and cultivating are still nightmares to most farmers."

Not content to wait for others to embrace mechanization, Massey, then 42, began manufacturing and importing implements that eased the workload for farmers and simplified the process of moving produce from field to kitchen table.

From this modest beginning sprang one of the largest and most important firms in Canada's history, the Massey Company, which under a new name more than a century later would be described as being as widespread and all-enveloping as Coca-Cola.

Massey was born in Windsor, Vermont, in 1798 and spent his early years near Watertown, New York, before moving across Lake Ontario with his family to Grafton, about 125 kilometres east of Toronto. After working on the family's 100-acre farm until he was 19, he rented his own land nearby, but instead of farming, he began working as a contractor clearing land.

Business was good as newcomers flocked to fertile areas on the north side of the lake. By 1830, Massey and his crews had cleared more than 1,000 acres and he began thinking about ways to ease the laborious task of trimming timber and rolling it by hand into piles for burning. His answer was to use oxen, an untried farming method in those days, author Peter Cook wrote in *Massey at the Brink: The Story of Canada's Greatest Multinational and its Struggle to Survive.*

In the meantime, Massey was busy building a family. In 1820, he married Lucina Bradley; a year later a daughter was born, and in 1823, son Hart Almerrin arrived. By age seven, Hart was handling teams of horses and making trips to the local grist mill. Daniel, meanwhile, was devoting more of his time to tilling the land and had developed an interest in farm mechanization.

In 1840, father and son imported a mechanical threshing machine — the first in Upper Canada — from Watertown, which reduced from 20 to 11 the number of workers needed to handle threshing. Soon, the large barn on the Massey property was being used as a workshop; eventually, Massey, 49, and a partner purchased a small foundry near the village of Newcastle, Ontario that had been used to produce ploughs and sugar kettles. They named their enterprise the Massey Manufacturing Company. The company soon expanded with a new building, new equipment, and more employees.

In his early 50s, Massey grew tired and was having trouble keeping up with the workload, so he asked Hart to join the business. The 28-year-old brought with him ambitious plans to import and sell the latest farm machinery, much of it imported from the U.S. Together, the Masseys developed a reputation for innovation and excellent workmanship, and four years after Hart came on board, Daniel retired. A year later, in November, 1856, Daniel Massey died at age 58, leaving behind a company that had grown fourfold in just 10 years.

With Hart at the helm, Massey Manufacturing used mergers, spirited sales and advertising techniques, and entry into foreign markets to become a dynamic farm-implement producer that would transform the productivity of Canadian agriculture. "If you ate a loaf of bread in the early 1920s, it's safe to say the grain was planted by a Massey seed driller," says Franz Klingender, curator at the Canada Agriculture Museum in Ottawa.

Massey Manufacturing became the first North American firm to successfully enter foreign markets. It relocated to Toronto in 1879 and in 1891 merged with its chief competitor, A. Harris, Son & Company, to form Massey-Harris Company Ltd., of which Massey was president until his death in 1896. Four sons, Charles Albert, Frederic Victor, Walter Edward, and Chester Daniel later were active in the company, which plunged into the tractor business in 1928 with the purchase of the J.I. Case Plow Works.

Alanson Harris, a native of Ingersoll, Ontario, was a sawmill operator in Brant County before buying a foundry in Beamsville, Ontario in 1857, where he began manufacturing farm implements. In 1872, he moved to Brantford, Ontario and seven years later began marketing his products in western Canada. His company merged with the Massey Manufacturing Company in 1891 to become Massey-Harris Company Ltd.

In 1953, Massey-Harris merged with the Ferguson Companies, operated by eccentric Irish inventor Harry Ferguson, to form Massey-Harris-Ferguson. The name Massey Ferguson was adopted in 1958 and in 1987 the corporation was reorganized into Varity Corp. In the early 1990s, Varity sold its Massey-Ferguson division to AGCO Corp., an American farm machinery maker.

Over the years, three members of the Massey and Harris families achieved considerable fame. Hart Massey's grandson Charles Vincent was president of Massey-Harris Company Ltd. from 1921 until 1925 and later became Canada's first native-born governor general. Another grandson, Raymond Massey, was an actor best remembered for his roles as Abraham Lincoln and Dr. Gillespie in the *Dr. Kildare* television series. Lawren Harris, son of Thomas Morgan Harris, secretary of the Harris farm machinery company, was a landscape painter and a member of Canada's Group of Seven self-proclaimed modern artists.

Massey Hall, on Shuter Street in downtown Toronto, was built by Hart Massey as a gift to the city.

# CHAPTER 15
# My Generation: From Boomers to Gen X

## QUIZ 1: THE 1980s

Join us as we recall the 1980s and everything from valley girls and Reaganomics to MTV's debut and the fall of the Berlin Wall. This quiz should help reacquaint you with the wild ride that was the eighties.

1.  In the mid-1980s, NBC's powerful "must see TV" lineup included four comedies. *The Cosby Show*, *Cheers*, and *Night Court* were joined by another sitcom starring Michael J. Fox. Name it.

2.  Fill in the blanks to complete the titles of these 1980s bestsellers (authors' names in parentheses):

    a) *Real Men Don't Eat* _____ (Bruce Feirstein)
    b) _____ *of the Vanities* (Tom Wolfe)
    c) *A* _____ *History of Time* (Stephen Hawking)
    d) *Clear and* _____ *Danger* (Tom Clancy)

3.  When Walter Mondale lost the 1984 presidential election to Ronald Reagan, who was Mondale's running mate?

    a) Geraldine Ferraro
    b) Gary Hart
    c) Lloyd Bentsen
    d) Michael Dukakis

4.  At the 1984 Academy Awards, Sally Field won the Best Actress Award and gave her memorable speech about how people in the audience "like me, right now you like me." What movie did she win for?

    a) *Norma Rae*
    b) *Murphy's Romance*
    c) *Places in the Heart*
    d) *Absence of Malice*

5.  Between 1980 and 1989, this NFL team won three Super Bowls, more than any other team during that decade. Was it the

    a) Washington Redskins
    b) Los Angeles Raiders
    c) New York Giants
    d) San Francisco 49ers

6.  Which one of the following performers did NOT sing on the 1985 mega hit "We Are the World," which was recorded to raise money to aid Africa?

    a) Michael Jackson
    b) Paul Simon
    c) Bruce Springsteen
    d) Tina Turner
    e) Madonna

7.  In 1982, Frank Sinatra did some promotional work for an American automaker and in recognition, the company named one of its models The Frank Sinatra Edition. Was the car company Ford, Chrysler, or General Motors?

8.  The spaceship *Challenger* explodes, the Red Sox lose the World Series to the Mets, nuclear disaster in Chernobyl, Haley's comet returns, America celebrates the national holiday Dr. Martin Luther King Jr. Day for the first time, and Turner

Broadcasting begins to colourize black and white classic movies. What year am I?

    a) 1984
    b) 1985
    c) 1986
    d) 1987

9.   Unscramble the following three words to reveal what was called the "Holy Grail" of children's toys for the 1983 holiday shopping season.

      bacgabe ctahp lsodl

10.  This musical debuted on Broadway in October 1982 and ran for more than 7,400 performances. Was it

    a) *La Cage Aux Folles*
    b) *Phantom of the Opera*
    c) *Les Miserables*
    d) *Cats*

11.  Which of these sporting successes by American athletes is known as The Miracle on Ice: the U.S. men's ice hockey team's gold medal win at the Olympic Winter Games in 1980 or Scott Hamilton's gold medal victory at the 1981 World Figure Skating Championships?

12.  At the 1985 Academy Awards, this Steven Spielberg film was nominated for eleven Oscars, but ironically Spielberg was not nominated in the Best Director category. Was this film

    a) *Empire of the Sun*
    b) *The Color Purple*
    c) *E.T.*
    d) *Raiders of the Lost Ark*

➡ **Answers on pages 353–354**

## QUIZ 2: THE OSCAR/GRAMMY QUIZ

You want glitz and glamour? Each February, acting and singing stars head down the red carpets for the Oscars and Grammys. If you know enough about these awards, you just may be giving your own acceptance speech.

1.   Only one of these groups won Grammys. Which one?

     a) Led Zeppelin
     b) The Kinks
     c) The Who
     d) Simon and Garfunkel

2.   Marlon Brando won two Academy Awards for Best Actor. One was for *The Godfather*, which he didn't accept. What was the other for?

     a) *A Streetcar Named Desire*
     b) *On the Waterfront*
     c) *Last Tango in Paris*
     d) *Mutiny on the Bounty*

3.   True or false. *Mary Poppins* won the Grammy over The Beatles' *A Hard Day's Night* for best motion picture soundtrack.

4.   Randy Travis received a 2009 Grammy nomination in the Best Country Album category for his album *Around The Bend*. What is his real name?

     a) Randy Ray
     b) Randy Brown
     c) Randy Traywick
     d) Frankie Travis

5. The 51st Grammy Awards were held at the Staples Center in Los Angeles for the ninth time since 2000. Who is the building named after?

    a) The Staple Singers
    b) the Staples office-supply company
    c) record producer Jerry Staples
    d) Barry Staples, who build the facility in the late 1990s

6. The Grammys have received their share of criticism over the years. Which artist made this scathing comment: "We called them 'The Grannys.' Snobs, we did not want to hear anything about music from anyone older than us."

    a) Paul McCartney
    b) Cher
    c) Bono
    d) Madonna

7. At the 1974, 1975, and 1976 Oscar ceremonies, two actors were in the running for Best Actor each year. One of them was Jack Nicholson. Who was the other?

    a) Al Pacino
    b) Dustin Hoffman
    c} Jack Lemmon
    d) Robert De Niro

8. Woody Allen achieved the rare feat of being nominated as Best Actor, Director, and Screenwriter for the same picture, in his case Annie Hall. The following year this actor/director/writer matched it. Who was he?

    a) Robert Redford
    b) Sylvester Stallone
    c) Warren Beatty
    d) Paul Newman

9.   Which comedian hosted the most Oscar ceremonies in the 1980s?

     a) Bob Hope
     b) Johnny Carson
     c) Chevy Chase
     d) Billy Crystal

➥ **Answers on pages 354–355**

 **QUIZ 3: ADVERTISING**

**Trivia BITE!**

The O-Pee-Chee company, which was famous in Canada for making such gum as Bazooka and Thrills, took its name from a line in the Longfellow poem "The Song of Hiawatha." O-Pee-Chee is a Native word meaning "robin."

Remember when you didn't (or couldn't) zap through TV commercials but actually paid attention to them? Then sit back in your comfiest TV-watching chair and try out this quiz on advertisements from baby boomers' early years.

1.   The 1970s ad for this brand of margarine told us "it's not nice to fool Mother Nature." Was it

     a) Chiffon
     b) Imperial
     c) Parkay
     d) Blue Bonnet

2.   Margaret Hamilton was best known as the Wicked Witch of the West in the *Wizard of Oz*, but in the 1970s she enjoyed a resurgence in the role of "Cora" pitching this brand of coffee.

a) Yuban
b) Sanka
c) Maxwell House
d) Nescafe

3. "A little dab'll do ya" of this hair product that peaked in the 50s and 60s but that has undergone something of a resurgence lately. It was once mentioned in a *Seinfeld* episode when George admitted to having some in his medicine cabinet. Name it.

4. Nothing came between Brooke Shields and this brand of jeans in these 1980s ads. Were they

a) Levi's
b) Calvin Klein
c) Lee's
d) Wrangler

5. A couple of actors pitching Polaroid cameras were so convincing, viewers mistakenly thought they were married. The guy was James Garner; who was his female counterpart?

a) Meryl Streep
b) Mary Tyler Moore
c) Michelle Phillips
d) Mariette Hartley

6. This product purported to consume forty-seven times its weight in excess stomach acid. How do you spell relief?

a) Tums
b) Rolaids
c) Alka Seltzer
d) Bromo Seltzer

7. Star-Kist Tuna always rejected this fish in its commercials by saying "Sorry, _____. (the character's name).

8. Madge the manicurist surprised her clients by telling them their hands were "soaking in it." What dishwashing liquid was it?

    a) Palmolive
    b) Lux
    c) Joy
    d) Dove

9. Karl Malden had a long and distinguished career as an actor, but he became even more familiar to TV viewers telling us "don't leave home without them." Were they?

    a) Pepto-Bismol pills
    b) Tylenol liquid capsules
    c) Foster Grant sunglasses
    d) American Express Traveller's Checks

10. Fill in the blanks on these popular slogans:

    a) Please don't _____ the Charmin.
    b) (Miller Lite) Tastes great, less _____.
    c) Bounty, the quicker picker _____.
    d) (Lay's potato chips) Betcha can't _____ just one.

➥ **Answers on page 355–356**

## Trivia BITE!

Until the 1960s, about 95 percent of milk consumed in Canadian homes was delivered door to door. With the advent of supermarkets and three-quart jugs, home delivery now accounts for about 1 percent of milk purchased.

## QUIZ 4: HOLIDAYS

Hang your ornaments, dig out the dreidel, or pop open some festive champagne. When the holiday season is upon us, it's time to celebrate. As part of the fun, sharpen your pencils and your wits and try our latest quiz.

1.  On December 31 of what year did Dick Clark's New Year's Rockin' Eve make its debut on ABC?

    a) 1970
    b) 1972
    c) 1976
    d) 1978

2.  Match the lead actor with the holiday-themed film he appeared in:

    a) Bill Murray    i) *The Santa Clause*
    b) Chevy Chase    ii) *Scrooged*
    c) Tim Allen    iii) *The Muppet Christmas Carol*
    d) Michael Caine    iv) *National Lampoon's Christmas Vacation*

3.  Name the holiday the Constanzas from the TV show *Seinfeld* celebrated instead of Christmas or Hanukkah.

4.  This children's toy was panned at the 1988 Toy Fair but by Christmas of that year sales had topped $40 million. Was it:

    a) Tickle Me Elmo
    b) The Pet Rock
    c) Super Ball
    d) Teenage Mutant Ninja Turtles

5.  Score a point for each singer or group you match correctly with their hit holiday songs:

a) "Jingle Bell Rock"                    i) Brenda Lee
b) "Rockin' Around the Christmas Tree"   ii) Band Aid
c) "Do They Know It's Christmas"         iii) Royal Guardsmen
d) "Snoopy's Christmas"                  iv) Bobby Helms

6. Which of the following celebrities did NOT die on Christmas Day?

   a) Dean Martin
   b) Ray Walston
   c) Charlie Chaplin
   d) James Brown

7. In a famous holiday episode of *Friends*, Ross tries to teach his son Ben about Hanukkah by dressing up as what kind of animal?

   a) aardvark
   b) alligator
   c) armadillo
   d) antelope

8. Shortly before he died in 1977, Bing Crosby recorded for a TV Christmas special a famous duet of "Little Drummer Boy" with this rock star. Was it

   a) Sting
   b) Bob Seger
   c) John Lennon
   d) David Bowie

9. Jimmy Buffet, Annie Lennox, and Sissy Spacek all share something in common with December 25. They

   a) were all born on Christmas Day
   b) all had a child born on Christmas
   c) all appeared together in the 1985 Bob Hope Christmas special
   d) all of the above.

10. On Christmas Day, 1971, the Miami Dolphins won the longest playoff game in NFL history with a field goal in the second over-time period. Which team did they defeat?

   a) Kansas City Chiefs
   b) Oakland Raiders
   c) New York Jets
   d) San Diego Chargers

 **Answers on pages 356–357**

 **QUIZ 5: MUSIC**

Disco, new wave, glam rock, punk rock, synth rock, and music videos. The 1970s and 80s were watershed years in pop music history. Think back to your dancing days or dig out those old albums — yes, albums — to see what your recall of that era in pop music.

1. Match these successful soloists with their former bands:

   a) Sting                 i) The Commodores
   b) Don Henley            ii) Wham!
   c) George Michael        iii) The Police
   d) Lionel Richie         iv) Eagles

2. Of the following 1970s songs by Elton John, which was the only one to reach Billboard's number one?

   a) "Your Song"
   b) "Rocket Man"
   c) "Philadelphia Freedom"
   d) "Daniel"

3. In the fall of 1975, what New Jersey-based rocker, though still relatively unknown at the time, landed on the covers of *Time* and *Newsweek* simultaneously?

4. Before the release of Michael Jackson's *Thriller*, this was the best-selling album of all time. Was it

   a) *Bridge over Troubled Water*, Simon and Garfunkel
   b) *Frampton Comes Alive*, Peter Frampton
   c) *Abbey Road*, The Beatles
   d) *Saturday Night Fever* soundtrack, Various Artists

5. In 1976, what singing duo became the first divorced couple to co-host a television variety series? (Hint: she later won an Oscar and he became a congressman).

6. Given its repetitive name, it only make sense that this band hit number one with "Broken Wings" in late 1985 and then repeated at number one a few months later with "Kyrie". Was it

   a) Mr. Mister
   b) Talk Talk
   c) Frou Frou
   d) Duran Duran

7. I used to be in the band Genesis, but in the early 1980s, "Against All Odds," I tried a solo career. I performed a lot more than "One More Night" during my career, and I resisted the urge for fans to "Take Me Home." A few years ago I won an Oscar for Best Song. Who am I?

8. What was Madonna's first number one single?

   a) "Papa Don't Preach"
   b) "Like a Virgin"
   c) "Material Girl"
   d) "Holiday"

9. The Paradise Garage, a notable club in the history of modern nightclub culture, operated from 1977 to 1987. Where was it located?

   a) Philadelphia
   b) New York City
   c) Detroit
   d) Atlanta

10. What did music industry personalities Jim Burgess, Walter Gibbons, John "Jellybean" Benitez, and Richie Kaczar have in common in the 1970s and 80s?

   a) rap pioneers
   b) DJs who popularized disco music
   c) Grammy-winning record producers
   d) members of the band Kool and the Gang

11. Of these musicians, who won Best New Artist at the 1980 Grammy awards?

   a) Rickie Lee Jones
   b) The Blues Brothers
   c) The Knack
   d) Dire Straits

➥ **Answers on page 357–358**

## QUIZ 6: MUSIC 2

The music we grew up with continues to play on radio stations and can often be heard in concert halls thanks to solo artists and bands that refuse to hang up their guitars. Test your power of recall with our 70s and 80s music quiz.

1.  Fill in the missing words from these popular songs (artists in brackets):

    a) "I've seen fire and I've seen rain. I've seen ____ days that I thought would never end." (James Taylor)
    b) "The Mississippi delta was _____ like a National guitar." (Paul Simon)
    c) "If you fall, I will catch you, I'll be _____, time after time." (Cyndi Lauper)
    d) "I'm easy ... easy like _____ morning." (The Commodores)

2.  This number one 1979 hit by Rupert Holmes was called "Escape" but most would remember it for the type of alcoholic drink he wondered if his would-be lover would like. Name the drink.

3.  The Bee Gees were three Gibb brothers. Two were named Robin and Barry. Name the third.

4.  In Billy Joel's 1973 hit single "Piano Man," we are told about an old man, who is making love in the bar. Who or what is he making love to?

    a) his tonic and gin
    b) the reflection in his beer glass
    c) his imaginary girlfriend
    d) his wife

**5.** Which of the following LPs was not released by Pat Benatar?

   a) *Crimes of Passion*
   b) *In the Heat of the Night*
   c) *Paradise Theater*
   d) *Precious Time*

**6.** Paul McCartney and Michael Jackson teamed up in the early 1980s for two hits songs, "The Girl Is Mine" and "Say Say Say." Which one of the two made it to number one?

**7.** In 1981 alone, Hall and Oates had three number one hits. Which one of the following "only" made it to number five?

   a) "Kiss on My List"
   b) "You Make My Dreams"
   c) "Private Eyes"
   d) "I Can't Go For That (No Can Do)"

**8.** Billy Ocean, who had a 1984 hit with the song "Caribbean Queen (No More Love On The Run)," was born in New Orleans. True or false?

**9.** When Dennis Wilson of the Beach Boys died in December 1983, President Ronald Reagan had to intervene to allow this to take place. Was it

   a) burial at sea
   b) scattering Wilson's ashes on Malibu Beach
   c) having Wilson buried at Arlington Cemetery
   d) awarding a posthumous Congressional Medal of Freedom

**10.** In 1979, this British band truly enjoyed its breakfast in America with three top fifteen singles including "Take the Long Way Home" and "The Logical Song." Name the group.

➥ **Answers on pages 359–360**

## QUIZ 7: TRAVEL

There's more to the holiday season than family gatherings, enjoying food, and unwrapping the odd gift or two. It's also a popular time for boomers to travel. With that in mind, we hit the research road to test your knowledge of all things travel related.

1. More than seven million visitors have walked through my doors since I opened in 1995. Am I:

   a) The Rock and Roll Hall of Fame
   b) The National Baseball Hall of Fame
   c) Canada's Wonderland
   d) Elvis Presley's Graceland Mansion

2. Match the following singers with the travel-related hit they had.

   a) Ricky Nelson        i) "Holiday"
   b) Ray Charles         ii) "On the Road Again"
   c) Madonna             iii) "Travelin' Man"
   d) Willie Nelson       iv) "Hit the Road Jack"

3. True or false? The founder of Hertz Rent-a-Car got his start in the taxicab business.

4. When packing for a holiday trip that involves air travel, which of the following does American Airlines NOT recommend?

   a) Placing contact information on the inside and outside of your bag
   b) Packing medications and other valuables such as cameras and electronics in your checked baggage
   c) Leaving gifts unwrapped in your luggage
   d) Using your camera phone to get a shot of your

parking location at the airport to ensure you can find your vehicle when you return.

5. If you take a ski vacation during the winter holidays, where would you find a resort that in 1936 installed the world's first motorized chairlift?

   a) Vermont
   b) Idaho
   c) California
   d) British Columbia

6. Unscramble the following letters to identify the former *Saturday Night Live* performer who was the star of *National Lampoon's Christmas Vacation* and other Lampoon vacation movies.

   vcyhe acshe

7. What occupation did budget travel expert Arthur Frommer give up in the early 1960s when he became the full-time publisher of the Frommer series of travel guides?

   a) book store owner
   b) cruise line operator
   c) lawyer
   d) hotelier

8. Las Vegas has 14 of the 15 largest hotels in North America. Where is the other one?

   a) New York City
   b) Orlando
   c) Honolulu
   d) Niagara Falls

9. Florida is the most popular winter destination in the eastern U.S. but what is the most popular in the western U.S.?

a) Las Vegas
b) Phoenix
c) Palm Springs
d) Aspen

 **Answers on pages 360–361**

 **QUIZ 8: TRIVIA HODGE PODGE**

1. For what movie did Jack Nicholson receive his first Academy Award?

   a) *Chinatown*
   b) *One Flew over the Cuckoo's Nest*
   c) *Five Easy Pieces*
   d) *The Last Detail*

2. Which of the following baby boomers has yet to celebrate his or her 60th birthday (as of March, 2009)?

   a) George W. Bush
   b) Patty Hearst
   c) Cher
   d) Dolly Parton
   e) Art Garfunkel

3. According to the Nielsen annual ratings, how many times was *The Mary Tyler Moore Show* the number one show on TV during its seven year run?

   a) four
   b) three

c) two

d) never

4. What sports team, in 1971, lost their first game in over eight years after winning 2,495 consecutive games?

5. Match the following British Invasion bands with their hit songs.

a) Herman's Hermits

b) The Kinks

c) The Zombies

d) Gerry and the Pacemakers

e) Dave Clark Five

i) "Bits and Pieces"

ii) "Don't let the Sun Catch You Crying?"

iii) "Can't You Hear My Heartbeat"

iv) "You Really Got Me"

v) "She's Not There"

6. While boomers remember Neil Armstrong being the first man on the moon in 1969, astronaut Gene Cernan has his own lunar claim to fame. Was he

a) the second man on the moon

b) the only astronaut to fly to the moon twice without stepping on the surface

c) the last man on the moon

d) the first man to orbit the moon

7. She was born Leslie Hornby, but this British supermodel, once christened "The Face of 1966," is better known by what one-word moniker?

8. In 1966, this group and the song they recorded held the number one spot for seven weeks, longer than anyone else that year. Was it:

a) The Beatles and "We Can Work it Out"

b) The Beach Boys and "Good Vibrations"

c) The Monkees with "I'm a Believer"

d) The Lovin' Spoonful and "Summer in the City"

9. In 1974, this former star of *The Honeymooners* beat out distinguished actors Albert Finney, Dustin Hoffman, Jack Nicholson, and Al Pacino for the Best Actor Oscar. Name him.

10. In 1946, James and Mary were the most popular baby names in the United States. Which of the following ranked number two?

    a) Robert and Linda
    b) William and Barbara
    c) Richard and Carol
    d) Kenneth and Karen

 **Answers on pages 361–362**

## QUIZ 9: BOOMER CAR QUIZ

If you want to put a little vroom into your boomer life, take a test drive with our auto quiz on everything from muscle cars to the music we played as we sailed down the highways.

1. What was Chevy's Camaro known as before the Camaro name was officially adopted?

    a) Cobra
    b) Panther
    c) Cheetah
    d) Lynx

2. True or false. The Beach Boys followed up their car-inspired 1963 hit "Little Deuce Coupe" with the even bigger song, "G.T.O.," the following year.

3.  To what film/television production company did Plymouth reportedly pay $50,000 for the rights to use the name, cartoon likeness and "beep-beep" horn for its Road Runner model?

    a) Warner Brothers
    b) MGM
    c) Looney Toons
    d) Hanna-Barbera

4.  Still with the Road Runner: True or false. The car was reputedly a favourite of moonshiners because it was faster than most police cars and built to handle practically any kind of bump.

5.  Unscramble the following letters to identify these car models from the 1970s:

    a) srdute
    b) mlegnir
    c) theron
    d) geav

6.  Appropriately enough, this rock band had a Top Five hit in 1984 with the song "Drive." Was it:

    a) The Cadillacs
    b) Bachman-Turner Overdrive
    c) The Cars
    d) The Highwaymen

7.  The engine of this 1970s small model car was described by John DeLorean as "noisy, expensive to manufacture, and top heavy." Was it the

    a) Astre
    b) Pinto
    c) Colt
    d) Vega

8.  The British have different automobile lingo than Americans. Match our terms with the corresponding British ones.

    a) trunk              i) wing
    b) gasoline           ii) boot
    c) hood               iii) damper
    d) shock absorber     iv) bonnet
    e) fender             v) petrol

9.  This car manufacturer was responsible for such 1970s model cars as the Hornet, Gremlin, and Pacer. Was it

    a) GM
    b) American Motors
    c) Ford
    d) Volkswagen

➥ **Answers on pages 362–363**

# CHAPTER 16
# Odds and Sods: From Eh to Zed

##  TRIVIA HODGEPODGE

- On average, Canadian households spend $257 a year on gaming, which includes the purchase of lottery tickets, casino gambling, and playing games of chance on video lottery terminals. Quebec leads the way, spending an average of $267 per family.

- The smallest, oldest jail in North America is found in Rodney, Ontario, southwest of London. Built in 1890 and now a tourist attraction, the 24.3-square-metre jail had two cells. Others have challenged Rodney's claim, but the town has refuted them.

- Canada's first grain elevator, a round structure, was built in Niverville, Manitoba, in 1879. It was the Ogilvie flour company that built the first of the rectangular, pitch-roofed grain elevators that became a common sight in communities across the Prairies. That elevator was built in Gretna, Manitoba, in 1881.

> **SNAPSHOT**
>
> **Suicides in Canada**
>
> 1950:  1,067
> 1970:  2,413
> 1990:  3,379
> 1995:  3,970
> 2004:  3,613

Photo by Sue Bandeen.

There is little elbow room in North America's smallest jail.

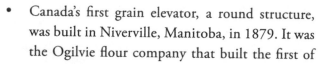
Photo by Harold Wright.

Canada's postal lighthouse.

- The only post office in a lighthouse in North America is found in Peggy's Cove, Nova Scotia. The lighthouse no longer serves its original purpose of guiding boats and is only used as a post office in the summer during peak tourist times.

- At a dinner meeting in Toronto of the Canadian Manufacturers Association, several speakers advocated the advantages of introducing the metric system to Canada. But this was no recent dinner; it took place in February 1901. The system was not adopted until 1971, and it was not used until April 1975.

### Trivia BITE!

In 1933 there were nearly 5,500 licensed primary grain elevators in western Canada, more than half of them in Saskatchewan. In 2006, fewer than 400 were still standing thanks to the grain industry's move toward increased efficiency. Some of the elevators were replaced with computerized concrete monstrosities with eight times the holding capacity.

### Trivia BITE!

The first formal advertisement in Canada is believed to have been an ad to help sell butter that appeared in 1752 in the *Halifax Gazette*. But the first advertising agency didn't open until 1889, when Anson McKim created a firm in Montreal.

- The Haskell Free Library and Opera House on the Vermont-Quebec border has the unique distinction of having a stage in Canada while the seats are in the United States. Construction on the building started in 1901 thanks to a bequest by Martha Stewart Haskell, a Canadian, to honour her husband, Carlos, an American.

Photo by Catherine Blake.

The Haskell Free Library.

# FIVE GREAT CANADIAN COMEBACKS

1. **The Great Lakes:** in the late 1960s and early 1970s Lake Erie was declared dead and lakes Ontario, Superior, Huron, and Michigan were on their way to becoming ecological wastelands. But since Canada and the United States signed the Great Lakes Water Quality Agreement in 1972, the lakes have returned to better health, as evidenced by the return of many species of fish and wildlife.

2. **The 1941–42 Toronto Maple Leafs:** After losing the first three games to the Detroit Red Wings in the 1942 Stanley Cup Final, The Leafs, under coach Hap Day, roared back with four straight wins to capture the cup, the only team in NHL history to come back from a three games to zero deficit in the finals.

3. **Chrysler Canada:** On May 10, 1980, the federal and Ontario governments provided $200 million in loan guarantees as part of a Canada-U.S. government restructuring program which saved the automaker from bankruptcy and salvaged more than 12,000 Canadian jobs.

4. **Silken Laumann:** The Canadian rower was the reigning world singles champion and the overwhelming favourite to win gold at the 1992 Olympics in Barcelona until her boat was accidentally hit by a German rowing pair prior to the Games, seriously injuring her right leg. Doctors said she would not compete in the Olympics but she recovered and won a bronze medal.

5. **The Whooping Crane:** In 1900 there were approximately 1,350 birds in Canada, but by 1951 only 15 remained because of hunting practices, destruction of prairie breeding habitats, and egg and specimen collection. By 1999, the population had rebounded to more than 250 birds, thanks to strong preservation methods and a captive breeding program.

### 📷 SNAPSHOT

**Annual Birth Rates:**

| Year | Births per 1,000 women | Babies Born |
| --- | --- | --- |
| 1921 | 29.3 | 264,879 |
| 1941 | 27.3 | 263,993 |
| 1961 | 34.1 | 475,700 |
| 1981 | 17.8 | 371,346 |
| 1995 | 12.8 | 378,011 |
| 1997 | 12.1 | 364,765 |
| 2004 | 10.5 | 337,072 |
| 2007 | 10.75 | 358,944 |

📷 **SNAPSHOT**

**Divorce Rates per 100,000 Population**

| 1921 | 1941 | 1961 | 1981 | 1995 | 2004 |
|------|------|------|------|------|------|
| 6.4 | 21.4 | 36.0 | 278.0 | 262.2 | 246.0 |

*Statistics Canada*

# 🍁 FIVE GREAT CANADIAN BUSTS: NOT SO FOND MEMORIES

1. **The Olympic Stadium, Montreal:** Without a doubt, one of the 20th century's biggest screwups. The Big O (or more appropriately, The Big Owe), had problems from the start, including a flawed design, poor workmanship, and a $52 million retractable roof that was not installed in time for the 1976 Summer Olympics. In subsequent years, roofs have been damaged by weather and by workmen; on other occasions pieces of the outside walls and a 55-ton beam crashed to the ground. And if that's not enough, the initial $120 million price tag had ballooned to close to $1.5 billion by the time the debt was paid off in December of 2006.

2. **Canadian Football League Expansion to the U.S.:** In 1992, the CFL announced plans to expand south of the border, and in 1993 the Sacramento Gold Miners became the first U.S. team to play in the league. Several other American teams were added the next year, and expansion did produce an exciting Grey Cup in 1994. But dogged by poor attendance and huge financial losses, the move to the U.S. ended in failure. By 1996, all American franchises had disappeared.

3. **The Bricklin:** A U.S.-designed sports car built in New Brunswick in 1974 and 1975 by American promoter Malcolm Bricklin. Only 2,857 were sold because the car was plagued by a high sticker price and technical problems with its unique "gullwing" doors. The company fell into receivership, owing the provincial government $23 million.

4. **Mirabel International Airport:** Known as Montreal's other white elephant (right behind the aforementioned Big O), Mirabel opened in 1975 but was soon declared a dud because its use was based on faulty assumptions about air traffic, it was too far from Montreal, and it was poorly designed. In the fall of 1997, the multi-billion-dollar facility was relegated to a cargo and charter terminal after all regularly scheduled international flights were consolidated at Dorval Airport in Montreal.

5. **Pickering Airport:** Known as the international airport that never got built, plans were announced in 1973 and scrapped in September of 1975 after fierce opposition from area residents. Over the years, with the federal government still the owner of the 7,530 hectares of land it expropriated for the airport, a few villages have become ghost towns, 19th-century farm houses have fallen into disrepair, and many buildings have deteriorated into firetraps. In 1997, Ottawa spent $3.5 million, mostly to maintain buildings on the site.

   In 2005, the Greater Toronto Airports Authority released a draft plan for the construction of a new airport, which would have two runways by 2012, serving first general aviation, but later a third runway, and full passenger and cargo services, by 2032.

# 🍁 GHOSTS AND GOBLINS ... CANADA'S TOP 10 HAUNTED LOCATIONS

1. **The Maritimes:** Phantom ships/ghost ships/Flying Dutchmen: the terms are synonymous and the phenomena are an important component to the folklore of Canada's Maritime provinces. These retrocognitive images are often so detailed that witnesses throughout the 20th century are still able to identify not only the long-ago sunken ship but, in some cases, even see what's happening on board.

2. **Oak Island, Nova Scotia:** This is the haunted site of treasure buried in the 18th century. Despite the enormous amounts of money, technology, and time spent trying to uncover the fortune, only disappointment, poverty, and unexplained deaths have resulted. The ghostly guardians of the cache have been the victors, despite concerted efforts by many determined souls over the last 60 years.

3. **Kingsmere in Quebec:** The summer residence of Canada's longest-serving prime minister, William Lyon Mackenzie King, was the venue for many ghostly visitations during King's lifetime. He and his friends frequently, and successfully, conducted

seances during which they summoned numerous spirits into their midst. Since his death in 1950, King's ghost has been seen there. The spirit reportedly conversed with journalist Percy J. Philip in June of 1954, at the property the deceased had so loved in life.

4. **The Hockey Hall of Fame:** Situated in a century-and-a-half-old Bank of Montreal building in downtown Toronto, it is haunted by the ghost of a former teller at the bank who killed herself during the early 1950s in response to an unrequited love affair. Her presence has been seen and felt amid the displays of hockey history as recently as the mid-1990s.

5. **Grand Theatre in London, Ontario:** Staff at the theatre are extremely fond of their resident ghost — Ambrose Small, the theatre's original owner. Small disappeared in December 1919 under suspicious circumstances and has never been seen since — alive, that is. His ghost continues to make regular appearances at his favourite theatre.

6. **The Hotel Fort Garry:** The Winnipeg hotel, which opened in December 1913, is home to several ethereal residents. The ghost of a woman wearing a formal gown has been reported by a guest. Employees once caught a glimpse of a male apparition enjoying a meal in the hotel's dining room, long after the room was closed for the day. Moments later the image vaporized.

7. **The Moose Head Inn at Kenosee Lake in Saskatchewan:** A much-investigated and well-documented ghost is frequently heard walking around the place. He has grabbed a worker's hand, borrowed small items, and caused plumbing and electrical fixtures to turn on and off independently. This ghostly activity continues today.

8. **Banff Springs Hotel:** Legend has it that this Alberta hotel is home to several ghosts. The manifestation of a dancing bride is said to be seen, even today, at the base of the stairs where she apparently fell to her death. A long-deceased bellman reportedly helped guests with their luggage a few years ago.

9. **Victoria Golf Course:** Doris Gravlin's ghost is only seen for a few weeks in the spring and so has been dubbed "The April Ghost." However, she's also known as British Columbia's most famous ghost. Since she died in 1936, Doris's image, wearing a number of different outfits, is seen on the fairways of the golf course located in Victoria, B.C. Every spring ghost-hunters gather there in hopes of catching a glimpse of her.

10. **The ghost town of Barkerville, British Columbia:** Even though many of the buildings currently standing are modern-day re-constructions, ghosts continue to be

both seen and felt there. The most poignant of the resident spectres is the ghost of an unidentified woman seen at a second-floor window of Madame Fannie Bendixon's Saloon.

*List prepared by Barbara Smith, author of* Ghost Stories of Alberta.

**Trivia BITE!**

Margarine has had a tough time establishing itself in Canada. Lobbying by dairy farmers led to margarine being banned by an Act of Parliament from 1866 to 1917. Butter shortages during the First World War led to margarine being legalized, but it was banned again in 1923. Margarine became permanently legal in 1948.

# ❦ TEN THINGS YOU DON'T KNOW ABOUT DIRT IN YOUR HOME

Spring, summer, winter, and fall, homeowners across the land are in house-cleaning mode in an effort to keep their residences clean and tidy. But to fight filth, they need to know the enemy. To help out, we're here to dish the dirt on, well, dirt.

So, while the year-round cleaning crusade defies dust bunnies, grapples with grime, and conquers cobwebs, here are 10 fabulous facts worth considering for Canadians who plan to attack household dust and dirt.

1. **The Dirt on Dust:** One kilogram of fine dust — the dirt we breathe in but can't see — accumulates in the average home every year, says J. David Miller, a chemistry professor at Carleton University in Ottawa. It consists mostly of human skin scales, pollen, fungi from leaves, grass, and pine needles, dust mite feces, and carbon from car exhaust. If sucking this into your lungs isn't disgusting enough, consider that the surface area of these tiny particles is more than 10 times the floor area of the average house.

2. **Dirty Laundry:** More than 60 percent of the laundry generated at home is soiled by the human body, says Procter and Gamble, maker of household cleaning products. Each day a person sheds more than a billion skin flakes, generates more than a litre-sized wine bottle of sweat, and produces tens of grams of "sebum," a mixture of triglycerides, fatty acids, wax esters, and cholesterol, most of which ends up on clothing. An average wash load contains 40 grams of dirt, or three large spoonfuls, while a heavily soiled load may contain more than 120 grams.

3. **Molly's a Canuck:** Household cleaning company Molly Maid's first customer was a home in Mississauga, Ontario, that was cleaned in 1979, with founders Adrienne and Chris Stringer pushing the mops and brooms. Over the past 30 years, the Stringers have expanded across Canada and into the United States, the United Kingdom, Japan, and Portugal. In 2009, Molly Maid expects to perform nearly two million home cleanings across Canada.

4. **You Dirty Duct:** A typical duct cleaning removes up to five pounds of dirt, equivalent to a good-sized bag of potatoes, from a home's air ducts. The crud consists of pet and human hair, pet droppings, toys, marbles, food, construction materials, and drink containers, among other things, says Direct Energy, a full services energy company. Although your ducts will be more pristine, experts say cleaning, in most cases, does little to improve energy usage and indoor air quality.

5. **Suck It Up:** He didn't invent the vacuum cleaner but W.H. Hoover's name is synonymous with the time-saving household device. The Hoover legacy began in 1907 when Murray Spangler of Canton, Ohio, developed a contraption that used a tin soapbox, a fan, a pillowcase, and a broom handle to pull dust away from air. His family friend, Susan Hoover, was so impressed she showed it to her husband, W.H., who bought the patent and began building the machines. He offered 10 days' free use of his machine to anyone who wrote and requested it and eventually established a business venture that definitely did not suck.

6. **Sleep on This ... or Not:** A University of Manchester study says a typical pillow contains more than a million fungal spores, and the most common fungi, *Apergillus fumigatus*, is the likeliest to cause disease. And if that doesn't give you nightmares, other research suggests this fungus is having sex. To remove that image from your dreams, scientists suggest putting allergen-impermeable covers on your pillow and washing bedding at least weekly in hot water.

7. **Vacuuming 101:** Heavy traffic areas in your home should be vacuumed daily, with seven strokes of the machine over all surfaces for thorough cleaning, says the Hoover Company. Areas less travelled on can be vacuumed once a week or every three or four days and three or four strokes should do the trick.

8. **Where Dirt is King:** Think the toilet bowl is the dirtiest spot in your home? Guess again. In reality, the cloth or sponge used to wipe your kitchen counter contains the most bacteria, says Reckitt Benckiser Inc., the manufacturer of Lysol products. Number

two on the list is your kitchen sink drain, followed by your bathtub and a distant fourth is the area beneath the rim of your toilet bowl. Wiping countertops with paper towels that can be tossed after use is the best way to avoid spreading bacteria, say the experts.

9. **And You Thought Rabbits Multiplied Quickly:** The bacteria found in kitchens, bathrooms, and other areas of a home can grow and divide every 20 minutes. A single bacteria cell can become more than eight million cells in less than 24 hours, says the maker of Lysol products.

10. **Mould Ain't Gold:** More than 270 species of mould have been identified as living in Canadian homes. Left unchecked, mould can result in wood rot and structural damage and can threaten the health of people prone to allergies and respiratory problems, says the Canada Mortgage and Housing Corporation.

# 🍁 FASCINATING FALL FACTS

Fall is a favourite season for many, highlighted by gorgeous leaf colours, crisp temperatures, and long walks. Unfortunately for many, though, it's followed by winter, which is enough to put many Canadians down in the dumps.

Fortunately we have a remedy to see you through the latter stages of fall: the following fascinating facts are sure to dazzle your friends and colleagues, and brighten up even the gloomiest of days.

First, allow us to put a little colour in your life. In fall, the leaves change from green to gold, red, and orange, but do you know why that happens? Leaf it to us to explain. Trees prepare for winter by reducing the moisture and nutrient supply that keeps their leaves green and they store it in more permanent parts of the plant. The green chlorophyll starts to break down and leaves begin to turn yellow.

With autumn's cool nights and clear sunny days, some trees also produce *anthocyanin*, a red chemical that mixes with the yellow of the leaves to create other colours. On the sugar maple, for example, a variety of colour can be found on a single tree as reds mix with yellow and orange leaves.

Of course, autumn for many sports fans means football. Speaking of football, do you remember the time the Hamilton Tiger-Cats beat the Buffalo Bills in a game? In 1961, during the pre-season, the Ti-Cats tangled with the Bills, of the old American Football League, in Hamilton, using Canadian rules. The Ti-Cats won 38–21, and after that game the AFL refused any more cross-border matches.

Canadian football teams had been playing their American counterparts from at least the 1930s. Several exhibition games between NFL and CFL teams took place in the 1950s, and one on record had the New York Giants defeating the Ottawa Rough Riders 27–6.

Football games aren't the only popular shows on the tube every fall. Fans usually settle in to watch their favourite shows when the new television season launches every autumn. They may also have their favourite stars, but did you know that a Canadian from Nelson, British Columbia, was the first professional television star? And that she made her debut back on November 2, 1936?

Joan Miller was a young actress who had achieved success in Canada and then went to Britain where she found work in radio. The BBC's first television producer liked what he saw and signed her on for his show *Picture Page*. Miller was the *Picture Page* Girl and was paid £12.10 per week for appearing on the show, making her the world's first professional TV performer. The show ran until the Second World War broke out, but Miller continued her career in Britain as a well-respected stage actress. She died in 1988.

If you're reading this in late fall, there's no getting around the fact that winter is just around the corner. With that in mind, consider this: As cold as the weather may get here in the "Great White North," it is never too cold to snow.

**They Said It!**

"I fear that I have not got much to say about Canada, not having seen much; what I got by going to Canada was a cold."

– *American author Henry David Thoreau, 1866, about a visit to Quebec.*

To produce the white stuff, the air must hold at least some moisture in gaseous form, says Environment Canada. The water vapour must be cooled beyond the freezing point at which snow crystals form. Because warmer air holds more moisture than colder air, the heaviest snowfalls and large flakes occur at temperatures close to freezing. As the air becomes colder the flakes become finer and finer. It is never too cold to snow, but the amount of snowfall is usually less the colder it is.

If that's any consolation.

# 🍁 JAVA JIVE

Anyone who has lined up for a double-double at a favourite coffee shop, languished over a latte, or perked up to the aroma of a fresh-brewed pot on a Saturday morning, knows Canada has a love affair with coffee.

Whether we sip it slowly on a lazy afternoon, or gulp it on our way to work, that daily jolt of java is an integral party of everyday life in this country. But what do we know about the cup of joe at the centre of Canada's coffee culture? The next time you enjoy a mug of your favourite blend, consider these 10 facts you may not know about one of Canada's most popular beverages.

1.  **Coffee a fruit?** You bet. Coffee beans are the pits at the centre of bright red coffee cherries, which grow on trees. The average coffee tree bears enough cherries each season to produce between one and one and a half pounds of roasted coffee.

2.  **Canada's coffee culture:** Sixty-six percent of coffee is consumed at home, 12 percent is consumed at work, 16 percent is consumed or purchased at eating places and 5 percent is consumed in other places such as hospitals, schools, hockey rinks and other institutions. Drinking coffee in-transit has increased from 2 percent in 1999 to 7 percent in 2003.

3.  **Coffee's roots:** Originally, the coffee plant grew naturally in Ethiopia, but once transplanted in Arabia, that country monopolized it. The Turks were the first country to adopt it as a drink, often adding spices such as cloves, cinnamon, cardamom, and anise to the brew. Today, coffee grows in more than 60 countries, says the Coffee Association of Canada.

4.  **Special species:** There are two key commercially important coffee species, Arabica, which accounts for about 75 percent of world production and Robusta. Arabica grows best at high altitudes, has a much more refined flavour, and contains about 1 percent caffeine by weight. Robusta coffee is a more robust species with a higher_resistance to disease, and a higher yield per plant. It flourishes at lower elevations and produces coffee with harsher flavour characteristics.

5.  **Coffee Queen:** American coffee heiress Abigail Folger made headlines in 1969, but her appearance on front pages had nothing to do with coffee. Folger, whose father, Peter, was president of the Folger Coffee Company, was murdered on August 9, 1969, by the Manson Family at Roman Polanski's Beverly Hills, California, home. Her friend Sharon Tate, a young Hollywood actress, was among the four others slain.

6.  **A real bargoon:** When Tim Hortons opened its first outlet in Hamilton, Ontario in 1964, a cup of coffee cost just 10 cents. A dozen doughnuts set customers back 69 cents. Today, depending on where you live, coffee prices at Tim's range from $1.13 for a small to $1.65 for an extra large, and 12 doughnuts can cost as much as $5.75.

7. **Cut the caffeine:** Health experts warn that caffeine found in coffee, tea, and other products could cause insomnia, headaches, irritability, and nervousness. To avoid these side effects, Health Canada recommends that the general population of healthy adults should drink no more than three eight-ounce (237- millilitre) cups of brewed coffee per day. Three cups contain a total of 400 to 450 milligrams of caffeine.

8. **Will that be Double-Double?** Forty percent of Canadian coffee drinkers drink their coffee with cream or milk and sugar. Thirty-three percent prefer cream or milk only, 20 percent drink it black, and 7 percent add nothing more than sugar, according to the Coffee Association of Canada.

9. **Bean battles:** Who drinks more coffee, Canadians or Americans? Canadians win by a fair margin. Sixty-three percent of Canadians over the age of 18 drink coffee on a daily basis compared to 49 percent of Americans.

10. **Roll it up:** Ron Buist of Oakville, Ontario, invented Tim Hortons' popular Roll Up the Rim to Win promotion. While working in marketing for the company, Buist, who is now retired, helped introduce the promotion on a trial basis in 1986. It eventually became an annual event that rewards coffee drinkers with prizes ranging from free doughnuts and coffee to vehicles and home entertainment systems.

# 🍁 TEN THINGS YOU DON'T KNOW ABOUT YOUR HOME

For many Canadians life revolves around their home and yard. But how many are familiar with the housing essentials that keep them comfortable and content, such as the roofing that keeps out the rain, the bulbs that light their rooms, and the birds that make their gardens a haven to appreciate?

Here are 10 things you may not know that just might make you appreciate your home even more as you embark on your spring or fall cleaning or spend long hours in the garden.

1. **Up on the roof:** The asphalt shingles on an average size home with 2,000 square feet of roof area weigh 2,106 kilograms, or about the same as two Honda Civic sedans. The tiny granules that coat the shingles weigh about 792 kilograms and the asphalt base contributes the remaining 1,314 kilograms. The granules, which number up to 1.3 billion on the average roof, are made from gravel that is ground into tiny pieces, then pigmented into hundreds of colours and cooked to achieve a ceramic finish. The

granules protect asphalt shingles from ultra-violet rays, says shingle manufacturer Emco Building Products.

2. **You know the drill:** Ever wondered how the Black & Decker name found its way onto the power tools in your home workshop? The company began in the United States in 1910 when S. Duncan Black and his friend Alonzo Decker powered up a business that produced industrial machines and tools. They diversified the company toolbox with power drills, sanders, and saws after learning during the Second World War that a significant number of workers were stealing power tools from United States defence plants. Seeing a market ripe for the picking, they launched their own line of household power tools in 1946. The rest is home do-it-your-selfers history.

3. **Down, down, down:** The Canada thistle commonly found in many lawns and gardens can in a single growing season produce 500 metres of root, which is equivalent to the length of three-and-a-half Canadian Football League playing fields. Most of the roots grow laterally but some have been known to drill 4.5 metres into the soil. You'll need a backhoe to pull out one of those!

4. **Ghosts use electricity, too!** Some appliances consume power even when they're turned off, a phenomenon known as "ghost" or "phantom" loads. A remote controlled 27-inch colour TV can use 115 kilowatt hours (kWh) of power per year when not in use and a remote controlled VCR 123 kWh per year. That's because the standby mode in some devices means some lights and displays stay on, infrared detectors stay alert for signals from your remote control, and some internal components keep running to stay ready for action. In addition, 120-volt AC transformers, the heavy black plugs that go into a wall outlet, consume power even if the device they're powering is off. Combined, the standby modes of all such devices can consume 5 percent of the average home's electricity, or approximately $54 per year for the average homeowner.

5. **Lives lived:** If your refrigerator's still running after more than 20 years, consider yourself lucky, even though it's eating up more power than today's energy efficient

**Trivia BITE!**

We say zed, they say zee, but another difference between Canadians and Americans is that more than 80 percent of freezers sold in Canada are chest style, while in the U.S., where warmer weather means fewer homes have basements, upright style freezers claim nearly 50 percent of the market.

models. Data from the U.S. Department of Energy says home appliances have life expectancies just like humans. The average life of a refrigerator is 14 to 19 years; dishwashers should last 11 to 13 years; ditto for clothes washers and dryers and microwaves for an average of nine years while most stoves head to the great kitchen in the sky after 11 to 18 years of service.

6. **It's cold down there:** They may be mostly below ground, but basements can account for up to 35 percent of a home's total heat loss, according to Natural Resources Canada. Here's the dirt: earth turns out to be a poor insulator and when you add to that all the air that can leak through basement windows and cracks you can be in for some serious chilling. Experts recommend insulating the walls of your basement to R-12 to keep it warm and cozy. Your wallet will appreciate it too.

7. **It wasn't Tom's bright idea:** Thomas Edison is often credited with the invention of the light bulb but Torontonians Henry Woodward and Matthew Evans beat him to the switch when they patented a bulb in 1875. When the two couldn't raise enough cash to make their product commercially viable, Edison, who like many others at the time had been working on a similar idea, bought the rights to their patent. Using different techniques and improvements, Edison's bulb was ready for patenting in 1879 and has remained in the spotlight ever since.

8. **Birdbrains they're not:** It's no fluke that birds keep returning to your backyard feeder; having a strong memory is a feather in these creatures' caps. Studies have shown relocating food, even to unfamiliar places, is a piece of cake (or suet) for many birds that may be using landscape features, memory, stars, and even the Earth's magnetism to find things to eat. The memory whiz king of the bird world could be the Clark's nutcracker, which can bury 22,000 to 33,000 seeds in up to 2,500 locations. Studies have shown the nutcracker finds two-thirds of its tasty treasures more than a year later.

9. **Down the drain:** Canadian homes occupied by four people send an average of 1,300 litres of sewage per day to municipal wastewater treatment facilities, which over the course of a year would fill more than seven 16 x 32-foot in-ground swimming pools. The sewage is 90 percent water; the remainder consists of fecal matter, urine, and tissue flushed down toilets, as well as grime and soap that exits the home via sinks, dishwashers, and clothes washers, says the Canadian Water and Wastewater Association.

10. **Put a lock on it:** On average, thieves break into a home or apartment every three minutes in Canada. The most sought-after goods are audio/video equipment, followed

by jewellery, cash, and cheques or bonds. Nine out of every 10 break-in artists are male and perpetrators that are nailed and jailed are usually back on the streets in six months. The good news is that Statistics Canada's most recent stats showed residential break-and-enters have decreased by about 30 percent in the past decade.

# Q AND A

**Q:** *Why do Canadians pronounce the last letter of the alphabet as "zed" while Americans say "zee"?*

**A:** The last letter of our alphabet is derived from the Greek *zeta*, which was later adopted by the French who pronounced it as *zed*. This pronunciation was also used in Britain where it remains the standard way of saying the letter.

In parts of Britain, however, such as Suffolk and Norfolk, the letter was further abbreviated in pronunciation to *zee*. It was from those regions of Britain that many people immigrated to the United States. In contrast, many settlers coming to Canada were Scots or Irish, or originated from English regions where the *zed* pronunciation was common.

In 1928, Noah Webster produced his famous *American Dictionary of the English Language*. Webster was very much in favour of making the American form of English distinct from British usage. He wrote "Our honor requires us to have a system of our own, in language as well as government." Thus, he adopted the pronunciation *zee* which was common in the United States by then.

Webster also dropped the *u* from many words such as *colour* and *honour*, turned *tyre* into *tire* and *theatre* into *theater*. Canadians remained loyal to the British spelling and pronunciations. Although we have since adopted or come to accept some of the American spellings, we still hang on to *zed*.

**Q:** *Is it true that the prisoner who spent the longest time on Alcatraz was a Canadian?*

**A:** Yes, Alvin "Old Creepy" Karpis has the dubious

### They Said It!

"Eh": An interjection or prompt spoken by Canadians. Equivalent to the American "huh?" or "right?" Usually used to prompt a person to respond to what was said or to indicate a lack of understanding.

– *entry on Urban Dictionary (www.urbandictionary.com)*

honour of having spent the most time in prison on Alcatraz Island. Karpis, who was born Albin Karpowicz in Montreal in 1908, spent a record 26 years in the island prison situated in San Francisco Bay. The average prison stay there was about eight to 10 years.

Although born in Canada, Karpis grew up in Topeka, Kansas, where his family moved when he was young. Despite living most of his life in the United States, Karpis remained a Canadian citizen. For that reason, he was deported back to Canada upon his release from jail in 1969.

Karpis was one of a number of gangsters who captured the public's imagination during the Depression. Karpis had first been arrested for burglary in 1926, but gained fame in the early thirties as a bank robber and kidnapper, often as henchman of the notorious Barker gang. To avoid detection for his crimes, Karpis had his fingerprints surgically removed. He was involved in the kidnappings of William Hamm Jr., president of the Hamm Brewing Company, and Edward Bremer, president of the Commercial State bank in St. Paul, Minnesota. Both kidnappings ended with the criminals getting their ransom money and returning the men unharmed.

By the mid-1930s, Karpis had become Public Enemy Number One; he was eventually arrested in New Orleans by the FBI in 1936. Although legend has it that J. Edgar Hoover personally arrested Karpis, the gangster mentions in his autobiography that several other officers were involved.

After spending time in Leavenworth prison, Karpis was sent to Alcatraz, where he was in the company of such notorious criminals as Al Capone, Robert Stroud (the Birdman of Alcatraz), and Baby Face Nelson. He left Alcatraz in 1962, shortly before the prison was shut down, and spent the rest of his time in a prison in Washington State. Karpis died in Spain in 1979.

## QUICK QUIZ FIVE-PACK

1. Although contraceptives didn't become legal in Canada until 1969, the first birth control clinic in the country opened in 1932. Where was it located?

    a) Hamilton
    b) Vancouver
    c) Winnipeg
    d) Halifax

2.  Which of the following games was *not* invented in Canada?

    a) Trivial Pursuit
    b) Scrabble
    c) Balderdash
    d) Scruples

3.  In which war did the battle of Vimy Ridge take place: The First World War or the Second World War?

4.  The February 1963 issue of *Imperial Oil Review* reported that a Canadian had invented a vehicle that was a "kind of scooter mounted on toy tracks and which growls like a runaway dishwasher." What kind of vehicle was it?

    a) a snowmobile
    b) an all-terrain vehicle
    c) a mini-bike
    d) a hovercraft

5.  Which province boasts Canada's longest coastline: Newfoundland or British Columbia?

➥ **Answers on page 364**

# CHAPTER 17
# On the Hill: Politicking in Canada

 YOUR POLITICAL FIX

- The motto "A Mari usque ad Mare" (From Sea to Sea) was first officially used in 1906, when it was engraved on the head of a mace in the Legislative Assembly of Saskatchewan. The phrase was adopted by the federal government in 1921, although another motto, "In memoriam in spem" (In memory, in hope), had also been suggested.

- James Gladstone was Canada's first Native senator. A member of the Blood tribe, Gladstone was appointed to the Senate in February 1958 and gave his first speech there in Blackfoot.

- Richard Bedford Bennett, prime minister from 1930 to 1935, is the only one to hold that post who is not buried in Canada. Bennett is buried in Surrey, England. Bennett, Canada's 11th prime minister, was the first millionaire to hold the country's top office. The New Brunswick native earned his fortune in Calgary on legal fees from the CPR and Hudson's Bay Company and through real estate investments and business ventures such as cement production, power, beer, grain elevators, and a flourmill.

- E.D. Smith was the first senator to resign from office. Smith, the founder of one of Canada's leading food manufacturing companies, based on Ontario's Niagara Peninsula, quit in 1946 because he felt he wasn't worth the money Canadian taxpayers were paying him.

- Sixteen of Canada's 22 prime ministers have been lawyers. Non-lawyer PMs are Alexander Mackenzie, a stonemason; Mackenzie Bowell, a printer and editor; Charles Tupper, a physician; Lester Pearson, a senior public servant and diplomat; Joe Clark, a journalist and university lecturer, and Stephen Harper, who has a Master's degree in economics from the University of Calgary.

- Sir John Joseph Caldwell Abbott was the first senator to serve as Canada's prime minister and was also the first PM born in Canada. He was the country's third PM, holding the office from June 16, 1891, to November 24, 1892. A former mayor of Montreal, he became prime minister when Sir John A. Macdonald died while in office.

- In addition to Macdonald, 316 members of Parliament have died while in office since 1867, including Sir John Sparrow David Thompson, who was the country's fourth prime minister when he died on December 12, 1894; John Diefenbaker, the country's 13th prime minister, who was a Progressive Conservative backbencher when he died on August 16, 1979; and Liberal-Conservative D'Arcy McGee, who was shot to death in Ottawa on April 7, 1868. An MP who died in more recent times while in office is Chuck Cadman, an Independent representing Surrey North in British Columbia, who died on July 9, 2005.

- Canada's longest serving member of Parliament is Sir Wilfrid Laurier, who was an MP for 44 years, 11 months, and 23 days in the late 1880s and early 1900s. For now, Laurier's record looks pretty safe.

- In 1951, Louis St. Laurent became the first prime minister to live at 24 Sussex Drive, official residence of Canada's prime minister. The 34-room residence was built between 1866 and 1868 for Joseph Merrill Currier, a prosperous Ottawa lumber mill baron.

- Pierre Elliott Trudeau is the first Canadian prime minister born in the 20th century. Born in Montreal on October 18, 1919, Trudeau held the nation's top political office from April 20, 1968, to June 3, 1979, and from March 3, 1980, until June 30, 1984.

- A buckskin jacket, a pair of beaded buckskin gloves, two canoes, and a paddle that belonged to Pierre Trudeau, are part of the collection at the Canadian Canoe Museum in Peterborough, Ontario, which bills itself as "home of the world's largest collection of canoes and kayaks."

  The Trudeau artifacts are by far the most popular items in the museum, said collection manager Kim Watson.

# 🍁 CANADA'S FIRST PRIME MINISTER: THE LEGACY OF SIR JOHN A. MACDONALD LIVES ON

Sir John A. Macdonald may be long gone, but Canada's first prime minister is certainly not forgotten in Kingston, Ontario, where he launched his political career.

Macdonald held the country's top elected post from 1867 to 1873 and from 1878 to 1891. Those with an interest in the flamboyant political leader will find plenty of landmarks in Kingston that commemorate the life and times of Macdonald, who, in addition to being on the city's municipal council and a member of the Legislative Assembly of Canada in 1844, was a successful lawyer and businessman, holding directorships with at least 10 companies.

In a career smattered with controversy, Macdonald's achievements include the confederation of the colonies of the United Province of Canada (Ontario and Quebec), Nova Scotia, and New Brunswick into the Dominion of Canada in 1867.

His policy of westward expansion resulted in a transcontinental nation in 1871 and the construction of the Canadian Pacific Railway by 1885. When the Glasgow, Scotland-born Macdonald died, the foundation for the nation had been well laid, despite his penchant for heavy drinking and his involvement in controversies, including his acceptance of large campaign contributions from Sir Hugh Allan, which were later considered bribes when Macdonald awarded Allan's syndicate the contract to build the CPR.

**They Said It!**

"This government can't afford two drunkards and you've got to stop."

*– Sir John A. Macdonald to colleague D'Arcy McGee*

**Kingston boasts all kinds of landmarks to its famous son:**

- 110–112 Rideau Street is the house where Macdonald lived as a teenager, and at age 15, began training for the legal profession as an apprentice. It's now a private residence marked with a plaque. Which reads:

  SIR JOHN ALEXANDER MACDONALD,
  1851–1891

  Statesman and Patriot. His boyhood days, those critical years that decide the character of the man, were spent in the Old Town, which has seen more than a Century of Canadian History. Erected by the National Committee for the Celebration of the Diamond Jubilee of Confederation, A.D. 1927.

- 169–171 Wellington Street became in 1835 Macdonald's first law office, where he later took in two law students, Oliver

Mowat and Alexander Campbell, both of whom later became Fathers of Confederation. The building, now a restaurant, has a plaque affixed to the outside, which notes its significance.

- Bellevue House, at 35 Centre Street, was Macdonald's home from August 1848 to September 1849. Staffed by costumed interpreters, the house and gardens were restored and are kept much as they would have been during the time that Macdonald lived there with his wife, Isabella, and infant son. A month after the couple moved into Bellevue House, their 13-month-old baby died.

Photo courtesy of Kingston Economic Development Corporation.

Sir John A. lived in Bellevue House in Kingston for about a year. It is now a popular tourist attraction.

- 180 Johnson Street was built in 1843. It housed Macdonald and his wife from 1849 to 1852. Their second son, Hugh John, was born in the house in 1850. The building is now a private home and is marked with a plaque.

- 343 King Street East served as Macdonald's law office between 1849 and 1860. Although he was away from Kingston for extensive periods in his role as MP, Macdonald retained his partnership in the Kingston law firm until 1871. The building is marked with a plaque and in 2009 housed a gourmet pizza restaurant.

- 79–81 Wellington Street. is marked with a plaque that indicates Macdonald rented this double house from 1876 to 1878 for his sister Louisa and his brother-in-law James

Williamson, a professor at Queen's. According to author Margaret Angus's book *John A. Lived Here*, the 1877 assessment roll lists Macdonald as a resident in this house, which was in his name.

- Macdonald is buried at the Cataraqui Cemetery on Purdy Mill Road in Kingston. The modern Sir John A. Macdonald Chapel, beside the cemetery office, features a dramatic stained glass window, commissioned in 1891 in memory of Sir John A. Installed in a tiny church at Redan, north of Brockville, the window was donated to the cemetery in 1980 when the chapel was built.

  His grave is marked by several plaques, all erected by the Government of Canada: one marking his grave as that of a Father of Confederation, one as a Canadian prime minister, and a third as part of a program by Parks Canada to mark the grave sites of Canadian prime ministers. A simple stone cross marks his grave.

- a statue in City Park at the corner of West and King Street East in Kingston commemorates Sir John A.

- the town hall erected in 1856 at 124 John Street, in nearby Napanee, Ontario, has been carefully preserved. Macdonald delivered his last campaign speech from its balcony in 1891.

Every year on June 6, the anniversary of Macdonald's death, the Kingston Historical Society organizes a memorial service in honour of Kingston's most famous son. For more information, visit www.heritagekingston.org.

## THEY SAID IT: MEMORABLE QUOTATIONS BY AND ABOUT CANADIAN POLITICIANS

"Canada appears content to become a second-tier socialistic country, boasting ever more loudly about its economy and social services to mask its second-rate status."
— *Stephen Harper, while leader of the Conservative Party*

"Mr. Day is a past master of reducing complex arguments to billboards. I'm not sure if he's running for prime minister or game show host"
— *former prime minister Joe Clark*

"Edmonton isn't really the end of the world — although you can see it from there"
— *Ralph Klein, former mayor of Calgary and premier of Alberta*

"Canada Post doesn't really charge thirty-two cents for a stamp. It's two cents for postage and thirty cents for storage"
— *former Nova Scotia premier Gerald Regan*

"Canadians can be radical, but they must be radical in their own peculiar way, and that way must be in harmony with our national traditions and ideals."
— *Agnes MacPhail, first woman elected to the Canadian Parliament, in a 1935 speech*

"In a world darkened by ethnic conflicts that tear nations apart, Canada stands as a model of how people of different cultures can live and work together in peace, prosperity, and mutual respect."
— *former American president Bill Clinton*

"In the long run, the overwhelming threat to Canada will not come from foreign investments or foreign ideologies or even foreign nuclear weapons. It will come instead from the two-thirds of the people who are steadily falling farther and farther behind in their search for a decent standard of living."
— *former prime minister Pierre Trudeau in 1968*

"The promises of yesterday are the taxes of today."
— *William Lyon Mackenzie King, 1916*

"I didn't know at first that there were two languages in Canada.
I just thought that there was one way to speak to my
father and another to speak to my mother."
— *Louis St. Laurent, former Canadian prime minister*

"We've marched together; we've won over and over again. The reason is
the rank and file, you men and women in the constituencies. And as
long as you remain true to the faith, this party, even though
predictions are made to the contrary, shall not die."
— *John Diefenbaker, leader of the Progressive Conservative Party, 1967, in a
speech to his supporters*

"I am publicity-prone, just as some people are accident-prone."
— *former Liberal MP and cabinet minister Judy LaMarsh
about her highly visible public profile in the 1960s*

"On the beach behind us, Canadians gave their lives so the world would
be a better place. In death they were not anglophones or francophones,
not from the West or the East, not Christians or Jews, not aboriginal
people or immigrants. They were Canadians."
— *former prime minister Jean Chretien, at Juno Beach, France,
on the fiftieth anniversary of D-Day*

"Everything points to Canada as being one of the key countries
in the new race for survival. If all politicians were like
Mr. (Pierre) Trudeau, there would be world peace."
— *John Lennon talking to the Parliament Hill media in 1969*

"I want to ask you gentlemen, if I cannot give consent to my own death,
then whose body is this? Who owns my life?"
— *Lou Gehrig's disease victim Sue Rodriguez, November 1992,
in a videotaped presentation to a House of Commons
subcommittee about assisted suicide*

# POLITICAL Q AND A

**Q: Can members of Parliament take their House of Commons chairs with them when they leave politics?**

**A:** They can, and several have. A spokesperson for the Commons Speaker affirms that MPs who are defeated or retire can buy the chairs they sit on in the Commons for $900.00, which is exactly what it costs the government to replace them.

The chairs, on which MPs sit at their desks in the Commons, are made of solid oak and have green leather or crushed velvet on the backs, seats, and arms. MPs have been permitted to purchase them since the conclusion of the 1988 federal election.

"They are souvenirs, mementos of a member's stay in Parliament," the spokesperson says. "MPs spend a lot of time in them. They are a little piece of history."

Among those who have doled out $950.00 for their chairs over the years are former NDP leader Ed Broadbent; former International Trade Minister Pat Carney of British Columbia; and former Environment Minister Tom MacMillan, an MP from Prince Edward Island. Carney and Broadbent retired, and MacMillan was defeated in the 1988 election.

**Q: Who was responsible for introducing Canada's first Medicare legislation?**

**A:** Although Tommy Douglas usually gets most of the credit, the first government-prepaid medical plan in Canada — and North America — was introduced in the rural municipality of McKillop, about seventy kilometres north of Regina, on June 1, 1939, by Matthew Anderson.

According to a privately published biography, Anderson, the long-time reeve of McKillop, became convinced in the late 1920s that a health-insurance plan similar to those of his native Norway was desirable. He began to quietly lobby for legislation to establish such a plan, and after watching the suffering caused by the Great Depression in the 1930s, he became even more convinced that such legislation was needed.

The biography, written by Harold A. Longman, observes that, in 1938, the outlines of Anderson's plan were submitted to the voters of the municipality in a plebiscite and received overwhelming approval. The Saskatchewan Legislature then introduced a bill officially known as An Act Respecting Medical and Hospital Services for Municipalities, which was often referred to as the Matt Anderson bill.

The bill allowed municipalities to collect taxes for health services, a procedure which was previously forbidden. It was passed by the legislature in March 1939 and went into effect a few months later. McKillop was the first to take advantage of this bill, thanks to Anderson's strong belief and lobbying.

Longman's book mentions that the initial annual cost per year was five dollars, with a maximum of 50 dollars per family, for which a patient received complete medical attention, including specialist services, surgery, hospital accommodations for up to 21 days, and prescription drugs.

**Political BITE!**

The prime ministers who served the shortest terms in office:

1. Sir Charles Tupper, Conservative. 69 days: May 1–July 8, 1896.

2. John Turner, Liberal. 80 days: June 30–September 17, 1984.

3. Arthur Meighen, Conservative. 89 days: June 29–September 25, 1926.

4. Kim Campbell, Conservative. 135 days: June 13–October 25, 1993.

When the bill was passed, the *Regina Leader-Post* praised Anderson in an editorial which said that "Matthew S. Anderson's name will go down in municipal history in Saskatchewan as one who had the courage and initiative to be the first to put a new idea into practice."

Douglas introduced the concept of Medicare on a province-wide basis in 1946, some seven years after Anderson's municipal initiatives.

**Q:** *On the first moon walk, Apollo astronauts left messages behind from every country. What did Canada's say?*

**A:** Astronauts Neil Armstrong and Buzz Aldrin left messages on the moon's surface on a grey disc the size of a half dollar. The Bilingual message from then prime minister Pierre Trudeau was: "Man reached out and touched the tranquil moon. *Puisse ce haut fait permettre à l'homme de redécouvrir la terre et d'y trouver la paix.*" The French translates as "May that high accomplishment allow man to rediscover Earth and there find peace."

**Q:** *How did a football once influence the outcome of a Canadian federal election?*

**A:** A football mishandled by Conservative leader Robert Stanfield during the 1974 federal election campaign is possibly the most famous pigskin in Canadian history.

Those in the know say the dropped ball was among the factors that caused Stanfield to lose the election to Pierre Trudeau.

Read on and see if you agree.

On May 30, 1974, Stanfield's DC-9 campaign airplane was flying from Halifax to Vancouver when it stopped for refuelling at North Bay where the leader's campaign staff and the trailing press corps embarked onto the tarmac to stretch their legs.

With the RCMP and airport security watching closely, Brad Chapman, director of Stanfield's campaign tour operations, produced a football and began playing catch with members of the media.

"I had carried the football as a means of exercise for the weary press corps, having to sit long hours in airplanes, buses, and bars, with little chance to loosen up," recalls Chapman, who with colleague Peter Sharpe was looking after the needs and wants of the press.

Unknown to Chapman, Stanfield had also decided to go for a stroll around the aircraft. Seeing the football being tossed, he slipped out of his suit jacket and called for the ball. To

## Political BITE!

Doug Ball, who took the famous Stanfield photograph and was rewarded with a National Newspaper award for feature photography, joined the Montreal Gazette photo desk in 1984. In 1987 he joined his friend, Trivial Pursuit co-inventor Chris Haney, to build two golf courses near Toronto, the Devil's Pulpit and the Devil's Paintbrush. Ball left the Pulpit in 1999 and since then has been a freelance photographer for a number of corporate clients. He is still a member of the Pulpit and in the fall of 2005 published two coffee table books, Life on a Press Pass, with his brother Lynn, which includes photos the pair took over forty years as photographers in the media, and The Greatest New Golf Courses in Canada with writer John Gordon. Life on a Press Pass includes Doug's photos of Stanfield catching and dropping the football.

the amazement of many, the leader began to throw thirty and forty-yard perfect spiral passes to willing receivers.

"Occasionally, a receiver dropped the ball. And the ball was thrown back to the leader. Occasionally, he dropped the ball. Most of the time, though, like the press receivers, he caught the ball," recalls Chapman.

Meantime, Canadian Press photographer Doug Ball was snapping away with his camera. Before the plane took off en route to the west coast, his roll of film, which contained photos of Stanfield catching and dropping the ball, was shipped to Canadian Press's photo desk in Toronto.

"The rest is history," says Chapman.

The next day a Ball photo of Stanfield fumbling the football was on the front page of the *Globe and Mail* and other newspapers across Canada. "Political Fumble?" said more than one newspaper caption that spring morning in 1974, when Stanfield's Conservatives were fighting to unseat Trudeau's minority Liberal government in an election forced by a non-confidence vote.

"The picture made him look really old," Don Sellar, who was covering the election for Southam News was quoted as saying. "The long boney fingers, the ball slipping through. He looked terrible. And yet he didn't look terrible on the tarmac.... He looked to be quite competent. He knew how to throw and catch: it's just that he dropped one."

Although the vote was still five weeks away, veteran Southam News reporter Charles Lynch told Ball: "Trudeau just won the election."

When the results were tallied on July 8, Canadians returned Trudeau to power with 141 seats, enough for a majority government. Stanfield's Conservatives won ninety-five ridings, 11 fewer than the party held when the election was called.

Few pundits blame the photo for Stanfield's defeat, but most say it played a role.

"It came at a particularly bad time, campaigning against Mr. Trudeau, who was perceived by the public as a very athletic guy — flips off diving boards and you name it," said Art Lyon, a lifelong Tory organizer who was working the campaign. "Then all of a sudden there's this one picture of a football and Mr. Stanfield, this crouched-over, bald guy in glasses. Put it this way: it didn't help."

Stanfield died in 2003 at the age of 89. The infamous football was kept by Chapman but during the 1980s and 90s, he went through several life transitions, during which time his personal goods were in storage and somewhere along the way "the" football went missing.

"Some young fella might have chanced through my goods and, seeing an old football, thought he might put it to good use. If it still exists, it's probably in pretty rugged condition. The last time I saw it in the 1980s, it had become pretty beat up. Like all good politicians, the ball has probably long since been recycled into anonymity."

## Political BITE!

Brad Chapman, went on to a variety of other political posts following the 1974 campaign including transportation director for the 1975 Bill Davis election campaign in Ontario, tour director for Michael Meighen's 1975 winning bid for the federal Tory Party Presidency and for the federal Tory leadership campaign in Alberta of Jim Gillies in 1976, tour operations director for both Joe Clark federal election campaigns of 1979 and 1980 and for the Ontario Tory leadership campaign of Alan Pope in 1985. In 1979 he was appointed Chief of Staff for John Fraser, Minister of the Environment and Postmaster General of Canada. In 1987, he managed a Bay Street analyst's tour to Hong Kong, Beijing, Nanjing, Shanghai and Shenzhen. After a tour with Saskatchewan Trade and Investment as Director of Investment Strategy and Policy, in 1992 during a sweat lodge ceremony on the Little Big Horn River in Montana, Chapman was given the Crow Indian name of "Shamrock." Soon after, he served as Director of Public Affairs for the late Senator and Sawridge Band Chief, Walter P. Twinn. In 1994, he managed the Juniper Lodge in Alberta where he coordinated a spiritual wellness program. He now lives in Toronto where he works in strategic investment banking, image marketing/consulting, and political history research and writing.

 **POLITICAL POSERS QUIZ**

Now it's time for a Question Period of our own. Take our quiz and test your Canadian political IQ. No catcalls, please!

1.  I was a champion of justice issues including women's rights when I was elected to the House of Commons in 1921. Who am I?

2.   Which Canadian prime minister was known as "Old Tomorrow"?

    a) Wilfrid Laurier
    b) John Turner
    c) John Diefenbaker
    d) Sir John A. Macdonald

3.   When Canada was formed in 1867, what was the maximum yearly salary a member of Parliament could earn?

    a) $300
    b) $600
    c) $1,200
    d) $3,000

4.   What was Joey Smallwood's occupation before he became premier of Newfoundland in 1949?

    a) cab driver
    b) journalist
    c) lawyer
    d) entrepreneur

5.   What is the name of the statue on the dome of the Manitoba legislative building in Winnipeg?

6.   What did the federal government outlaw in September 1972 for safety reasons?

    a) firecrackers
    b) open-wheeled go carts
    c) smoking in airplanes
    d) expense accounts for politicians

7.   Where in Canada did women first have the legal right to vote?

    a) Quebec
    b) Ontario

c) Nova Scotia

d) Manitoba

8. Where did MPs meet after fire gutted the Centre Block of the Parliament Buildings in 1916?

   a) the East Block at Parliament Hill
   b) Ottawa City Hall
   c) the Museum of Nature
   d) Lansdowne Park

9. Unscramble the following letters to form the name of one of Ontario's Conservative premiers:

   Ibil vidas

10. What was Sir John A. Macdonald's middle name?

   a) Albert
   b) Arthur
   c) Alexander
   d) Allan

➥ Answers on page 366

# CHAPTER 18
# Our Game: Hockey Heroes

 **GREATEST PLAYERS OF ALL TIME**
(in order of position)

## Goalie:

1. **Terry Sawchuk:** Many consider him the greatest ever. His crouching style was innovative and helped him get his name on the Vezina Trophy four times. He recorded 103 shutouts during his 21-year career.

2. **Jacques Plante:** A creative and talented goalie who won seven Vezina trophies, six with the great Canadiens' teams of the 1950s, and one jointly with Glenn Hall of the St. Louis Blues. He was at the top of his game in the 1950s and early 1960s, but was superb enough to later help less-talented teams such as the St. Louis Blues and the Toronto Maple Leafs.

3. **Glenn Hall:** He was called "Mr. Goalie" and his Calder Trophy, seven first-team all-star berths, 84 shutouts, and three Vezina trophies solidify him as one of the best.

4. **Ken Dryden:** A cool performer who played his best when the pressure was on, Dryden was a five-time first team all-star and winner of the Vezina Trophy five times in a relatively short, eight-year career.

5. **Bill Durnan:** Durnan was one of the best goalies in hockey's "old days," thanks to lightning-quick hands and the ability to stymie shooters by changing hands with his goal stick. He won six Vezina trophies and had six first-team all-star berths in just seven NHL seasons.

6. **Patrick Roy:** This Quebec native was one of the best in the league in the 1980s and 90s. He played in 11 all-star games and earned three Vezina Trophies over 19 NHL seasons. During the 2000–01 season he surpassed the legendary Terry Sawchuk for the most NHL career wins. His record of 551 victories between the pipes stood until March,

2009. He was also the first goalie to play in 1,000 career NHL games and had 12 30-win seasons. He retired in 2003.

7.  **Martin Brodeur:** With his unique style, sharp reflexes, puck-handling abilities, and reliability, Brodeur well deserves to round out this list. He has been honoured with four Vezina Trophies and has 10 all-star game appearances. Still a key member of the New Jersey Devils at the time of printing, he is within reach of Sawchuk's record for most career shutouts and has surpassed Patrick Roy's record for career victories.

# Defence:

1.  **Bobby Orr:** Some consider him the perfect hockey player, and though he won the Norris Trophy as the best defenceman eight times, he also changed the game with his offensive skills. Bad knees kept him from having a longer and probably greater career.

2.  **Doug Harvey:** A seven-time winner of the Norris Trophy, even though such an award didn't exist for the first six years of his career. Many consider him the best defenceman ever.

3.  **Eddie Shore:** A fearless and talented player with great skating skills that made him an offensive threat as well. And he did it long before Orr.

4.  **Denis Potvin:** Some consider him the equal to Orr during the years they were in the league together. Potvin had similar offensive skills, but was a better bodychecker.

5.  **Ray Bourque:** A superb all-round defenceman with five Norris Trophy wins. He has been favourably compared to Orr. He holds the current records for all-time points scored by a defenceman with 1,579, and for goals scored by a defenceman with 410. He also had an amazing 13 first-team all-star berths and a league-high number of consecutive appearances at all-star games with 19 (surpassing Wayne Gretzky's previous record).

6.  **Larry Robinson:** Creative with the puck, a decent goal scorer, and able to deliver devastating bodychecks, Robinson was a six-time all-star and double Norris Trophy winner. His 20-year career saw him win six Stanley Cups.

7.  **Red Kelly:** Though he also excelled as a forward, he was a great defensive defenceman early in his career and played on many Stanley Cup-winning teams.

8. **Paul Coffey:** A great all-round defenceman who was a superb skater, playmaker, and goal-scorer. He has four Stanley Cup rings and has won the Norris Trophy three times.

9. **Brad Park:** Overshadowed during his career by Orr, Park was a five-time first-team all-star who had exceptional defensive skills.

10. **Dit Clapper:** The NHL's first 20-year player, this six-time all-star made the smooth transition from right wing to defence 11 years into his career. Power, precision, and a knack for avoiding mistakes were Clapper's hallmarks.

# Centre:

1. **Wayne Gretzky:** He's called "The Great One" for good reason. Gretzky hold so many records and has won so many awards it's hard to keep track, and even in the twilight of his career he was still outshining most everyone in the game.

2. **Mario Lemieux:** The only player who has come close to matching Gretzky's offensive skills, he was also a great playmaker, skater, and leader.

3. **Jean Beliveau:** A smooth and majestic player who was not only a perennial all-star, but a great leader who won 10 Stanley Cups during his career.

4. **Howie Morenz:** A speedy skater who had a flair for scoring dramatic goals. One of the best players in the first half of the 20th century.

5. **Mark Messier:** The man they called "Moose" is known as much for his leadership and dressing room presence as his ability to score big goals that turn around games. He is a six-time Stanley Cup winner and has five all-star selections and two Hart Trophies to his credit.

### Hockey BITE!

Approximately 4.5 million Canadians are involved in hockey as coaches, players, officials, administrators, or direct volunteers. More than 540,000 players are registered with Hockey Canada, and between them they play more than 1.5 million games every season and take part in two million practices at Canada's 3,500 arenas.

## Left Wing:

1. **Bobby Hull:** "The Golden Jet" was the dominant player of his time, a great skater, legendary goal-scorer, and underrated checker and penalty killer.

2. **Ted Lindsay:** One of the toughest players in the game, a great goal-scorer, and first-team all-star eight times.

3. **Frank Mahovlich:** A gifted skater and stickhandler with a huge slapshot, "the Big M" could turn a team into a champion, as he did on several occasions. He won the Calder Trophy in his first season with the Toronto Maple Leafs and played on six Stanley Cup winners.

4. **Dickie Moore:** Although his career was plagued by injuries, Moore persevered to win two Art Ross Trophies, including in 1957–58 when he played with a broken wrist for the final three months of the season. Maurice Richard once called him the best left-winger he ever played with.

5. **Johnny Bucyk:** Often lost in the shadow of Bobby Orr and Phil Esposito, hard-hitting Bucyk was one of the league's premier wingers but not until later in his career. After turning 32, he had seven 30-goal seasons, including his first 50-goal year. He won the Lady Byng Trophy twice and retired in 1978 as the fourth-leading NHL goal and point producer of all time.

## Right Wing:

1. **Gordie Howe:** Until Gretzky came along, most considered him the greatest player ever. And with the kind of record he piled up over 34 incredible years he's certainly the greatest right winger in the history of the game.

2. **Maurice Richard:** "The Rocket" was the dominating player of his day, an exciting and excellent goal-scorer who played with intensity and skill rarely matched.

3. **Guy Lafleur:** One of the dominant players of the 1970s, he was fast, scored a bucket of goals, and was a winner.

4. **Mike Bossy:** The New York Islander winger was one of the most prolific scorers in NHL history, notching 50 or more goals in nine consecutive seasons and helping his team to four consecutive Stanley Cups.

5. **Charlie Conacher:** Six feet one inches of determination and possessing the hardest shot in the league in the 1930s. Conacher was a hockey legend. He was a five-time all-star, won two Art Ross Trophies, scored more than 30 goals in four of his 12 seasons, and held or shared the league goal-scoring lead five times.

 # WHERE ARE THEY NOW?

 ## Dave Schultz

### Vital Stats

Dave Schultz was born on October 14, 1949, in Waldheim, Saskatchewan, and grew up in Rosetown, about an hour west of Saskatoon. For three years he played with the Swift Current Broncos, including during the team's first year in the Western Hockey League. He finished his junior career with the Sorel Blackhawks of the Quebec Major Junior Hockey League and was selected by the Philadelphia Flyers in round five, number 52 overall, in the 1969 NHL Amateur Draft. He played for Roanoke and Richmond and the Quebec Aces of the American Hockey League before cracking the Flyers' roster in 1972. He was a member of the Flyers for four seasons and also patrolled the wing with the Los Angeles Kings, Pittsburgh Penguins, and Buffalo Sabres. He retired in 1980 from Sabres affiliate, the Rochester Americans of the AHL.

### Claims to Fame

In 535 regular season NHL games, Schultz scored 79 goals and had 121 assists and added

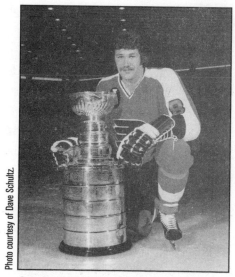

Photo courtesy of Dave Schultz.

Schultz helped the Flyers win back-to-back cups in 1974 and 1975.

another 20 points in the playoffs. He helped the Flyers win Stanley Cups in 1974 and 1975 and make it to the finals in 1976. He's best known, however, as an enforcer who racked up 2,294 regular season penalty minutes in the NHL and averaged 25 fights a season in his prime. He holds the NHL record for most penalty minutes in a season, 472 in 1974–75. Nicknamed "The Hammer," he was part of the infamous Flyers' teams known as the "Broad Street Bullies" whose rosters included tough guys Don "Big Bird" Saleski, Bob "Hound Dog" Kelly, and Andre "Moose" Dupont. Schultz and his tough-guy teammates deserve plenty of credit for turning a lacklustre early 1970s Flyers expansion team into a Cup winner. Schultz was more than an enforcer: he scored 20 goals for Philadelphia in 1973–74 and fired the series-clinching goal in overtime in the first round of the 1974 Stanley Cup playoffs against the Atlanta Flames.

### Style
The six-foot, one-inch, 195-pound left-winger was known for his aggressive play and penchant for dropping his gloves to protect his teammates.

### Where is He Now?
After retiring as a player, Schultz for three years coached teams in the United Hockey League and the East Coast Hockey League. He managed a hockey rink for 10 years and for 22 years has operated a limousine service in the Philadelphia area. He is a comedic and motivational speaker and in 2009 was running a website offering an online collection of vintage NHL hockey autographs and signed sports memorabilia; he was also working as a consultant to help companies streamline their operations. He lives in the Philadelphia area and has two sons, one of whom has written a movie script about the Hammer's life in pro hockey.

Photo courtesy of Dave Schultz

Dave Schultz is now a motivational speaker.

### Quotable Quote
"I hated fighting in junior … when a brawl started I would go to the bench and be glad to be there but that all changed. I got in a few fights in my first year out of junior … in the NHL tough guys were always needed and the fans certainly appreciated it when some guy was doing something to one of my teammates and I'd go and challenge them. It was the code — enforcers would do the policing ourselves."

## Fabulous Fact

Schultz was anything but a tough guy during his junior career, which saw him involved in just two fights. In his final year of junior, he scored 50 goals in 80 regular season and playoff games.

 # Yvan Cournoyer

## Vital Stats

Yvan Cournoyer was born on November 22, 1943, in Drummondville, Quebec. He played minor hockey in his hometown before graduating to Junior B with the Lachine Maroons at age 13. Between 1961 and 1964, he played three seasons with the Montreal Junior Canadiens and first played with the Montreal Canadiens in the 1963–64 season when he was called up for five games.

## Claims to Fame

During his junior career, Cournoyer racked up 115 goals and 91 assists in 121 regular season games. As a member of the Canadiens for 16 seasons, he scored 428 goals and 435 assists during the regular season and bagged another 64 goals and 63 assists in 147 playoff contests. In 11 seasons he scored 25 goals or more, with his most prolific season being 1968–69 when he recorded 87 points on 43 goals and 44 assists. He helped the Canadiens win 10 Stanley Cups, including 1972–73, when he was awarded the Conn Smythe Trophy as the most valuable player in the playoffs. He was captain of the Habs from 1975 to 1979. In 1972, Cournoyer scored three goals as a member of Team Canada during the Canada-Russia Summit Series, including the game winner in game two and the game-tying goal in game eight. In 1998, he was ranked number 98 on *The Hockey News* list of the 100 Greatest Hockey Players. The Canadiens retired uniform number 12 in honour of both Cournoyer and Dickie Moore in 2005.

## Style

Dubbed "The Roadrunner" for his blazing speed and small stature (five-foot, eight inches, 179 pounds.), Cournoyer was an offensive-minded winger who used his speed to find openings and take passes that often turned into breakaways or odd-man rushes. Few players in NHL history have been as exciting to watch.

### Where is He Now?

Cournoyer and his second wife live on a golf course in Blainville, Quebec, a Montreal suburb 25 minutes from the Bell Centre. The couple's son was attending Georgian College in Barrie in 2008. Cournoyer also has three other children, two girls and a boy, from his first marriage. He coached the Montreal Roadrunners roller hockey team in 1994–95 and in 1996–97 was an assistant coach with the Canadiens. Along with former teammates Henri Richard, Jean Beliveau, Rejean Houle, and Guy Lafleur, he is an "ambassador" for the Canadiens, regularly attending banquets and golf tournaments and visiting hospitals on behalf of the team and through his Toronto agent is often booked to speak and sign autographs at corporate functions. He attends about half of the Canadiens' games. In the summer he plays golf three times a week. In September 2008, he had an operation to repair a nerve problem in his back.

Cournoyer was one of seven legendary Canadiens alumni and team ambassadors introduced to the crowd during the NHL All-Star Game held in Montreal in January, 2009.

### Quotable Quote

"We did it, we did it," were Cournoyer's jubilant words when he embraced Henderson after the latter scored the winning goal against Russia in the 1972 Summit Series.

### Fabulous Facts

Cournoyer acquired his nickname from a *Sports Illustrated* writer after scoring two break-away goals against the New York Rangers early in his career. He attributes his blistering shot to practising his shooting in summer in the family garage using heavier than normal pucks he made in his father's machine shop. Cournoyer could shoot left and right, a talent that often dumfounded opposing goalies.

##  Danny Gare

### Vital Stats

Danny Gare was born in Nelson, British Columbia, on May 14, 1954. He played his minor hockey in the Nelson area before joining the Calgary Centennials of the Western Canada Hockey League in 1971 for three seasons. His Centennials' teammates included future NHLers Bobby Nystrom, John Davidson, and Jimmy

> **They Said It!**
>
> "Most young Canadians … are born with skates on their feet rather than with silver spoons in their mouths."
>
> — *former prime minister Lester B. Pearson*

Watson. Gare was selected by the Buffalo Sabres in round two, 29th overall, in the 1974 NHL Amateur Draft and also by the Winnipeg Jets of the World Hockey Association in round three, 36th overall in the former league's amateur draft. He chose Buffalo, where he played until the 1981–82 season when he joined the Detroit Red Wings for five seasons. A sore back convinced him to retire in 1987 after just 18 games with the Edmonton Oilers.

## Claims to Fame

During 17 NHL seasons, Gare played in 827 regular season games, notching 354 goals and 331 assists. In 64 playoff games he added another 25 goals and 21 assists. He was never on a Stanley Cup-winning team but on two occasions with the Sabres he reached the 50-goal mark, notching 50 in 1975–76, while playing on a checking line with Don Luce and Craig Ramsay, and 56 in 1979–80. He scored the first goal of his career at the 18-second mark of the first period in a game against Boston. It was the second fastest goal ever scored by a rookie. In 1976, Gare helped Canada win the Canada Cup on a team stocked with superstars, including Bobby Hull, Darryl Sittler, Phil Esposito, and Bobby Orr.

Courtesy of Columbus Blue Jackets/Jamie Sabau.

Danny Gare.

## Style

The five-foot, nine-inch, 175-pound forward was known for his quick wrist shot and status as a small, yet scrappy and fearless player.

## Where is He Now?

After retiring as a player, Gare dabbled in several careers including restaurant ownership and a computer company. He was involved in broadcasting and marketing in the initial years of the Tampa Bay Lightning franchise and for four years was the team's assistant coach. He worked as a studio analyst and ice level reporter on Sabres broadcasts from 1987 to 1992 and 1995 to 2004; since 2006, he has been the colour commentator for the NHL's Columbus Blue Jackets on Fox Sports Ohio, handling about 75 televised games a season. He spends summers in the Nelson area and regularly visits his two daughters and two grandchildren in Buffalo. He plays in the occasional Sabres Alumni hockey game. He lives in Columbus, Ohio, about 10 minutes from Nationwide Arena, home of the Blue Jackets.

## Quotable Quote

"The key to a good colour commentator is being able to analyze the play and have stories to tell. I have many stories and I try to relate those to what comes up in the game."

## Fabulous Fact

Gare's father, Ernie, was a solid senior hockey player who for 20 years was athletic director at Notre Dame University (now Selkirk College) in Nelson. The elder Gare started the first athletic scholarship program in Canada, and possibly North America. Ernie Gare also coached the university's hockey team, which regularly defeated the team from the much larger University of British Columbia in Vancouver.

 # Dickie Moore

## Vital Stats

Dickie Moore was born in Montreal on January 6, 1931, and grew up in a family of nine boys and one girl. Despite a badly broken leg at the age of seven, he developed into a solid minor hockey player. In 1947–48 he played a partial season with the Montreal Junior Royals and a year later his offensive prowess helped the Royals become the first Memorial Cup champions from Quebec. He also starred with the Montreal Junior Canadiens and helped that team win a Memorial Cup. After becoming property of the Montreal Canadiens, he first skated with the Habs in 1951–52, registering a respectable 18 goals and 15 assists in 33 regular season games. After brief stints with the Royals and the AHL's Buffalo Bisons, Moore graduated to the Canadiens for good in the 1954–55 season.

## Claims to Fame

Moore played in the NHL until 1967–68, skating in 719 regular season games and notching 261 goals and 347 assists over 14 seasons, several of them on a line with Rocket Richard and his brother Henri. In 135 playoff games he scored another 110 points. He helped the Canadiens win six Stanley Cups, including five in a row with the great Canadiens teams of the late 1950s, and won the league scoring championship in both 1958 (84 points) and 1959 (96 points). He was inducted into the Hockey Hall of Fame in 1974. In 1998, he was ranked number 31 on *The Hockey News*' list of the 100 Greatest Hockey Players.

### Style

The five-foot-10-inch, 185-pound left-winger was known for his offensive prowess.

### Where is He Now?

After brief stints with the Toronto Maple Leafs and St. Louis Blues, Moore retired in 1968 and has dedicated most of his energy to Dickie Moore Rentals, a Montreal-based company that he launched in 1961 while still playing hockey. The company rents construction equipment, storage containers, and office trailers and has branch offices in Toronto, Ottawa, and Longueil, Quebec. Moore lives in Montreal with his wife and regularly attends Canadiens' games.

### Quotable Quote

On former Canadiens coach Toe Blake: "When Toe became coach, I was elated. He kept me on the team. I was lucky to have a guy who believed in me. You're only as good as how somebody can lift you up to the heights where he thinks you can play."

### Fabulous Fact

Although he grew up in Montreal, Moore did not cheer for the Canadiens at that time, ironic considering his later affiliation. He was a big fan of the Leafs and idolized Gordie Drillon, a productive winger who, like Moore, won two NHL scoring titles.

Photo courtesy of Ron Ellis.

 # LEGENDS OF THE GAME

 ## Ron Ellis: Mr. Dependable

Ron Ellis is still involved in hockey with the Hockey Hall of Fame in Toronto.

If there has ever been a winger who gave his all at both ends of the ice, while rarely being caught out of position, it's Ron Ellis.

"Under coach Punch Imlach, it was not a good idea to wander off of your wing. If you did, you might be watching the rest of the game from the end of the bench," says Ellis.

Ellis was born on January 8, 1945, in Lindsay, Ontario, northeast of Toronto, and played his minor hockey mostly in Toronto and Ottawa. When he was 14 and attending high school in Ottawa, Toronto Maple Leafs coach Punch Imlach and general manager

## Sports BITE!

Prior to the 1968–69 season, former Maple Leafs great Irvine "Ace" Bailey insisted that Ellis wear his retired number 6 because he admired his high-calibre yet clean style of play. Ellis's father, Randy, played with the Toronto Marlboroughs under Harold Ballard, coach of the team at the time and later owner of the Leafs.

King Clancy visited his home and asked him to join the Toronto Marlboroughs junior hockey organization the following season.

He developed into a pro prospect and led the Marlies in goals during his Memorial Cup-winning year in 1963–64. He joined the Leafs in 1964, scoring 23 goals and narrowly losing the Calder Trophy for rookie of the year to Detroit netminder Roger Crozier. Ellis spent his entire career with the Leafs and retired in 1980 after playing in 1,034 games and notching 332 goals and 308 assists.

In game six of the Stanley Cup finals in 1967, Ellis provided the crucial first goal to help the Leafs win the game 3–1 and take the Cup. In the 1972 Canada-Russia Summit Series, the five-foot-nine, 190-pounder was a member of the Team Canada squad that beat the Russians on Paul Henderson's dramatic goal with only seconds remaining in the final game. He was on a line with Henderson and Bobby Clarke.

After retiring from pro hockey, Ellis worked in the Toronto area as a teacher and in the insurance business and ran his own sporting goods store for six years. In 1993, he joined the Hockey Hall of Fame, where he is the director of public affairs and assistant to the president.

He supports the work of Christian Athletic Ministries and lives in Caledon East near Toronto with his wife, Jan.

## Garry Monahan: Drafted First

As professional hockey players go, Garry Monahan was never a household name. But when he was selected by the Montreal Canadiens in the National Hockey League entry draft in 1963, he became a part of hockey history.

Garry Monahan wearing the blue and white.

Photo courtesy of Garry Monahan.

Monahan, who was born October 20, 1946, was the first player picked in the first ever National Hockey League draft of amateur players 17 years of age and older.

The Barrie, Ontario, native, best known as a defensive forward in the NHL, played junior hockey with the St. Michael's College organization, which has spawned many hockey greats, including Joe Primeau, Dave Keon, Red Kelly, Frank Mahovlich, and Eric Lindros.

He also skated for the Peterborough Petes and minor league teams in Houston and Cleveland before jumping to the NHL, where he played for the Canadiens, Detroit Red Wings, Los Angeles Kings, Vancouver Canucks, and Toronto Maple Leafs.

During his 12-year career, Monahan played in 748 regular season games and scored 116 goals and 169 assists. After retiring from the NHL in 1979, he played amateur hockey in Japan for three years with the Seibu Bears. While in Japan he earned his teaching degree. When he returned to Vancouver he earned his stock broker's licence and worked within that field for five years before getting his real estate licence; Monahan became a real estate agent in 1990. He lives in West Vancouver, where he is an agent with Royal LePage Garry Monahan Realty Ltd.

After staying off skates for 20 years, he tied up the blades in 2003 as a member of the Canucks alumni. He also plays golf and tennis and spends many winter weekends skiing at Whistler.

**Sports BITE!**

The second player taken in the 1963 draft was Peter Mahovlich, who later joined the Detroit Red Wings. Coincidentally, about three years into their careers, the two swapped teams, with Monahan going to Detroit and Mahovlich to Montreal.

## Willie O'Ree: Cracking the Colour Barrier

Willie O'Ree became the first black athlete to play in the National Hockey League when he debuted with the Boston Bruins in 1958.

But breaking down the colour barrier in hockey, an accomplishment that often saw him referred to as "the Jackie Robinson of Hockey," was not the New Brunswick native's only claim to fame.

Unknown to many, O'Ree played pro hockey for more than two decades without any vision in his right eye. Despite his disability, he was usually among the top scorers in the leagues he played in.

O'Ree was born in Fredericton on October 15, 1935, the youngest of 13 children, and like many Canadians, he learned to play hockey on a backyard rink made with a garden hose by his father. He skated with the Fredericton Capitals Senior A team before playing junior hockey with the Quebec Frontenacs and Kitchener-Waterloo Canucks in the mid-1950s.

In 1956, after being scouted by Punch Imlach (later coach and general manager of the Toronto Maple Leafs), he turned professional with the Quebec Aces of the Quebec Hockey League and went on to a 21-year pro career, which included parts of two seasons as a winger with the Boston Bruins.

When he played for the Bruins on January 18, 1958, wearing sweater number 22, he became the first black man to play in the NHL before being shipped back to the Aces. He played in two games with the Bruins that season.

In 1956–57 he helped the Quebec Aces win the Duke of Edinburgh Trophy as QHL champs. In 1960–61, he was called up to the Bruins again, this time skating in 43 games. In 45 games with Boston he notched four goals and 10 assists.

Much of his career was spent in the Western Hockey League, where he topped the 30-goal mark four times.

Despite losing 97 percent of the sight in his eye after being hit by a puck while playing with the Kitchener-Waterloo Canucks, he won two WHL scoring titles — in 1964–65 when he notched 38 goals and 21 assists for the Los Angeles Blades and in 1968–69 when he scored 38 goals and 41 assists for the San Diego Gulls. He was named to the WHL all-star team three times.

Remembering his days playing hockey in all-white leagues, O'Ree says, "I heard the racial remarks from players and fans … I wanted to concentrate on hockey and I soon found that the names never hurt unless you let them. I told myself 'I am proud of who I am and I can't change the colour of my skin.'"

## Sports BITE!

Following his eye injury, doctors told O'Ree his career was finished. But he continued to play, and the only people who knew about his disability were his younger sister, Betty, of Montreal, and a close friend, Stan Maxwell, of Truro, Nova Scotia. His bad eye was replaced with a prosthesis in the early 1980s.

Courtesy of NHL images.

Willie O'Ree made history when he donned the Bruins uniform in 1958.

O'Ree retired following the 1978–79 season, in which he played in 53 games with the San Diego Gulls of the Pacific Hockey League. Since then he has lived in the San Diego area, where he has dabbled in a handful of careers, including construction, athletic equipment sales, fast food outlet management, automobile sales, and security. A new career dawned in 1995, when he was hired as an ambassador for the NHL's diversity program.

O'Ree is director of Youth Development for NHL Diversity, a job that involves on- and off-ice clinics, speaking engagements, and personal appearances to introduce children with diverse ethnic backgrounds to hockey and help them pay for hockey equipment.

Since 1995, the program has involved more than 40,000 children in the United States and Canada, including goalie Gerald Coleman of Illinois, who played for the London Knights of the OHL and was drafted by the NHL's Tampa Bay Lightning in 2003.

O'Ree lives in La Mesa, California, a suburb of San Diego, with his wife, Deljeet, and daughter, Chandra. In 1999 he published a children's book *The Autobiography of Willie O'Ree: Hockey's Black Pioneer*. A documentary, *Echoes in the Rink: The Willie O'Ree Story*, recounts his life.

In October 2005, he was among 10 people named to the Order of New Brunswick and in December of 2008, he received the Order of Canada.

## Denis Potvin: Stellar NHL Blueliner

When the New York Islanders drafted Denis Potvin first overall in 1973, it was hoped the young defenceman from Ottawa would be a good foundation to improve the lowly expansion team that finished in last place in its first two years of play.

Potvin surpassed these expectations: during a 15-year career played entirely with the Islanders, he was one of the cornerstones that held the franchise together and eventually turned the team into a dynasty.

The former star of the Ottawa 67's of the Ontario Hockey Association (now the Ontario Hockey League) quickly became one of the most complete defenders to step onto the ice, helping the Islanders win four straight Stanley Cups from 1980 to 1983, along the way becoming the first NHL defenceman to score 1,000 career points.

Potvin's wealth of natural talent allowed him to jump into the offensive rush while serving as a tough physical presence in his own end of the rink. His mean streak caused many an opposing forward to stay off his side of the ice.

At age 14, Potvin broke into the OHA with the 67's and played five seasons, beginning with the 1968–69 campaign. In his last season with Ottawa, he broke the scoring record for OHA defenceman with 123 points. He won two consecutive Kaminsky Awards as the league's premier rearguard.

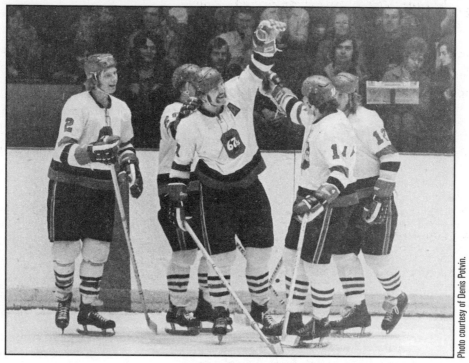

Photo courtesy of Denis Potvin.

Denis Potvin started his career with the Ottawa 67's.

As an NHLer, he played in 1,060 regular season games, notching 310 goals and 742 assists, plus another 56 goals and 108 assists in the playoffs. In addition to four Stanley Cups, he won three Norris Trophies as the league's best defenceman, plus the Calder Trophy in 1974 as the league's best rookie.

In 1991 he was inducted into the Hockey Hall of Fame and Canada's Sports Hall of Fame. On March 31, 1988, a cheering crowd at the Nassau Coliseum on Long Island paid homage to his stellar career when his number 5 sweater was hung from the rafters.

After retiring from the Islanders in 1988, he worked in New York City as a commercial real estate agent and stockbroker. He also worked part-time as an in-studio hockey analyst with the Sports Channel New York. In 1993, he became a colour analyst for the NHL's Florida Panthers and now works with the Fox Sports Network.

Potvin was living in the Fort Lauderdale, Florida, area with his wife, Valerie, daughters Madeleine and Annabelle, and son Christian. The family vacations from June to September at their summer home in Mont Tremblant, Quebec.

## ⊕ Manon Rheaume: Breaking the Ice

Manon Rheaume hasn't faced a blistering slapshot since 2000, but the woman who broke ground in North American sport by becoming the first female to play in a National Hockey League game is still close to the game she loves.

When the native of the Quebec City suburb of Lac Beauport inked a deal to play goal with the Tampa Bay Lightning in 1992, she became the first woman to sign a professional contract, the first to try out for an NHL team, and the first to play on a major men's professional team.

Rheaume, who was born on February 24, 1972, played in parts of two exhibition games with the Lightning — one period against the St. Louis Blues in 1992 and one period in 1993 against the Boston Bruins. In both games she allowed two goals.

She also helped backstop the Team Canada women's team to a silver medal at the 1998 Winter Olympics in Nagano, Japan, allowing four goals on 54 shots, and won gold medals at the World Championships in 1992 (1.72 goals-against average in four games) and 1994 (0.67 goals-against average in five games). She was named to the all-star team both years.

Rheaume began skating on her family's backyard rink at the age of four, and by five was dressed up as a goaltender (snow pants, goalie gloves, and sometimes a helmet) so her two brothers could practise their slap shots. Her first stint as a goalie in organized hockey was in 1978 when she tended the nets for her brothers' team, coached by her father, Pierre.

She played with various boys' teams in the Quebec City area, and in 1984, at age 10, practised with the Quebec Nordiques of the NHL and became the first girl to play in the Quebec International Pee Wee Hockey Tournament. She was regularly cut from top-level AA teams in favour of less talented male goalies.

At 19, she became the first woman to play in a Junior A men's hockey game when she tended goal for the Trois-Rivières Draveurs of the Quebec Major Junior Hockey League, allowing three goals in the 17 minutes she was between the pipes.

When she appeared in the Atlanta Knights' 4–1 loss to Salt Lake City in the International Hockey League on December 13, 1992, Rheaume became the first woman to play in a regular-season professional game.

Her pro career spanned 1992 to 1997 and saw her play 24 games for seven pro teams, the Atlanta Knights, Knoxville Cherokees, Nashville Knights, Las Vegas Aces, Tallahassee Tiger Sharks, Las Vegas Thunder, and Reno Renegades.

At five feet seven inches tall and 130 pounds — compared to male goalies who are often six feet tall and 200 pounds — Rheaume used quickness and a butterfly style to compensate for her smaller size.

Her pioneering efforts and good looks attracted worldwide attention. At one point she turned down an offer to pose for *Playboy* magazine.

After leaving hockey in 2000, Rheaume worked as director of marketing for Mission Hockey in Irving, California, for three years, where she helped market and develop hockey equipment for girls. She then worked for two years in Milwaukee as director of girls' hockey/ marketing for POWERade Iceport, a sports complex that included rinks for hockey, figure skating, and roller hockey.

When the POWERade project stalled she looked for a new challenge and was hired in August 2005 as director of sales and marketing for the Central Collegiate Hockey Association in Farmington Hills, Michigan. Her job involves attracting corporate partners and demonstrating the potential of marketing their products and services in conjunction with the 12-team college hockey association.

She knows she has helped the cause of women in the male-dominated world of sport but insists she is one of many females who have done their part, including golfers Annika Sorenstam and Michelle Wie and racing car driver Danica Patrick.

"I am one of a lot of women including the entire Canadian women's national [hockey] team who has helped the cause of women in professional sports … but when I hear about young girls who say they have a poster of me in their bedroom and they want to be like me, it is most satisfying to think that I may make a difference in a girl's life."

She formed the Manon Rheaume Foundation in 2008, which "provides scholarships for young women to assist them as they seek to fulfill their aspirations."

She currently resides with her family in Northville, Michigan, about 50 kilometres from Detroit.

## Hockey BITE!

In 2004, Rheaume coached a girls' all-star team that competed with boys' teams in an international Pee Wee tournament in Quebec. Her team reached the semifinals but was not invited back the following year.

## STANLEY CUP QUIZ

The Stanley Cup, the supreme trophy in all of hockey, has been hoisted by some of the most famous names in the history of the game. Let's see how much you know about hockey's most elusive prize.

1. What was original name of the Stanley Cup?

    a) The Upper Canada Cup
    b) The Dominion Hockey Challenge Cup
    c) The Macdonald Trophy

2. Approximately how much did it cost to make the first Stanley Cup?

    a) $100
    b) $50
    c) $1,050

3. Which Canadian team last won the Stanley Cup? (as of May, 2009)

4. True or false? The Stanley Cup has been to the White House.

5. What was the Montreal Victorias claim to fame in Stanley Cup history?

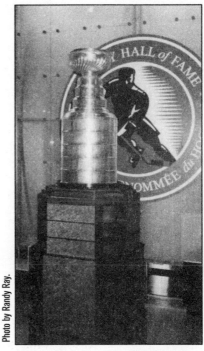

Lord Stanley's Cup.

    a) They won the cup with a team consisting of only seven players.
    b) They won the cup in 1899 but refused to accept it.
    c) They were the first team to accomplish a "hat trick" by winning the cup three years in a row.

6. What do Brendan Shanahan, Brett Hull, and Howie Morenz have in common?

      a) All have scored Stanley Cup-winning goals.
      b) All were captains when their teams won the cup.
      c) None have ever played on Stanley Cup-winning teams.

7. Where was the first Stanley Cup made?

      a) Toronto
      b) Halifax
      c) Sheffield, England
      d) Boston, Massachusetts

8. Which team was the first winner of the Stanley Cup?

      a) Toronto Arenas
      b) Montreal Amateur Athletic Association
      c) Ottawa Senators

➡ **Answers on page 367**

# CHAPTER 19
# Setting up Shop: A History of Canadian Retailers

## $ James Grand and Samuel Toy (Grand & Toy)

From the start James Grand was a stationer who wasn't stationary.

When he started his office supplies business in Toronto in 1882, he would gather orders, buy paper on credit, and deliver products by wagon door to door. In fact, Grand is believed to be the first person in Toronto to sell stationery to customers this way.

He was the eldest child of an officer of the Regiment of Royal Engineers from England who settled in Toronto. At age 14, Grand began working in the publishing business. By 1882, Grand had a wife and infant son to support and decided that going into business for himself was the solution.

When he started his stationery/office supplies business, Grand used his mother's kitchen table as a counter and set up shop on the second floor of a building at 4 Leader Lane. By August 1883, business was so hectic he realized he couldn't continue single-handedly. Enter Samuel Toy, Grand's brother-in-law. The two formed the partnership Grand & Toy and within three years, total annual sales cracked the $15,000 mark.

By 1895, Grand & Toy moved to better headquarters at Wellington and Jordan streets, and four years later they had about 12 employees, including Grand's son Percy. The company expanded their delivery area beyond Toronto's downtown. Then what was a catastrophe for the city in 1904 turned into a bonus for Grand & Toy.

In April that year, a fire raged through the city's core, destroying buildings and causing $10 million in damage. Thanks to Percy's vigilance in dousing any flaming debris from the Grand & Toy roof, the company's store was not damaged. That left Grand & Toy as the only office supplier in the downtown area, and customers flocked there to replenish their supplies. They were handed wastebaskets to hold their supplies as they moved around the store, likely making it the first time self-serve shopping occurred at a stationery store.

Toy was the brains behind introducing the company's catalogue that same year, which also helped boost sales. Despite Toy's death two years later, the firm continued to flourish. James Grand's health began to fail in 1913, and Percy took over more responsibilities. In 1922, when James died, Percy became president, with his brothers, Arthur and Ernest, placed in senior roles. Grand & Toy opened its first branch store in Toronto in 1926, and as skyscrapers became popular in the following years, the company began landing contracts to furnish these new office centres.

When Percy died in 1954, his son, James R. Grand, succeeded him as head of the firm, and a year later the company opened a store in Hamilton, the first one outside of Toronto. Grand & Toy continued to blossom and expand through the next couple of decades, especially in western Canada. In 1995, it was purchased by Boise Cascade Office Products, and today there are 43 Grand & Toy locations, 22 commercial sales offices, and seven distribution centres in Canada employing 2,200 people. Sales are in excess of $120 million. From its humble beginnings on the second floor of a Toronto building, it is now North America's leading office products dealer.

## $ Theodore Pringle Loblaw

Anyone with well-stocked cupboards has likely shopped at Loblaws, a company launched by Theodore Pringle Loblaw. The Alliston, Ontario, native moved to Toronto in 1889 with just 20 dollars and the dream of following in the footsteps of department store mogul Timothy Eaton.

Soon, however, he found the grocery trade more delicious. He plunged into groceries in the late 1800s, taking night courses in accounting and bookkeeping, and eventually became one of the millionaire co-owners of Loblaws. In the early 1900s, he felt it was time to launch a food store chain. For a time, he operated 19 traditional-style grocery stores in Toronto but eventually sold out and formed a partnership with Milton Cork. Together, they opened two self-serve Loblaws stores. Ten years later, the company had expanded to 95 outlets in Ontario, with annual sales of $18.4 million.

Loblaw innovations included: abandoning the pre-First World War system whereby food processors and producers set retail prices; opening self-serve, cash-and-carry stores, and the introduction of systems that tracked sales and bought most products with cash direct from farmers or manufacturers to get the best discounts. Loblaws also manufactured many of its own brands of butter, bacon, coffee, and other products, an early version of the "no-name" products trend that became popular years later.

### Biz BITE!

The next time you use a pencil, think of Percy Grand. In 1927, he was looking for a pencil that wouldn't roll off his desk, like the hexagonal ones that were popular at that time. But he wanted one that was more comfortable to use. He filed down the sharp edges of a hexagonal pencil to create the Roundedge Pencil, which was smoother to hold but still didn't roll. It's the prototype for virtually all pencils today and is still sold in vast quantities by Grand & Toy.

In 1933, with more than 100 stores, Loblaw died suddenly at age 61 from an infection acquired after a minor sinus operation.

In 1947, the firm was sold to Toronto-based George Weston Ltd. These days, the smallest Loblaw store is about five times the size of a typical outlet operated by Loblaw in 1928.

Today, there are more than 1,000 corporate and franchised Loblaws stores operating from coast to coast and the company employs more than 140,000 people.

## $ John Holt and G.R. Renfrew (Holt Renfrew)

Sometimes the person who starts a company isn't part of its famous brand name. While the name Holt Renfrew today conjures up a sense of quality clothing, it was actually William Samuel Henderson who got the firm started. Messrs. Holt and Renfrew would show up later.

Henderson came from Londonderry, Ireland, in 1834 to Quebec City to sell a variety of hats and caps. The first firm he worked for was Ashton and Company, but by 1837 he had taken control and set up shop on rue Buade.

Business was good, and 12 years later Henderson began expanding the company by getting into the fur business. Three years later, he sold the shop to his brother John. In 1860, G.R. Renfrew, an employee, became a partner to form Henderson, Renfrew & Co. After another change in partnership in 1867, John Holt joined the company, and he too, eventually took a controlling interest. The two bought Henderson out, and the name Holt Renfrew & Co. Ltd. would become official in 1908.

In the 1880s, the company was appointed Furrier-in-Ordinary to Her Majesty Queen Victoria, and its association with the British royalty continued with three other monarchs. In fact, in 1948, Holt Renfrew was asked to create a Labrador wild mink coat as Canada's gift for then-Princess Elizabeth's wedding.

By 1889, Holt Renfrew had opened a second store in Toronto at Yonge and Adelaide Street. More stores in other cities followed and to meet their shoppers' sophisticated tastes the company became the exclusive representative of such haute couture lines as Christian Dior and Valentino. In fact, in the 1930s and 1940s Holt Renfrew secured the oldest existing contract with the house of Christian Dior. When Yves Saint Laurent opened his own maison in Paris, Holt Renfrew promptly procured the exclusive rights in Canada for Saint Laurent Haute.

Ownership of the firm changed hands a couple of times between American companies in the 1960s, but in 1986 Holt Renfrew returned to its Canadian roots when it was purchased by Wittington Investments Ltd., chaired by Galen Weston, whose company, George Weston Ltd., of Toronto, has vast holdings, including Canadian companies Weston's Bakery, Loblaw, Neilson Dairy, and Connors Brothers Ltd. fish processors.

Several stores were renovated and different marketing styles were introduced to appeal to a broader range of shoppers.

Today, patrons can buy a wide selection of designer and private label women's and men's fashions, cosmetics, fragrances, jewellery, accessories, and home furnishings. In addition to several stores in Montreal and Toronto, there are others in Ottawa, Quebec City, Vancouver, Calgary, and Edmonton.

## $ John Inglis (John Inglis and Sons)

If you've done a load of laundry or cooked a meal, you've met John Inglis in a round-about way.

Since the end of the Second World War, his surname has been a fixture in Canadian kitchens and laundry rooms, where it can be found on washing machines, clothes dryers, stoves, refrigerators, and dishwashers built by the company he founded in 1859.

But Inglis is known for more than just household appliances. His name is connected to a diverse range of goods, including guns and fishing equipment, which have played a role in the lives of generations of Canadians since before Confederation.

In 1850, at age 36, Inglis immigrated to Canada from England and worked in Hamilton, Oakville, and the Niagara Peninsula, where he honed the metalworker and patternmaker's skills he'd learned in England and Scotland. Nine years later, he moved to Guelph, Ontario, and with two partners founded Mair, Inglis & Evatt, which built machinery for grist and flour mills.

Within 10 years, Inglis and his counterparts were also making pulleys, fly wheels, steam engines, and water wheels — the basic technology of Canada's industrial revolution — as well as chains, window grates, and manhole covers. A decade later, Inglis, a native of Castleton, Roxboroughshire, Scotland, and a new partner, Daniel Hunter, were making engines and mill machinery under the name Inglis & Hunter.

### Biz BITE!

Inglis's Toronto plant on Strachan Avenue has been called "Canada's most important factory." Few Canadian factories ever manufactured the range of products this one did; few have seen as many generations of workers pass through the same factory gates; few have played such a major role in equipping other industries as this one did; it was one of a small number of plants to have witnessed so many changes in manufacturing over the course of their existence. The plant was a snapshot of worker history over 108 years in the same location.

Having outgrown its Guelph factory, the company moved to Strachan Avenue in Toronto in 1881 and soon took advantage of the city's growing manufacturing sector. Within a year, output was five times that of the Guelph enterprise; by 1885, a new factory had been built that eventually dwarfed everything in the neighbourhood but the churches.

Two years later, Hunter left and the company's name was changed to John Inglis and Sons, with William Inglis, one of John's five sons, playing a large role. At the time, John Inglis was a prominent member of the Canadian Manufacturers' Association.

In April 1899, with his company growing by leaps and bounds and in the midst of diversifying its products, John Inglis died. William took over and, under his direction, John Inglis and Sons began manufacturing marine steam engines and waterworks pumping engines, at the same time discontinuing production of its other products. In 1904, the company was forced to rebuild after a major fire.

In 1935, when Inglis was a key manufacturer of equipment used by other industries, William Inglis died. Reeling from the effects of the Depression, and without an Inglis at the helm for the first time in 75 years, the company closed the doors of its Toronto factory, which over the years had provided jobs for thousands of Torontonians. Shortly after, American-born industrialist Major J.E. Hahn purchased the company and obtained the right to use the name John Inglis Co. Limited. In 1938, Inglis began manufacturing guns for Canada and other countries.

**Biz BITE!**

Toronto's Central Prison was located next to John Inglis's early Toronto factory on Strachan Avenue. More than once, public hangings and lashings were conducted during factory hours. Prisoners made brooms in the prison.

When the Second World War ended in 1945, Inglis continued to make heavy equipment such as boilers, pumps, and tanks for the mining, brewing, and steel industries.

And for the first time, the company began manufacturing consumer products, such as fishing tackle, house trailers, lipstick holders, and home appliances.

In the late 1940s, John Inglis and Co. affiliated with the company that evolved into American-owned Whirlpool Corporation, eventual owners of Inglis. The product line changed to wringer washers, and later, automatic washers, electric and gas dryers, dishwashers, and refrigerators.

In 1972, Inglis produced its one-millionth automatic washer and began manufacturing appliances under the Whirlpool brand name. The next year, the company name became Inglis Limited. In the mid-1980s Whirlpool Corporation of Ohio assumed majority ownership and in 1989 closed the Toronto plant, which at the time made only washing machines.

Factories in the Ontario communities of Stoney Creek, Cambridge, and Mississauga were also closed. Since 2001, Inglis has been known as Whirlpool Canada Ltd. Despite the new name, plants in Quebec and the U.S. continue to build and sell appliances which bear John Inglis's name.

## $ Timothy Eaton (Eaton Department Stores)

The name Timothy Eaton evokes treasured memories of gaily decorated store windows, a parade that delighted generations of children every November, and the company's famous mail-order catalogue.

And it's no exaggeration to say Eaton is Canada's version of retailing superstars Rowland Macy in the United States and Charles Harrod in the United Kingdom. All founded tremendously successful department stores that became central to the lives of those who love to shop.

Eaton's climb to department store stardom began in 1854, when he arrived in Canada and took a job as a junior clerk in a general store near Georgetown, Ontario. Two years later he and his brother James, sons of an Irish tenant farmer, started the J. and T. Eaton General Store in a log building in Kirkton, a small community near Stratford, Ontario. In 1860, they moved to nearby St. Marys to sell dry goods, boots, farm tools, and kitchenware. Timothy married Margaret Wilson Beattie in 1861.

Eight years after tying the knot, Timothy decided to try his luck in the big city. When his business partnership with his brother James dissolved in 1868, Timothy took his storekeeping experience and his wife to Toronto and in 1869 purchased a dry goods store at 178 Yonge Street for $6,500 in cash.

Before long, the shop was taking advantage of a growing market brought on by increasing urbanization and industrialization in Toronto, not to mention rising living standards.

Timothy Eaton.

City of Montreal, Document and Archives Management Ægidius Fauteux fonds (BM1), P0643.

In 1883, Eaton moved to larger quarters on Yonge Street and three years later the store doubled in size. To meet the product needs of his rapidly expanding business, Eaton in the

1880s and 1890s set up his own companies to manufacture clothing, paint, and chemicals and purchased farms to supply dairy products to his store and feed for his delivery horses.

In the years that followed, Eaton and his company were an integral facet of daily Canadian life as a full-line department store with a broad selection of goods, including jewellery, carpets, sporting goods, clothing, and appliances. A visit to an Eaton's store was a major happening for generations of Canadians, especially around Christmas when the stores' windows were filled with lights and holiday scenes.

Known as a pious, teetotalling Methodist who could be abrupt, gruff, and outspoken, Eaton was an innovator from the start: he was the first merchant in Toronto to sell goods for cash only and at one price; he coined and stood by the motto "Money refunded if goods not satisfactory" and he shortened store hours to ease his employees' long work week. He manufactured products under various house brand names; introduced the Santa Claus parade; and in 1884, launched the Eaton's catalogue, which came to hold a position second only to the family Bible in many Canadian households.

Originally called The Wishing Book, the catalogue carried just about everything, from farm tools, wedding rings and lace, to prefabricated homes, home remedies, and clothing. The 1896 version included a hand-powered washing machine for $3.75 and a year's supply of food for a man going on the Klondike gold rush for $68.69.

> **They Said It!**
>
> "A man who works longer hours than meets his needs will have a margin of profit; that gives him comforts and he and the whole country prosper."
>
> – *Timothy Eaton, when asked about the slim margin between cost of living and wages.*

As Eaton's business prospered, his wife and five children (three other children died in infancy) adopted the comfortable lifestyle of other well-off Torontonians. They lived in a large home at the corner of Spadina Road and Lowther Avenue and spent summers at a lakefront property in Muskoka, north of Toronto, where they owned several steam yachts. Despite its wealth, the family never gave up its simple ways, which meant social vices such as cards, dancing, drinking, and smoking were no-nos.

In January 1907, about two years after opening a second store in Winnipeg, Eaton died of pneumonia. He left behind an estate worth $5.3 million and an empire that author Rod McQueen wrote in his book *The Eatons: The Rise and Fall of Canada's Royal Family*, "would weave itself into the very fabric of the land and the vital fibre of its people."

The company was taken over by Timothy's son John Craig and later by several of Timothy's relatives, who until the 1980s kept Eaton's at the forefront of Canadian department stores. In the 1950s, Eaton's laid claim to more than half of all department-store spending in Canada; in the 1990s, the company had 85 stores; and at one point, sales hit $2.1 billion.

But like its renowned catalogue, which disappeared in 1976, the business Timothy Eaton founded was erased from Canada's retail landscape, the victim of years of mismanagement, stiff competition from aggressive American retailers such as Wal-Mart, and an economic downturn in the late 1980s and early 1990s.

On February 27, 1997, the department store chain announced that after 128 years as a Canadian institution, it could no longer pay its bills. Twenty-one stores were closed, and on May 18, 1999, Eaton's hung a for sale sign on its remaining assets, including its flagship store in Toronto's Eaton Centre. As McQueen noted in his book, the family's Irish luck had run out.

"If Timothy Eaton were alive and saw this he'd be a pretty sad man," one bargain hunter said during an auction where cash registers, desks, and well-worn chairs from Eaton's better times were up for grabs.

Despite the company's downfall, the Eaton name survived, though only briefly. When Sears Canada Inc. acquired 16 Eaton's stores in 1999, it kept the Eaton banner on upscale department stores reopened a year later in Toronto, Ottawa, Winnipeg, Calgary, Vancouver, and Victoria. But early in 2002, Sears dropped the Eaton name.

## Biz BITE!

On January 1, 1985, Nancy Eaton, the great-great-granddaughter of Timothy Eaton, was found dead in her Toronto apartment, a victim of multiple stab wounds.

## Biz BITE!

When Timothy Eaton's private rail car the Eatonia was destroyed by fire a new car was built in 1916. The Eatonia II was 78-feet-long, had four staterooms panelled in Cuban mahogany, an observation area, a dining room with seating for 10 on leather chairs, a full kitchen, and servants' quarters. The car was eventually sold to Canadian National Railways for use by VIPs such as royals and cabinet ministers. In 1972 Eaton's repurchased and restored the car, before donating it to Calgary's Heritage Park.

## $ Samuel and Beatrice Irwin (Irwin Toy Limited)

He could sell just about anything while she had a knack for figures. What started out as a two-person operation in 1926 selling souvenirs and other small items eventually became the number one toy company in Canada.

Anyone growing up in the 1950s and beyond probably knows the Irwin name. Among the toys the company has sold over the years are the Slinky, the Yo-Yo, Pound Puppies, and Pro Star tabletop hockey games.

Samuel Irwin grew up on a farm near Orangeville, Ontario. He would visit future wife Beatrice Whiteside, who lived in Alliston, Ontario, by driving his jalopy over the rough roads of the time. As a young man, he worked as clerk for Hill's General Store in Orangeville and then moved to Toronto, where he was an employee at Eaton's, Simpson's, and then a wholesale dry goods firm.

After serving overseas in the First World War, Sam found work selling business courses. That led to a job selling specialty items such as souvenirs for Rumsay & Company, and Sam thought he could make more money with a similar business of his own. He and Beatrice married in 1924 and decided two years later to open their shop, Irwin Specialties, near Yonge Street and St. Clair Avenue in Toronto.

"My dad was really a salesman and good at it," Arnold Irwin told us from his winter residence in Florida. "My mother was more meticulous and kept the records."

By 1935, there were five salesmen employed to cover the country, and the firm was specializing in selling toys, games, and souvenirs. The company did well, due in part to Sam's knack for taking chances and his penchant for travel that took him around the world seeking business opportunities. In the late 1930s, while in England, he bought up old and unwanted souvenirs of King George VI's coronation ceremony at a cheap price. Employees back home were surprised at how much he shipped back, Arnold says, but by placing them in Christmas stockings that the firm sold to other companies, Sam managed to move all the merchandise.

The Irwin Company, which was a wholesale firm, had other successes thanks to Sam's knack for spotting bargains. After the Second World War broke out, there was a lot of public pressure on stores not to sell German- and Japanese-made goods. Samuel saw this as an opportunity. He bought up the goods, mostly toys, at bargain prices, and within a year the shops realized they were low on stock and had to buy the merchandise back from him. "He made a fortune," Arnold says.

After the war, however, the company was running into financial difficulty and Sam suffered a nervous breakdown. A friend suggested that Sam bring his two sons, Mac and Arnold, into the business. Both were still in university and managed to finish their studies even after they went to work for their father around 1950.

It was Mac and Arnold who started moving the company even more into the toy business. They allied themselves with several strong manufacturers and secured rights early on to sell products that became successes. As the company grew, both Sam and Bea continued to take an active role. Both worked hard and would often take work home with them on weekends and holidays, Arnold says.

But tragedy struck in 1968. Sam, who was always a "hesitant swimmer," drowned in the swimming pool at his North Toronto home. It was never clear what happened.

Arnold says his father, like many of his generation, quit school at an early age, but "he was very much in awe of people who had an education." When Samuel died, his sons set up a fund that would help pay for employees' children to attend university.

Irwin Toy went public in 1969 and had a long string of profitable years. Like their parents, Arnold and Mac, who were president and vice-president respectively in the company, believed in putting in an honest days' work. "We were really hard working. We spent a lot of time in the business. We thrived on it, and we enjoyed it. It didn't seem like work."

Arnold describes the company of that era as one big family, with low turnover and many long-term employees. His mother stayed on as a company director for several years, and when she got older they made her an honorary director. She died at age 89.

Irwin Toy, meanwhile, continued to expand, initiating direct sales of toys in the United States in 1991, and setting up in Australia in 1997. In April 2001, an affiliate of Livgroup Investments Ltd. bought the company and turned it back into a private company.

Known as IToys since 2003, the toy and game manufacturer is now led by the Irwins' sons, George and Peter, who have effectively reshaped the business for a new generation of children. In just five short years, Itoys Inc. has emerged as a leading international manufacturer of homegrown and licensed toys available at leading retailers around the globe.

### Biz BITE!

The education fund set up by the Irwins proved to be a blessing many years later when Arnold's wife had to be rushed to the hospital. The doctor who treated her was an employee's son who had had his schooling paid for partially by the company.

## $ Herman and Sarah Reitman (Reitmans Canada Limited)

It wasn't exactly rags to riches, but like many prosperous Canadian companies, Reitmans, the large chain of women's wear stores, had humble beginnings.

Herman and Sarah Reitman were both born in Romania and came to Canada for a better life. In the early 1900s, they operated a small shop called American Ladies Tailoring and Dressmaking Company in Montreal. It catered primarily to the dressmaking needs of ladies, specializing in made-to-measure garments.

About 1914, they decided to move away from the dressmaking field and turn their business into a dry goods general store. They sold hosiery, gloves, some house furnishings and housewares, clothing, fabrics, and ribbons by the yard, all from a small department store of about 15,000 square feet.

Their second store in 1926 was located on St. Lawrence Boulevard in Montreal, and the couple got help from their children, Louis, Sam, John, and Jack. It soon became apparent that the most popular items in the dry goods store were hosiery, gloves, and lingerie, so the Reitmans decided to specialize in ladies' wear.

It was a good decision. Under the simple name Reitmans the store prospered, and by 1929 the family had four outlets in Montreal. The company expanded, first to Ottawa in 1936, and then three years later it opened a store in Toronto. By this time, Reitmans had 22 stores with annual sales of almost $1 million.

Herman died in 1941, while Sarah's death came nine years later, but the company was firmly in family hands. In 1947, with sales exceeding $2 million, the company went public and was listed for trading on the Montreal Stock Exchange. By 1950, Reitmans had 15 stores in Quebec and 20 in Ontario. A year later the head office and distribution centre was moved to a 25,000-square-foot facility at 3510 St. Lawrence Boulevard, across the street from the first store.

Reitmans opened its first store in western Canada in 1958 in Calgary and the following year moved into eastern Canada with an outlet in Halifax. The company continued to grow and prosper from the 1960s onward, opening Smart Set stores and acquiring others such as Penningtons, which caters to larger-sized women. In the fall of 2008, the women's wear retailer launched a new chain called Cassis that caters specifically to 45- to 60-year-old women, what they view as a growing and potentially lucrative market. The stores will provide shoppers with ampler sizing, better quality, and higher prices. So far, 16 stores have opened under the name in Ontario, Quebec, and New Brunswick.

Today, president Jeremy H. Reitman oversees an operation that has over 900 stores operating under eight divisions, and of which more than 350 bear the Reitmans name. Annual sales in 2008 were in excess of $1 billion.

# $ Rolland Dansereau and Napoléon Piotte (RONA L'entrepôt/RONA Warehouse/RONA Home & Garden)

The next time you're shopping for two-by-fours at a home improvement centre with RONA on the sign, think of Rolland Dansereau and Napoléon Piotte. The two Quebeckers founded the RONA chain back in 1939, and it's their names — in part, at least — that are in front of retail building supply stores in many parts of Canada. RONA is a combination of the first two letters of each man's first name.

The firm's foundation dates back to 1939 when several Quebec hardware stores led by Dansereau and Piotte formed Les Marchands en Quincaillerie Ltée (The Hardware Merchants Ltd.). Twenty years later, they incorporated as Quincaillerie Ro-Na Inc. with a mandate to promote business collectively.

The company moved outside Quebec in 1982 by acquiring the Botanix network and negotiating purchasing alliances with Canada's Home Hardware stores and the Do-it-Best chain in the U.S. In 1988, Ro-Na merged with Dismat, which specialized in the building materials sector and the name was changed to Groupe Ro-Na Dismat Inc.

In 1994, RONA L'entrepôt (RONA Warehouse big box outlet) was launched and soon after, the RONA name was officially adopted. Seven years later, RONA purchased Ontario-based Cashway Building Centres and a year after, took over the British Columbia-based Revy Network, which included stores formerly operated in B.C. and Ontario under the Revelstoke, Revy, Lumberland, and Lansing Buildall banners.

Today, the company founded by Mssrs. Dansereau and Piotte is known as RONA Inc. and is based in the Montreal suburb of Boucherville. It is the largest distributor and retailer of hardware, renovation, and gardening supplies in Canada, operating stores in eight provinces. RONA and its dealer-owners run a Canada-wide network of over 600 home improvement stores operating under 15 different banners, including RONA L'entrepôt, RONA Warehouse, RONA Home & Garden, RONA Revy Home Centres, RONA Revelstoke Centres, and RONA Lansing.

With more than 16,000 employees and some 10 million square feet of retail space, the stores ring up annual sales of nearly $3 billion. About 62 percent of the company's shares are held by RONA dealer-owners and employees. Dansereau and Piotte have not been associated with RONA since the 1960s.

## $ Robert Simpson (Simpson's Department Stores)

For the better part of 100 years you couldn't mention Eaton's department stores without mentioning Simpson's in the same breath. Eaton's stores continued on until 2002, but the Simpson's name disappeared before the 20th century ended.

Robert Simpson was born in Speymouth, Scotland, in 1834, the son of a general store owner. When he was about 20, he arrived in Upper Canada, having apprenticed to a shopkeeper in his homeland. He worked in a general store in Newmarket, Ontario, and in 1858 he and two others bought the business and sold dry goods, boots, hardware, and groceries. It was the trend at the time to deal only in cash, and the partners offered the lowest prices around.

The partnership only lasted four years, but Simpson soon linked up with another businessman, M.W. Bogart. Two fires caused damage to the enterprise and in the mid-1860s Bogart left Simpson to run the business on his own. Fortunately economic times were good during that decade, and Simpson opened a new shop said to be the finest north of Toronto.

Hurt by still another fire and some slack accounting, Simpson once again regrouped before selling his store to a cousin in 1872. He moved his family to Toronto and opened a dry goods store, this time on Yonge Street north of Queen. Simpson's business grew along with Toronto, which was becoming increasingly industrialized during those years. Like his rival Timothy Eaton, Simpson established a wholesale operation to complement his retail store. By 1881, however, he had abandoned the wholesale business and concentrated on his retail business in premises that were adjacent to Eaton's.

Though the two competed for business, both were able to prosper in busy Toronto, and by 1885 Simpson's employed 60 clerks and sold a variety of goods. Simpson, who was reportedly a heavy drinker, managed to keep his firm profitable through the rest of his life.

## Biz BITE!

The connection between Canada and the Sweet Marie candy bar that's smothered with chocolate and nuts began in 1893 when American-born author Cy Warman was living in London, Ontario, and walked his girlfriend Marie to her home at Queen's Avenue and Colborne Street. The book *The North and the East* by historian John Lutman says Warman then strolled to Victoria Park in the city's downtown and wrote a love poem to her called "Sweet Marie." It opens with the lines "I've a secret in my heart, Sweet Marie/A tale I would impart, love to thee /Every daisy in the dell/Knows my secret, knows it well/And yet I dare not tell Sweet Marie."

A few years later a composer named Raymon Moore put the words to music, and the result was a hit song that became popular across North America. It was said that Marie was the best-known London resident on the continent thanks to the tune, which was later featured in the 1947 film *Life with Father* starring William Powell and Irene Dunne.

A chocolate company capitalized on the song by naming one of its products the Sweet Marie bar. Today, you can still wander into most shops that sell candy and buy a Sweet Marie, which is made by William Neilson Ltd. and bears the Cadbury name.

As for Marie and Warman? The poet proposed to Marie and they married and settled in London, raising four children. Their house still stands in the city's north end on Cheapside Street.

When he moved the company into new headquarters in 1896, there were 500 staff, a restaurant on the premises, and a mail order department.

Simpson died suddenly on December 14, 1897. Eaton and his son attended Simpson's funeral and flew flags at their stores at half-mast that day. Simpson had a daughter, but in those days business usually didn't get passed on to female heirs. So without a son to inherit the business, Simpson's was sold a few months later to three Toronto businessmen.

Simpson's thrived as a major department store with outlets across the country for most of the 20th century. It was bought by the Hudson's Bay Company in 1979 and some years later the Simpson's name was removed from the storefronts. But for older shoppers the name remains memorable as one of the most famous retail stores in Canadian history.

## $ Thomas Bata (Bata Shoe Organization)

Thomas Bata was a young entrepreneur with a head for shoes.

Bata and his son Thomas are behind an Ontario-based company that has put footwear onto the feet of millions of people and provided jobs for thousands more.

The Bata Shoe Organization dates back to 1894 when Thomas (sometimes spelled Tomas) Bata was an apprentice in his father's shoemaking shop in the small community of Zlin in the former Austria-Hungary Empire (now the Czech Republic).

He persuaded his elder brother and sister to use $350 bequeathed by their mother to launch their own shoemaking company in Zlin, and despite a brush with bankruptcy in the first year, the business was soon thriving under Bata's leadership. Six years later it had a staff of 120.

As a youthful shoemaker, Bata's business concept was to use assembly line technology and innovative human resources in footwear manufacturing. He was driven by a desire to provide shoes to people around the world and the business goals of selling shoes where they were not available, reducing production time, and supplying stylish footwear at affordable prices.

In 1904, Bata spent six months working at a mechanized New England shoe factory. When he returned to Czechoslovakia he introduced the assembly line to his company, and soon the firm grew so large that Zlin resembled a company town. In 1905, Bata was making 22,000 pairs of shoes per day. Eventually, factories were established in Poland, Yugoslavia, Holland, Denmark, the United Kingdom, Switzerland, and the United States.

Bata's moral testament was that his business was not to be considered as simply a source of personal profit but rather as a vehicle of public trust: "We were motivated by the knowledge that our enterprise was providing an entire region with new previously unknown advantages, that its growth was contributing to the wealth and the education of the nation."

Unfortunately, Bata would not live to see his vision come to fruition in its entirety. In July 1932, he was killed in a plane crash while flying to Switzerland, leaving behind his son Thomas Jr. and his wife Marie. "Every nation has its heroes," read the eulogy at Bata's funeral. "The Czech nation's hero was a shoemaker." The company was left in the hands of his half-brother Jan and was later taken over by Thomas Jr.

The Canadian connection to Bata Shoes was made in 1939, as the Nazis steamrolled their way across central Europe at a time when the company was making 10 million pairs of shoes annually. Recognizing that the family empire was in danger, the young Bata, then in his mid-20s, smuggled the company's equipment to Canada where a new company town called Batawa was built near Trenton, Ontario, on land purchased from farmers.

In his book *Bata: Shoemaker to the World*, Bata said he picked Canada because it was "the best of two worlds, a blend of British traditions with the progressiveness and dynamism of the United States."

From its new base 160 kilometres east of Toronto, Bata began building the empire he and his Swiss-born wife Sonja would run for years from the company's headquarters in Don Mills, Ontario. Bata, who like his father began his working life as an apprentice, rebuilt the business by tapping into a huge global market for practical, sturdy shoes. One story says he once fired a salesman who returned from Africa with the gloomy view that the shoe market there was minimal because everyone walked around barefoot.

The company grew rapidly in the 1940s and 1950s by setting up fully integrated shoe industries, from tanneries to shoe shops, across Asia, Africa, and Latin America. Many of the factories were located in company towns in rural areas.

The company prospered despite its share of troubles, including slow times, which forced the closure of the Batawa factory in 2000. Bata's son Thomas George Bata took over the shoe company in 2001 but the elder Bata remained active in its operations.

In 2005, Bata closed the last of its retail outlets in Canada and decided to concentrate instead on its 160 Athlete's World outlets. Thomas Bata died at age 93 in September 2008. At the time, Bata continued to operate over 5,000 retails stores worldwide, employed 40,000 people, and managed a retail presence in over 50 countries. The company is based in Lausanne, Switzerland.

The Bata name is also found on the popular and world-renowned shoe museum set up in downtown Toronto by Sonja Bata. In September 2008, the museum welcomed its one millionth visitor.

## Biz BITE!

Batawa, the eastern Ontario community where Bata Shoes set up shop, is a combination of the Bata name and the last syllable of Ottawa. A buyer from the Eaton's department store chain suggested the name.

## $ Alex Tilley (Tilley Endurables)

Alex Tilley had no special love of hats as a boy growing up in such places as Kitchener, Sudbury, and Vancouver. But in his mid-20s, he owned a favourite coat and got someone to make him a "Mississippi Gambler" style hat to match.

Little did he know that years later, hats would earn him a fortune and worldwide acclaim.

In 1980, Tilley was a self-employed art consultant and avid sailor. One day while sailing in his 30-foot sloop in Lake Ontario, his hat blew off and got soaked — again. Enough, he thought. Tilley put on his thinking cap and started researching ways to make better, longer-lasting headgear. With the help of a sailmaker, Tilley came up with the first of more than 1.5 million hats that bear his name.

Shortly afterwards, he tried the hat out on a trip to Belize but still experienced problems when the wind blew. While lying in bed one Sunday morning, Tilley came up with the idea of affixing a cord that went around the back of the head.

Within a year, Tilley had branched into sailing shorts and pants for travellers that would wear well and be comfortable. Today more than 13,000 retailers in 17 countries, including Australia, Finland, and Turkey sell Tilley Hats. The first one he ever sold, to Horst Berlin of the National Yacht Club in Toronto, is still around.

Most of Tilley's clothing is manufactured in Don Mills, Ontario. "The hat represents me," says Tilley of why he put his name on the product. Some 200,000 Tilley hats are made in Canada annually and come in more sizes than any others in the world. They're known for their indestructibility; a hat belonging to Michael Hackenberger of the Bowmanville Zoo, for example, was still wearable after being eaten by an elephant three times. Among the celebrities who have worn Tilley hats are legendary mountaineer Sir Edmund Hillary, former president George Bush, and members of the royal families in Great Britain and Denmark.

And Tilley still owns that Mississippi Gambler hat. "It's interesting that even way back when, I was somewhat hat conscious."

## $ Karim Hakim (Hakim Optical)

Karim Hakim has been helping people see more clearly since he was nine years old.

The founder of Hakim Optical got his start as a young boy in Iran, grinding magnifying glass from old windows to help support his family. He was

### Biz BITE!

Tilley Hats were worn by all of Canada's armed forces during the Gulf War in 1991 to help protect them from harsh desert conditions, and the U.S. Coast Guard Auxiliary has adopted the product as its official sun hat.

obviously skilled at it because by age 19, Hakim was working in Germany grinding lenses for various instruments. He did the same work in Switzerland before immigrating to Canada in the mid-1960s.

Hakim set up a lab in the old Elmwood Hotel in Toronto and eventually began selling his lenses to opticians and optometrists. When people wanted to buy lenses directly from him, he saw a business opportunity and began making frames as well. Today, there are more than 100 Hakim Optical outlets in Ontario, Nova Scotia, New Brunswick, Manitoba, Saskatchewan, and Alberta selling as many as 1,000 pairs of glasses a day. In fact, since he began operations in Toronto, Hakim has sold more than 14 million pairs of glasses.

Now that's a man with a vision.

A Hakim Optical outlet in south Ottawa.

## $ Harry Rosen (Harry Rosen Inc.)

Harry Rosen's sense of style and design in men's clothes can be traced to lunchtime pinochle games when he was a high school student.

Rosen worked summers at a clothing manufacturer in Toronto and wanted to find out more about clothing design. That area of the business was off limits to most employees, but Rosen said he liked "sticking [his] nose into everything that was going on." He started playing cards over lunch with the company's designer and peppered the man with questions about how to make suits and what made for a good shirt.

By the time he returned to school, Rosen was starting to think the clothing business might be the right fit. The following summer he branched off into retail and "inside of a few weeks I was able to compete with the hotshot salesman on the floor. I made it my business to understand what the features (of a clothing item) were that the consumer would see as a benefit, and I knew how to articulate it."

Sam Lelo, the store's owner and Rosen's mentor, wanted him to stay on staff, but the young man had another dream — to run his own shop. With a $500 loan from a relative, Rosen opened a small clothing store in 1954 on Parliament Street, which at the time was not the best location for that type of business because it didn't have the kind of shops that would attract high-end shoppers. His brother Lou soon joined him.

Rosen, who was born in Toronto on August 27, 1931, had not been a clothes horse as a child, but once he got into the business he approached it with passion and zeal. In his first year of business, he did about $70,000 in sales as word spread about the store's quality and service.

He soon met up with people in the publishing and advertising businesses who brought their money to his store and made it something of a hangout. Rosen recalled how they'd gather in late afternoons to "tell lies, drink coffee, and have a fitting. It was a warm, hospitable place."

Rosen was adept at following up prospects and soon customers from outside Ontario started showing up. By 1961, Rosen had moved to larger, more upscale headquarters on Richmond Street. As the company prospered, Rosen's name and quality men's wear attracted attention across North America and beyond. Among his more famous clientele were actors Alan Bates and Christopher Plummer and newscaster Peter Jennings.

In 1982, he expanded outside of Ontario by opening a store in the West Edmonton Mall, and five years later opened his flagship store on Bloor Street in Toronto, introducing the idea of grouping clothing lines together in kind of a shop-within-a-shop concept that has been copied by others many times since.

Having dealt with customers for more than 50 years, Rosen once said that men today are more self-assured about their style, but "are still learning a lot about clothing. Men are essentially lazy, they don't care to shop."

Harry Rosen Inc., which has more than 20 stores across Canada and sales of about $200 million annually, carries such designers as Hugo Boss, Armani, and Versace.

Rosen himself prefers the Kiton line from Italy with its soft, understated look and likes shades of blue, grey, and green/khaki. His business skills have led him to be on the advisory board of the Richard Ivey School of Business in London, Ontario, he

### Biz BITE!

Rosen's successful Ask Harry ad campaign was introduced as a way of answering men's questions about how to select and buy clothes. Because of his contacts in the business, Rosen was able to get top-notch advertising early on by bartering clothes. "I got the finest talent money could possibly buy for two suits per ad," he once said with a chuckle.

was named Retail Marketer of the Year in 1987, and he received the Lifetime Achievement Award from the Retail Council of Canada in 2001.

Harry was also presented with an Honorary Doctorate in Commerce from Ryerson University in 2003 and was appointed as a Member to the Order of Canada in 2004. When he's not selling clothes, Rosen likes to read, play chess, study history, and play the mandolin, "an instrument I love."

When we spoke with him several years ago, he said, "I delight in looking after customers. I remember what most of them purchased from me." Then he added with a laugh, "I don't remember my wife's birthday, but I remember the wardrobes I've provided to people over the years."

Harry's son Larry took over as president in 1997 and was appointed chairman and chief executive officer in 2000. The company sponsors annual charity runs in Toronto and Vancouver, both called "Harry's Spring Run-Off," that raise thousands of dollars each year to support prostate cancer research.

## $ First Flagship Canadian Tire Store: More than Just Tires

We take Canadian Tire for granted these days. With some 460 retail stores across Canada and a national presence as one of the country's leading retailers, Canadian Tire is part of our culture. Who hasn't gone off to one of these stores to buy auto parts, barbecue tools, or sports equipment? Who hasn't stashed Canadian Tire money in a car's glove compartment or made fun of the know-it-all actor featured in the company's television commercials until early 2006?

But the road to becoming a national icon is long. Back in 1922, brothers John W. and Alfred J. Billes bought out Hamilton Tire and Garage Ltd. at the corner of Gerrard and Hamilton streets in Toronto, the first step in establishing the Canadian Tire company. The shop sold repair parts, tires, batteries, and homemade antifreeze at a time when there were about 40,000 cars in the city.

The brothers then moved operations to Bloor Street West, then to Yonge Street, installing a gas pump at the first of two Yonge and Isabella locations. In 1927, they incorporated the company as Canadian Tire, a name they chose "because it sounded big," according to the company's history. As other Canadians became interested in ordering from the store, Canadian Tire launched its first catalogue in 1928. The catalogue is still a common browsing material in millions of Canadian households today.

Although the company set up an associate store in Hamilton in 1924, it was three years later that it reached a notable milestone by establishing its first flagship store at 837 Yonge Street in Toronto. Canadian Tire gained a reputation as the store where clerks wear

Photo by Mark Kearney.

Part of our culture.

roller skates, a technique used in the store to speed up service from the large stock floor to the sales counter.

From then on the company rarely looked back, eventually spreading across Canada. As for that first flagship store, it was renovated and transformed in 2002 into a new, larger Canadian Tire on the same site. The new flagship store was officially opened April 24, 2003, with 65,000 square feet of retail space.

For more information on Canadian Tire visit www.canadiantire.ca.

# CHAPTER 20
# Sports Time Out

 ## WHO'S ON FIRST? 12 BEST CANADIAN-BORN BASEBALL PLAYERS
(in order)

1.  **Ferguson Jenkins:** The greatest player to come from Canada and the only Canadian in the Baseball Hall of Fame in Cooperstown, New York. Jenkins, from Chatham, Ontario, won 20 games a year six seasons in a row, was awarded the Cy Young Award in 1971, and finished with 284 wins and 226 losses. He threw more than 3,000 strikeouts in his career.

2.  **Larry Walker:** A perennial league all-star, batting champion in 1998, and National League Most Valuable Player in 1997, the only Canadian to achieve this honour. Over his career, the Maple Ridge, British Columbia, native hit 383 home runs, had 2,160 hits and posted a .313 batting average. He is being considered for induction into the Baseball Hall of Fame in Cooperstown as this book is being written.

3.  **Jeff Heath:** A two-time all-star who had seven seasons in the late 1930s and early 1940s batting .300 or better. Heath, from Fort William, Ontario, had a career average of .298, had 1,447 hits, and 194 home runs.

4.  **Terry Puhl:** The Melville, Saskatchewan, native had three seasons batting .300 or better, a career .993 fielding average, played more than 1,500 games in 15 seasons with the Houston Astros, and had the most career stolen bases by a Canadian with 217 until Larry Walker surpassed him in 2003.

5.  **John Hillier:** In his 15 years with the Detroit Tigers, Hillier, from Toronto, compiled 125 saves, including a then-record 38 saves in 1973. He threw more than 1,000 strikeouts and finished with an 87–79 record.

6.  **George Selkirk:** In nine seasons with the Yankees, from 1934 to 1942, he batted .290,

including five seasons of .300 or better. Born in Huntsville, Ontario, Selkirk played in two all-star games and hit 108 home runs during his career.

7. **George Gibson:** The London, Ontario-born catcher played 1,213 games between 1905 and 1918. Although he only batted .236 during his career, he was a superb defensive player who later managed in the big leagues.

8. **Russ Ford:** A three-time 20-game winner, including winning 26 for the New York Yankees in 1910, Ford, of Brandon, Manitoba, finished with a 99–71 record over seven seasons.

9. **Pete Ward:** The Montreal-born player won the *Sporting News* American League Rookie of the Year Award in 1963 and over 973 games in his career hit .254 and slugged 98 homers.

**Sports BITE!**

Jack Graney was the first ex-ballplayer to broadcast a game on the radio.

**Sports BITE!**

Justin Morneau, from New Westminster, British Columbia, is well on his way to a highly successful career in Major League Baseball. Since he joined the Minnesota Twins in 2003, he has already won the Home Run Derby during the All-Star game (2008), received the Tip O'Neill Award from the Canadian Baseball Hall of Fame, which honours the country's top player, not once but twice (in 2006 and 2008), won the American League Most Valuable Player Award in 2006 and was second in voting in 2008. In 2006, he was second in the league in RBIs and tied Larry Walker's 1997 total for the most RBIs in a season by a Canadian. For his hitting, he won the 2006 American League Silver Slugger Award representing first basemen, only the fourth player in Twins history to do so. With these stats he is well on his way to cracking the Top 12 list.

10. **Reggie Cleveland:** The first Canadian to pitch in the World Series, Cleveland, from Swift Current, Saskatchewan, amassed a 105–106 record over 13 seasons , from 1969 to 1982.

11. **Frank O'Rourke:** He had more than 100 hits in six different seasons, led American League second basemen in fielding percentage one year, and had a career .254 batting average over 14 seasons, between 1912 and 1931. O'Rourke, from Hamilton, Ontario, was later a baseball scout for many years.

12. **Jack Graney:** During his 14 seasons, from 1908 to 1922, he batted .250 and twice led the league in bases on balls. The St. Thomas, Ontario, native was also the first person to pitch to Babe Ruth in the major leagues.

# 🍁 IT HAPPENED IN CANADA: 23 CANADIAN SPORTS FIRSTS

1. George Orton of Strathroy, Ontario, may have been competing for the Americans, but he was the first Canadian to win an Olympic gold medal when he captured first place in the 2,500-metre steeplechase event in Paris, in July 1900. Montreal policeman Étienne Desmarteau was the first to win Olympic gold while competing for Canada when he won the 56-pound hammer throw at the St. Louis Olympics in September 1904.

2. Babe Ruth hit his first professional home run as a member of the Providence Grays, during a game in Toronto on September 5, 1914.

3. The voice of hockey, play-by-play man Foster Hewitt, announced his first hockey broadcast over Toronto radio station CFCA on March 23, 1923.

4. Lela Brooks of Toronto won a world speed skating championship in Saint John, New Brunswick, becoming the first Canadian woman to be a sports world champion, in 1926.

5. Clint Benedict of the Montreal Maroons was the first goalie to wear a mask in a hockey game in the 1929–30 season.

**They Said It!**

"How would you like a job where, every time you make a mistake, a big red light goes on and 18,000 people boo?"

– *legendary NHL goalie Jacques Plante*

269

### Sports BITE!

When Marilyn Bell became the first person to swim across Lake Ontario, she took more than 20 hours to accomplish the task. But while the lake is 51 kilometres across, Bell had swum the equivalent of more than 64 kilometres because currents prevented her from swimming in a straight line.

Courtesy of City of Toronto Archives, f1244_it2128

Marilyn Bell, the first to swim across Lake Ontario.

**6.** Detroit Red Wings great Gordie Howe scored his first NHL goal on October 16, 1946.

**7.** The Toronto Huskies of the Basketball Association of America became Canada's first major professional basketball team: 1946.

**8.** Marilyn Bell became the first person to swim Lake Ontario, a distance of 51 kilometres, on September 9, 1954.

**9.** The first Canadian Football League regular season game that was played in the United States. The Hamilton Tiger-Cats beat the Ottawa Rough Riders 24–18 in Philadelphia on September 14, 1958.

**10.** Northern Dancer became the first Canadian horse to win the Kentucky Derby: May 2, 1964.

**11.** Dave Bailey became the first Canadian to break the four-minute mile (3:59.1) on June 11, 1966.

**12.** During a bout at Maple Leaf Gardens, George Chuvalo became the first professional boxer to go the distance with American boxer Muhammad Ali in 1966. Chuvalo was never knocked out in 97 career heavyweight fights.

**13.** Montreal was awarded Canada's first major league professional baseball franchise on May 27, 1968.

**14.** Sandra Post became the first foreign player to win the LPGA Championship on June 24, 1968.

**15.** Cindy Nicholas was the first woman to complete a return, non-stop swim of the English Channel on September 7, 1977.

**16.** Steve Podborski won the men's downhill skiing World Cup, the first non-European to do so, on March 5, 1982.

**17.** Vicki Keith was the first marathon swimmer to swim the English Channel using the butterfly stroke on July 10, 1989.

## They Said It!

"I was absolutely thrilled. I remember feeling extremely exhausted and my legs were like rubber. Then we had to jog back to the hotel."

*– David Bailey, recalling the race when he became the first Canadian to break the four-minute mile.*

## Sports BITE!

The NBA and Canada was always a natural match, as James Naismith the famed inventor of the sports was a Canadian. However, after the Toronto Huskies folded after the NBA's first season in 1947 it was more than 50 years before the NBA returned to Canada. The Vancouver Grizzlies only lasted six seasons, moving to Memphis at the end of the 2000–01 season. The Raptors are still going strong in Toronto.

**18.** Kurt Browning became the first Canadian male to win successive world figure skating championships in March, 1990.

**19.** Wayne Gretzky became the first National Hockey League player to score 2,000 points on October 23, 1990.

**20.** The Toronto Blue Jays were the first team based in Canada to win baseball's World Series on October 24, 1992.

**21.** The Toronto Raptors and the Vancouver Grizzlies both played their first regular season games in the National Basketball Association (NBA) on November 3, 1995. Toronto beat the New Jersey Nets 94-78 at SkyDome (now Rogers Centre) and the Vancouver Grizzlies beat the Portland Trail Blazers on the road 92–80.

**22.** Steve Nash, superstar player for the Dallas Mavericks of the National Basketball Association, became the first Canadian ever named to the NBA All-Star Team in February 2001.

**23.** Mike Weir became the first Canadian golfer to win the Masters on April 14, 2003.

## SPOTLIGHT: A Sports Entrepreneur

## Louis Garneau (Louis Garneau Sports Inc.)

Wherever there are cyclists and cross-country skiers, you're likely to see Louis Garneau's name.

After racing for Canada in the 1984 Los Angeles Olympics and winning 150 races worldwide, the Quebec-based cyclist bought a sewing machine and started making bicycle shorts for his friends on the Canadian cycling team. The company, now known as Louis Garneau Sports Inc. was launched in his father's garage in Ste. Foy, Quebec.

These days, the company is run by Garneau in St-Augustin-de-Desmaures, Quebec, and is a major manufacturer of clothing, helmets, and accessories for cycling; cross-country ski wear; children's apparel; bicycles; and fitness equipment. The firm has a manufacturing plant in the United States and most recently set up shop in Mexico. Louis Garneau Sports Inc. has a presence in 35 countries.

As a racer, Garneau gained the experience to lead a company and the will to succeed. He beat legendary Canadian cyclist Steve Bauer in an individual race at Montreal's Velodrome, was a member of the Canadian cycling team for seven years, and at his peak in 1982 was ranked 11th in the world in the 100-kilometre team time trial event.

Garneau drives his business the way he would cycle a race, by focussing on goals and working with his team. From 1984 to 1990, his vision ran like a well-tuned racing bike: sales doubled every year and by 1985 he was in a 5,000-square-foot factory with 16 employees. By 1989, there were 118 employees in a 32,000-square-foot facility and he was also running a plant in Newport, Vermont.

The recession of 1990–91 showed Garneau the need for innovation. After studying all bike helmets on the market, he designed his own helmet line, which retails in the $30 to $140 range and is among the top three best-sellers in the world. In 2002, helmets made up nearly 40 percent of his business.

The firm has about 50 percent of the market in cycling and cross-country accessories in Canada and is the only company making bicycle helmets and sunglasses in Canada.

Louis Garneau Sports Inc. has 20 distributors in the world and 25,000 accounts in the U.S. and Canada alone. Its lines sell in Canada, the U.S., Europe, South America, Japan, and Australia. Olympic and world champions such as Myriam Bedard, Lance Armstrong, and Curt Harnett wear Garneau products.

Garneau was able to make the leap to international sales because of the helmets and his passion. "I was not a world champion in cycling and some of my friends were, so I decided to be a world champion in business," he told the *Financial Post* in 1996. In 2006, Louis Garneau launched his biography entitled *Ne jamais abandonner* (*Never Give Up*). All profits are donated to support Little Brothers, Friends of the Elderly.

Louis Garneau.

Louis Garneau Sports Inc. continues to expand and the company celebrated its 25th anniversary in 2008.

# GREY CUP FACTS

Innovative plays, charismatic players, and a handful of outrageous incidents — including the time an over-zealous spectator prevented a touchdown — have highlighted the Grey Cup's long and colourful history.

Over the years, the annual fall classic has been dubbed the "Grand National Drunk," because it brings easterners and westerners together for a Canadian party that's rarely matched. Take a few minutes to revel in some of the trivial and not-so-trivial items that continue to make the Grey Cup a major national happening:

- Most Canadians know the Cup was named after Lord Grey, Canada's governor general from 1904 to 1911, but were you aware that he also donated an Earl Grey Trophy to horse racing? Grey was an avid sportsman who enjoyed skiing, curling, and golf. He provided prizes for music and drama and tried unsuccessfully during his term to bring Newfoundland into Confederation. The Grey Cup cost $48 to make and, according to Grey, was supposed to be contested "always under purely amateur conditions." But his intentions didn't last long: over the years, professionals began infiltrating the game and for much of its history the Grey Cup has pitted professional teams against one another in a bid to win Canada's top football prize.

- Canadians were playing a brand of football long before the first Grey Cup in 1909. As you watch the next game being played under the lights, don't for a minute think artificial lighting is a recent innovation. According to the Canadian Sports Hall of Fame, the first night football game on record was back in 1879. The game was played under lights between the Brittania and Montreal football clubs in Montreal. Football was a much different game then, and there was a quaintness about the announcement of the match. An ad told fans there would be "Ice Cream and Strawberries Supplied on the Ground."

- Anyone who thinks we simply borrowed an American game and adapted it to our style would be wrong. In fact, Canadians actually had a hand in teaching Americans about the game that evolved into what we now know as football. In the mid-1800s, the games of soccer and rugby were played here. The two balls used for the sports were slightly different, with the soccer ball being round and the rugby ball being slightly oblong. Students from McGill University introduced the game of rugby to players from Harvard University in 1874. Two matches had been set up between the two teams. In the first one, the Harvard round ball was used and in the second the McGill oval ball was to be used. However, the oval ball was lost and the round one was used again, but played under McGill's rules. The game ended in a scoreless tie, but the Americans were impressed enough to adopt the sport, and the editor of the *Harvard Magenta* called it better than "the somewhat sleepy game now played by our men." Football spread throughout both countries with different rules being used.

- The Americans can take credit, however, for introducing the forward pass to the game. And the first forward pass thrown for a touchdown in a Grey Cup? That would be Warren Stevens to Kenny Grant of the Montreal Winged Wheelers in the 1931 Cup game against Regina.

- Many great sports heroes have shone during the Grey Cup, but for all-round ability, Lionel Conacher has to receive plenty of credit. Canada's best all-round athlete of the first half of the 20th century scored 15 points for the Toronto Argonauts in the 1921 Grey Cup game before leaving to play hockey that night for the Toronto Aura Lee of the Ontario Hockey Association Senior League.

- If that seems weird, who can ever forget the Grey Cup of 1962 when Winnipeg defeated Hamilton 28 to 27. Known as "The Fog Bowl," it was the great Cup game that few people saw. The two teams staged an exciting game that saw the lead change hands, but fog rolling in from Lake Ontario reduced visibility to the point where few people could see what was happening on the field. With only a few minutes left, and Hamilton trailing by a point, the game was stopped and the remaining time played the next day. The contest ended with Hamilton trying to score a single point, but the punt fell short of Winnipeg's end zone.

- Speaking of weird, how about the Ray "Bibbles" Bawel incident during the 1957 Grey Cup? Bawel, of the Hamilton Tiger-Cats, was running toward the Winnipeg goal line with no one in front of him when a spectator near the sidelines tripped him and prevented him from getting a touchdown. Winnipeg was penalized half the distance to the goal line, and Hamilton later scored and eventually won 32 to 7. The spectator later apologized to Bawel and sent him a gold watch.

- Finally, a gold watch award to one of the great Grey Cup quotable quotes. Running back Vic Washington of the Ottawa Rough Riders, while discussing his 80-yard run that was a crucial turning point in the Riders winning the 1968 Grey Cup against Calgary, said: "All I could think as I ran was, I hope I don't get a cramp."

## Ian Millar and Big Ben

Big Ben, originally named Winston, after British Prime Minister Winston Churchill, came to Canada in 1983 from the Hooydonk Farm in northern Belgium. His owner, equestrian Ian Millar, purchased and brought the 17.3-hand chestnut to Millar Brooke Farm in Perth, Ontario.

In 1984, Big Ben started competing in show jumping events with Millar in the saddle. The pair made a glorious tandem, with 40 Grand Prix victories, the World Show Jumping Championship two years in a row, and $1.5 million in prize money.

In 1994 Big Ben retired to the Millar Brooke Farm. He was the second horse inducted into the Ontario Sports Legends Hall of Fame (Northern Dancer was the first) and in 1999 was honoured by Canada Post with a stamp.

At the age of 23, Big Ben was euthanized at Millar's farm on December 11, 1999, after veterinarians said nothing could be done to ease suffering caused by a persistent case of equine colic. He was buried on a knoll overlooking the farm.

On May 22, 2005, a full-size bronze sculpture of Big Ben and Millar by sculptor Steward Smith was unveiled in Perth at the corner of Wilson and Herriott streets, overlooking Stewart Park.

Millar, a native of Halifax and a nine-time Olympian and show jumping legend was named to the Order of Canada in 1986. He continues to run his farm and also spends time in Florida, where he shows horses. He competes in as many as 25 show jumping events a year and recently participated in the 2008 Olympic Games in Beijing, this time atop In Style, where the Canadian team picked up a silver medal.

## Betsy Clifford: Champion Downhill Skier

Betsy Clifford will never forget her second-place finish in the World Downhill Skiing Championship in 1974 at St. Moritz, Switzerland. "I was neck-in-neck with Annemarie Moser-Proell of Austria," she recalled. "It came down to one turn and I lost by 2/100ths of a second. There was nothing I could have done better … it was a great race."

While she lost by the slimmest of margins, Clifford, a native of Old Chelsea, Quebec, just north of Ottawa, still managed to bring home a silver medal to add to a string of honours she would win after learning to ski in the Gatineau Hills of southwestern Quebec at age three.

In 1968, at the age of 14, Clifford became the youngest Canadian skier ever to compete at the Olympics. In 1970, in Val Gardena, Italy, she became the youngest skier to win a medal at the World Championships when she earned gold in the giant slalom; she was named most newsworthy woman in sports in 1971 after winning the special slalom in Schruns, Austria, and the slalom in Val D'Isere, France, to finish second in overall Slalom World Cup standings.

## Sports BITE!

Betsy Clifford's late father, John, was often referred to as a ski pioneer and "the father of popular skiing." The Ottawa native spent seven decades as a racer, ski centre developer, instructor, and ski resort owner. He is credited with bringing snowmaking technology to Canada in the mid-1950s, adding nearly two months to the downhill ski season each year. "Thanks to John, people now ski into mid-April until they are bored and want to play golf," said his long-time friend Keith Nesbitt. John Clifford passed away in 2002 in Almonte, Ontario, at the age of 79.

Photo courtesy of Canadian Ski Museum, Le Musée canadien du ski, Ottawa, ON.

Betsy Clifford demonstrates her championship style at Val Gardenia, 1970.

In 1972, she broke both heels while training for a World Cup race at Grindelwald, Switzerland, and vowed to retire. The accident forced her to miss the 1972 Olympics. In 1973, she returned to competitive ski racing and dominated the Can-Am series with five victories, finishing 72 points ahead of her nearest competitor.

Now in her mid-50s, she is a member of the Canada's Sports Hall of Fame and the American National Ski Hall of Fame.

Clifford has married for a second time and lives in Lanark, Ontario, a town 70 kilometres west of Ottawa. She's a certified Level 3 ski instructor and has worked as a ski patroller at nearby Mount Pakenham, which was developed by her late father, John Clifford, and is currently owned by her sister Joanne.

Clifford, whose married name is Whitehall, has worked for the federal government since 1981. In 2006 she was working in human resources with the Department of Fisheries and Oceans, Canadian Coast Guard section.

The bib and Rossignol skis she was wearing in Val Gardena in 1970 when she won the gold medal are in the collection of the Canadian Ski Museum in Ottawa.

For more information, visit www.skimuseum.ca.

## Russ Jackson: The All-Canadian Quarterback

No one wants to see a homegrown quarterback shine in the Canadian Football League more than Russ Jackson — if only because it'll mean people will stop asking him about the issue.

There are many reasons why it hasn't happened in recent decades, says Jackson, but if it ever does happen "he's going to have to be someone really special."

Someone like Jackson. In a brilliant career that saw him lead the Ottawa Rough Riders to three Grey Cup victories, including one in his last season, 1969, Jackson set the standard, not only for Canadian-born quarterbacks, but for quarterbacks, period.

The Hamilton native won three Most Outstanding Player awards, something unprecedented for a homegrown player in the CFL. Given that he started with the Rough Riders in 1958 as defensive back, Jackson's accomplishments were all the more unexpected. "At that time to think you might make it as a Canadian quarterback was unheard of," Jackson said in an interview from his home in Burlington, Ontario.

But when two other quarterbacks got injured, Jackson got his chance and proved that being a Canadian at that position was no handicap. But since he retired from the game in 1969, there have been few Canadians who've been given the chance to play quarterback. Jackson, however, helped Ottawa to a Grey Cup win in 1960 and led the team to victory again in 1968 and 1969. He picked up his Most Outstanding Player awards at intervals along the way, which he recalled with pride: "winning it over a period of time because you maintained a degree of excellence" was satisfying, he said.

Jackson saved his best for 1969, the year he announced he would be retiring. He enjoyed a stellar season, including a playoff victory over the Toronto Argonauts, whose coach Leo Cahill had claimed it "would take an act of God" for his team to lose to Ottawa after the Argos won the first of a two-game total points playoff. Jackson responded with a memorable performance that saw his team trounce the Argos 32–3 and win the series 46–25. Ottawa then defeated Saskatchewan in the Grey Cup. "To go through that year and end on a high note, that had to make it special," Jackson recalled.

The quarterback stuck to his word, though, and said farewell to the game. He had been a teacher and vice-principal during his playing days but wanted to be a principal and believed he could do that only away from football. He became principal of an Ottawa high school soon afterward and held that position in different schools in both Ottawa and the Peel Region of Ontario until his retirement in 1992.

He also did a stint as a CFL colour commentator with the CBC in the 1970s and tried coaching for a couple of years in the middle of that decade with the Argonauts. Coaching wasn't a successful fit for Jackson and he was let go from the team in 1976. He enjoy the commentating, however, noting it was far less stressful than coaching ever was. But of the Argo job, he said that while it was upsetting at the time, "I'm glad I tried it."

Jackson spoke more enthusiastically of his years as a principal, during which he helped one high school make the transition from being English to unilingual French, saved some programs at another, and helped a new school in Peel get started. "There was always something neat about the schools I was at," he said.

Jackson coached basketball during his years as an educator and occasionally helped mentor some high school quarterbacks, but when he stepped down, he recalled, "It was time, I was ready. It was like football."

He did some colour commentating for Hamilton Tiger-Cats games after that and still attends their home games. Ever the quarterback, Jackson watches the action on the field trying to analyze what the defence might do on a particular down. "I enjoy watching the game from the aspect of being the quarterback. It's kind of fun for me that way."

Since moving to Burlington, Jackson has kept busy playing golf at nearby Credit Valley Golf & Country Club, skiing in the winter, and doing a great deal of charity work, including raising funds for the football program of his alma mater, McMaster University. He's still an avid fan of the CFL and thinks the players are better trained and better coached than in his day. Fans still recognize him just about everywhere he goes, and he's happy to answer questions and talk about the game. "And they recognize my voice which is always interesting."

Jackson was appointed an Officer of the Order of Canada and was voted one of the top 50 CFL players of all time in 2006 by Canadian sports network TSN.

As for the quarterbacks that came after him, Jackson believes there were many good ones but that Doug Flutie in particular stood out. "He had that leadership that made him special. He made good teams into great teams. That's what a quarterback can do."

Not unlike Russ Jackson.

## Lui Passaglia: Hometown Boy Gets His Kicks

As a young boy, Vancouver native Lui Passaglia remembers hearing the sound of fans cheering on the B.C. Lions wafting over the walls of the old Empire Stadium. His father, who had emigrated from Italy, became a fan of the Lions and would occasionally sneak Passaglia in to watch games.

Fast forward to 1994, and the Grey Cup in another Vancouver stadium, BC Place, featuring the Lions and an all-American team, the Baltimore Stallions, battling it out. With the score tied at 23 and the last seconds of the game ticking off the clock, the hometown boy, Passaglia, steps on the field to try to win it with a 38-yard field goal. In the first Grey Cup to feature an American-based team, Canadian fans hold their collective breath as Passaglia makes contact.

Like he did so many times in his 25-year career, the Vancouver kicker nailed it through the uprights, making the Lions CFL champions. In what was a long and fruitful career for the place-kicker/punter, Passaglia's 1994 last-second field goal is what most Canadians remember about him.

But as he told us a few years back from his office with the Lions club, where he worked as director of community relations, you can't define a career by one kick. He acknowledged that the 1994 Grey Cup game was "a standout" and that it took on special meaning because it was Canada versus the U.S. "It was here in Vancouver, it was a pretty good spectacle, and we were the Cinderella team."

But Passaglia remembered other key moments in his career just as fondly: making the team for the first time in the mid-1970s after graduating from Simon Fraser University and being introduced as a player in his first game; his first Grey Cup played at BC Place in 1983; and the Lions winning in 1985 and the again in 2000 in Passaglia's last season.

When it was all over, Passaglia had set a CFL record (and, in fact, an all-pro football record) of 3,991 points, one that would stand up for some time. In his final year, as a 46-year-old, the kicker notched 40 of 44 field goals for an astounding 90.9 percent success rate.

As was the case with several CFL players in the 1980s, Passaglia received offers to go to the NFL. He declined, saying that the money wasn't much better south of the border in those days and that B.C. had made him a good offer. In 1988, he did try out for the Cleveland Browns and was also thinking of retiring, but the Lions still wanted him and offered a series of one-year contracts until he did retire.

Although he lasted longer than most kickers, by 2000 Passaglia says his body was telling him it was time to retire. He went to work for the Lions after retirement and found he missed playing the game for that first year. In his post with the Lions, he had a significant presence in Vancouver, which included the team's involvement with literacy programs in elementary and high schools as well as connections with amateur football and charities throughout the province.

It's a position he enjoyed. "Even though I'm removed from the game I'm still involved with the players," he told us. He resigned from the Lions at the conclusion of the 2007 CFL season to devote his time to his family property development business.

Passaglia, who was inducted into the CFL Hall of Fame in 2004, looks back fondly at his career. He admitted he got butterflies before the games, but once he stepped on the field to make a crucial kick he stayed focussed. "I was never nervous to go in and do my job. Once I was on the field, I thought I could make a difference."

And the Vancouver boy who dreamed of playing for the Lions and helping them win the Grey Cup certainly did.

"You couldn't ask for a better script," he said. "And to do it all in your hometown."

# CHAPTER 21
# Strange Brew: A History of Canada's Potent Potables

##  Alexander Keith's Brewery

When Alexander Keith arrived in Halifax in 1817, he had all the tools necessary to run his own brewery. When it came to brewing, some said he was a perfectionist.

As a teenager in Halkirk, Caithness, in northern Scotland, his father, a highly respected farmer, financed his business education to prepare him for the world of commerce. At age 17, he was sent to Sunderland in northern England to learn the basics of brewing and malting from an uncle. He later gained practical experience in London and Edinburgh.

By the time he landed in North America, Keith's recipe for beer-making had the ring of a modern-day television advertisement: Brew beer slowly and carefully and take the time to get it right, using only the finest pure barley malt and hops. At age 22, he was practising what he preached as a brewmaster and business manager at a small Halifax brewery owned by Charles Boggs.

Three years later, he purchased the business and began brewing under the name Nova Scotia Brewery.

Legendary for his hospitality and known as a devoted husband and father to his eight children, Keith was confronted by his first major business challenge when the economy weakened after the War of 1812. Although land and buildings were devalued and business stagnated, he decided to take a gamble by expanding his brewery. His hunch paid off: the economy improved and headed into a 10-year boom.

Keith made a name for himself as a brewer of strong ales and porter, as well as conventional ginger and spruce beers, which were milder brews with a distinctive taste that was popular in North America at the time. Prosperous times enabled him to move to larger quarters on Lower Water Street in Halifax.

When the boom ended and a cholera epidemic struck, the city was again in a slump. Keith again threw caution to the wind and enlarged his brewery; his instinct proved correct. In 1833, abolition of the slave trade in the sugar islands of the West Indies sent rum prices skyrocketing, making ale the most affordable and popular drink in Halifax.

In 1853, Keith's only son Donald became a full partner in the firm and the brewery name was changed to Alex Keith & Son.

Although brewing his famous India Pale Ale was his first love, Keith always found time to play a leading role in Halifax's social and business communities. He held directorships with the Bank of Nova Scotia, the Halifax Fire Insurance Company, the Halifax Gas, Light and Water Company, the Provincial Permanent Building, and the Investment Society. He helped found the Halifax Marine Insurance Association.

He served as commissioner of the Court of Common Pleas for Halifax before its incorporation and was a member of the city's first council from 1843 to 1854. He served as mayor of Halifax three times. In the 1840 general election, he lost his bid to win a seat for the Conservative Party in Halifax. At the time of Confederation he was offered a Senate seat but declined. He was a leader of the Freemasons, and in 1869 became grandmaster of the Nova Scotia Freemasons. Keith was a respected philanthropist who was involved in several charitable and cultural societies. He died in Halifax in 1873, leaving an estate worth $271,000.

Following his death, Keith's son continued to run the brewery, which maintained its family ties until 1928, when his granddaughter sold it to the Oland & Sons brewery. Keith's and its India Pale Ale became part of the Labatt family in 1971, when the London, Ontario-based brewery acquired Oland. Keith's continues to be Atlantic Canada's best-selling brand and the company has launched a new product, Keith's Red, which is made exclusively at the Oland Brewery in Halifax.

##  Molson's Brewery

John Molson was an 18-year-old farm boy with few skills when he arrived in Montreal in 1782. Thirty years later, he was an established entrepreneur who helped Montreal develop into a major Canadian city.

Though known to most Canadians as the name behind beers such as Molson Canadian and Molson Export, the founder of North America's oldest operating brewery was also involved in lumber, distilling, steamboats, a railway, a foundry, banking, politics, public libraries, hotels, and the founding of Montreal General Hospital.

Molson's pioneering efforts laid the foundation for one of Canada's most enduring and well-known business dynasties, a multi-million-dollar conglomerate with interests that later would include hockey, auto racing, music, building supplies, chemicals, and office products.

The eldest son of an English gentleman farmer, Molson was born on December 28, 1763 in Lincolnshire, England, where it appeared he was destined for a life in the country. That changed in 1772 when he was orphaned and became the head of his family at the tender age of eight. Eventually, he became the sole beneficiary of his father's small estate.

When Molson stepped onto the shores of the New World, his ambition and thirst for opportunity more than made up for his lack of skills. His introduction to brewing began by sharing duties at a small brewery owned by Thomas Lloyd (also spelled Loid), a fellow Englishman who was 20 years his senior. The combined malting and brewhouse was strategically located on a 40-foot plot of river frontage where a broad rapids known as St. Mary's Current met the St. Lawrence River, just east of what was then the walled city of Montreal. With a population of about 8,000, Montreal was the market centre of the fur trade, the colony's principal export.

At the time, the economics of brewing were especially attractive. Land was cheap and the water, barley, and hops needed to produce beer were readily available at little or no cost. Locally brewed beer was not subject to tax or duties and most sales were made for cash. These factors, plus the lack of competition, attracted Molson to the brewing trade.

In January of 1785, Molson secured title to the property from Lloyd. He then returned to England to liquidate his assets and buy equipment for his new brewing enterprise, returning to Montreal in June of the following year. He brought with him 46 bushels of barley and seeds, a small quantity of hops, wooden casks, brewing equipment, and a copy of *Theoretical Hints on an Improved Practice of Brewing*, written by John Richardson in 1777.

Test runs on the ale started in September, and by Christmas, Molson began brewing. On July 28, 1786, the 22-year-old officially opened his brewery in Montreal. Brewing was limited to four months of the year during winter. Over the summer, because there was no refrigeration, the ale was stored in stone underground vaults kept cool with ice taken from the river in winter. In his first season, Molson produced a modest 4,000 Imperial gallons of beer.

At five cents a bottle his ale sold quickly and thirsty Montrealers clamoured for more. Additional property was purchased, buildings were added or enlarged, and a new stone building was erected to house more brewing equipment brought from England. By 1791, Molson was brewing about 30,000 gallons a year.

In 1801, after several years in a common-law relationship, he married Sarah Vaughan, with whom he had already had three sons, John Jr., Thomas, and William.

In the years leading up to his marriage, Molson had begun a pattern of diversification which later generations of Molsons continued long after he was gone. He started a lumberyard on his brewery property; launched the *Accommodation*, Canada's first steamboat; formed the St. Lawrence Steamboat Company, also known as the Molson Line; and owned a large hotel. He was involved in a profitable family banking business, which in the 1850s became Molsons Bank, and from 1826 to 1830, he was president of the Bank of Montreal.

Molson entered politics in 1816 as the representative of Montreal East in the legislature of Lower Canada and that year opened the Mansion House, a large hotel in Montreal that housed the public library, a post office, and Montreal's first theatre. He later invested in the construction of Canada's first railway, the Champlain and St. Lawrence, which ran 16 miles between Montreal and Lake Champlain so that traffic could move freely to and from the Atlantic Coast via the Hudson River.

Gradually, Molson's sons became active in the family's growing enterprises and the business prospered. Soon the Molsons were among Montreal's well-to-do families and were known to have explored almost every business opportunity 19th-century Canada had to offer. They were among the largest distillers in British North America, and their interest in steamboats involved heavy manufacturing and a small foundry next to the brewery. It was this diversification, however, that created disagreements that often pitted one brother against the other and father against son.

In 1828, John Sr. retired from his active role in the brewery and a partnership was drawn up between sons John and William, who alternated as brewmasters. Money was invested in new equipment, and a short time later, the senior Molson asked Thomas to return to the business. The brothers were united once again.

John Molson died in January 1836, on the 50th anniversary of the brewery's founding. An obituary in Quebec City newspaper *Le Canadien* remembered Molson as "at all times a zealous supporter of every important commercial and industrial enterprise. Few men have rendered better service to their country in connection with its material development."

## They Said It!

"Character is the real test of manhood. Live within your income no matter how small it may be. Permanent wealth is maintained and preserved by vigilance and prudence and not by speculation."

*– John H.R. Molson, grandson of the founder of Molson's brewery, dictating a message for his descendants.*

Following Molson's death, Thomas and William purchased their brother John's interest in the brewery and an agreement was signed to conduct business as brewers and distillers under the company name of Thomas and William Molson and Company. Over the years, other members of the family ran the operation.

The company became Molson's Brewery Ltd in 1911. By the middle of the century, Molson was producing an average of 1.5 million bottles of beer a day. In 1957, the Montreal Canadiens hockey team was purchased, and between 1968 and 1972 Molson went on a major diversification binge, purchasing Anthes Imperial Ltd., a company that specialized in office furniture and supplies, construction materials and public warehousing; Canada's Beaver Lumber chain; and American companies that manufactured chemical cleansers and other chemical specialty products.

In 1993, the brewing company was partially owned by Australian and American companies, but in 1998, Molson bought out its foreign partners and the brewery was once again 100-percent Canadian.

In 2001, Molson's sold 80 percent of the beloved Canadiens to a Colorado businessman.

Molson Inc. sponsored the Molson Indy car race in Toronto from 1986 to 2005 and the Molson Indy car race in Vancouver until 2004. The family name is found on the Molson Amphitheatre at Ontario Place in Toronto.

Molson operates six breweries across the country, including the Creemore brewery in Ontario, and is involved in various charitable initiatives and sports and entertainment sponsorships. In 2005, the company merged with the Coors Brewing Company to form the Molson Coors Brewing Company. Its major markets are Canada, the U.K. and the United States.

## Biz BITE!

In his will, John Molson stipulated that an oil painting of himself must hang in the boardroom at the Montreal brewery for as long as the Molson family retained control. His will also states that should the brewery pass into the hands of strangers, the portrait must be removed.

 ## O'Keefe Brewery

In a country famous for such brewmasters as Molson, Labatt, and Carling, Eugene O'Keefe is a different case. Though he ran one of the most successful breweries of the late 19th and the 20th century, O'Keefe knew almost nothing about the business when he started.

With banking and accounting as his career specialty, O'Keefe decided to get into brewing because he thought it was an industry with unlimited growth potential. It was a wise move.

The O'Keefe Brewery Company of Toronto Limited made him a wealthy man; in fact, he was one of the wealthiest in that city. Born in Ireland in 1827, O'Keefe came to Canada with his family while still a child. He received a private school education, was an accomplished sportsman, and from an early age had strong ties to the Catholic Church — not an enviable position in what was then a predominantly Protestant Toronto.

His shrewdness in business helped make him a successful brewery owner. O'Keefe was innovative and aggressive in introducing new ideas to the business, becoming the first in Canada to install a mechanically refrigerated storehouse and using motorized vehicles to transport his product.

When his son died young in 1911, O'Keefe sold his shares in the business and became as well known as a philanthropist to many charities and the Catholic Church as he was for his beer. He died October 1, 1913, but the brewery that bore his name remained a popular one for most of the rest of the 20th century. O'Keefe ale is still sold today by Molson's.

## 🍸 Gooderham and Worts Distillery

Making spirits was a family affair for the Worts and Gooderham clans. In the early 1830s, brothers-in-law James Worts and William Gooderham founded a milling business in Toronto which eventually became the Gooderham and Worts Distillery. In later years, the founders' sons would play key roles in the company.

Worts, a mill owner in Suffolk, England, immigrated to Toronto with his son in 1831 and built a 70-foot-tall wind-driven flour mill at the mouth of the Don River in what was then York. A year later he was joined by Gooderham, son of a Norfolk, England farmer, and they formed the partnership of Worts and Gooderham.

In 1834, two weeks after his wife Elizabeth died in childbirth, Worts drowned himself in the mill's well.

With his partner gone, Gooderham forged on, adding a distillery to the business in 1837 to process surplus grain. In 1845, he made Worts's eldest son, James, a partner in the

### Biz BITE!

The Liquor Control Board of Ontario (LCBO) is the largest single retailer of beverage alcohol in the world, offering more than 12,000 products for sale through its stores, catalogue, and private ordering service from more than 60 countries. According to its latest annual report, the LCBO has more than 700 stores and some three billion dollars in annual net sales.

LCBO stores attract millions of customers each year.

Photo by Mark Kearney.

enterprise, which they renamed Gooderham and Worts. In 1861 the pair built the largest distillery in Canada West, also at the mouth of the Don River.

Most of James Worts's time was spent managing the distillery, which experienced rapid growth. Eventually, Worts and Gooderham diversified their interests. Worts invested heavily in the Bank of Toronto, which Gooderham had helped found, and over the years both served as its president. Their other interests included railway building, livestock yards, retailing, and woolen mills.

Distilling, however, continued as their mainstay. In the 1870s, the company's 150 workers were producing one of every three gallons of proof spirits manufactured in Canada. Gooderham was one of Toronto's most prominent businessmen when he died in August 1881, leaving the distillery he and James Worts had started to their sons, James Worts and George Gooderham.

The two men, and in later years other members of their families, ran the distillery until it was sold in 1923 to wealthy Torontonian Harry Hatch. In 1926, Gooderham & Worts purchased distiller Hiram Walker & Sons of Walkerville, Ontario.

**Biz BITE!**

"Honest Henry Corby," of Corby's Distilleries Ltd., was mayor of Belleville in 1867 and sat in the Ontario legislature, representing the people of East Hastings from 1867 to 1875. Corby died in 1881 but his name lived on; the town where his distillery was located was named Corbyville.

**Biz BITE!**

Officially opened in December 2002, the Mill Street Brewery is housed in an original tankhouse within the historic Gooderham & Worts Distillery complex, now known as the Historic Distillery District. Mill Street was named Canadian Brewery of the Year in both 2007 and 2008.

Gooderham & Worts whisky is marketed today by Corby's Distilleries Ltd. Its historic Toronto distillery, which was closed in 1990, has been redeveloped. For years the site was a hot spot for movie producers, who used the 5.2-hectare property and its buildings to shoot more than 700 movies. The site was then purchased in 2001 by Cityscape Holdings Inc. and in May 2003, The Distillery was officially opened as a pedestrian-only village entirely dedicated to arts, culture, and entertainment. The cobblestone streets are lined with restaurants, art galleries, artist studios, cafes, and theatres and the area has become a cultural Mecca for the city of Toronto.

## Y Seagram's Spirits & Wine

Even if he'd only stuck to politics and horse breeding, Joseph Seagram would probably be well remembered today. It was his wizardry with whisky distilling, however, that made the Seagram name world famous.

Joseph Emm Seagram was born April 15, 1841 near New Hope, Upper Canada, the son of an English immigrant who owned two farms and a tavern in the area around what is now the southwestern Ontario city of Cambridge. Seagram's father died when he was seven and his mother died just four years later, which put Joseph and his brother Edward in the care of an Anglican clergyman nearby.

Seagram studied at a business college in Buffalo for a year before taking a job as a junior bookkeeper at an axe-handle factory in what was then Galt, Ontario. He had a fist fight with another bookkeeper, however, and left for other jobs. When he hooked up with Wilhelm Hespeler a few years later in a milling operation, Seagram got his first taste of the distilling business. It was also where he met his future wife, Hespeler's niece, Stephanie Urbs.

In 1868, seeing the potential for the distilling business, he bought out Hespeler's share in the business and then acquired another partner's share a few years later. He changed the name of the business to Seagram and Roos (named for William Roos, another partner), and then two years later owned the company outright. He renamed it the Joseph Seagram Flour Mill and Distillery Company.

By the 1880s, Seagram had developed his best-selling brand, Seagram's 83, and also sold Seagram Old Rye and Seagram's White Feather. His distillery prospered, and he began selling to customers in the United States and Britain. His success south of the border soon surpassed the business in Canada.

By 1911, the company, now known as Joseph E. Seagram and Sons Limited, was established firmly as a family-run business. In fact he had a special whisky blend created, known as Seagram's V.O., which stood for "very own," to celebrate his son Thomas's wedding.

Thanks to his business success, Seagram was able to

Photo by Randy Ray.

pursue his hobby of horse racing and breeding throughout the late 19th century and into the 20th until his death. He imported horses from the U.S. and Britain to improve the quality of animals in Canada and had several winners. By 1900, he was dubbed "perhaps the greatest Canadian horse-breeder."

He also entered politics beginning in 1881. Starting as a member of the Waterloo Town Council, Seagram eventually became a federal MP and an MPP for Ontario. It was said that his campaign contributions against a young William Lyon Mackenzie King in 1911 were a major reason for King's defeat that year.

Seagram also had his philanthropic side, supporting the Berlin and Waterloo Hospital and the local branch of the Canadian Association for the Prevention of Tuberculosis. He remained active in his business and hobbies until his death on August 19, 1919. In 1928, the Seagram Company was bought by the Bronfman family of Montreal, who led it to even greater prosperity. Among the products they introduced was Crown Royal, which was commissioned in 1939 in honour of King George VI and Queen Elizabeth's visit to Canada that year.

In December 2000, it was announced that Seagram's Spirits & Wine was sold to a consortium of Diageo plc, based in London, England, and Pernod Ricard of Paris, France, for $8 billion. At the time of the announcement Seagram's was generating revenues of $5.1 billion annually and its products were sold in 190 countries and territories around the world.

### Biz BITE!

Joseph Seagram's success as a horse breeder was never more evident than at the Queen's Plate. He first tasted victory there in 1891, and his horses would win the renowned race 10 times before his death.

 **Q AND A**

**Q: How did my favourite drink, Newfoundland Screech, get its name?**

**A:** Jamaican rum has long been a mainstay in Newfoundland, having been acquired originally in exchange for salt fish. According to the Newfoundland Liquor Corporation, the government took over control of the liquor business in the early 20th century and began selling rum in unlabelled bottles.

During the Second World War, an American serviceman was having his first taste of the rum and downed a drink in one gulp. Apparently, he let out such a loud howl that many locals came running to see what was the matter. An American sergeant arrived on the scene and demanded to know what "that ungodly screech" was. The serviceman's Newfoundlander host replied "The screech? 'Tis the rum, me son."

The legend surrounding the drink's origin was born. The liquor board pounced on the new name and began labelling the rum "Screech."

## GOOD FOR WHAT ALES YOU QUIZ

Canadians love their beer, eh? Here's a case of 20 we hope you'll find refreshing. Cheers!

1.  True or false? John Carling, who ran the Carling Brewery & Malting Company of London Ltd. in the late 19th century, never drank beer because it disagreed with his system.

2.  In the 1990s, Interbrew S.A. became owner of the Toronto Blue Jays. In what country is this brewery based?

    a) Germany
    b) Luxembourg
    c) Ireland
    d) Belgium

3.  Name the Waterloo, Ontario-based brewery that brought stubby beer bottles back to the market in spring 2002.

4.  According to the Brewers Association of Canada, one of the main reasons American beer tastes different from the Canadian variety is that ours contains more malt barley. What do American brewers use more of?

    a) corn
    b) wheat

c) rye

d) oats

5. John Labatt Ltd. says its founder, John Kinder Labatt, is responsible for introducing the idea of a certain national holiday. Which
one?

    a) Thanksgiving

    b) Victoria Day

    c) Labour Day

    d) Canada Day

6. Before Eugene O'Keefe started the brewery that bears his
name, he had a background in a different business. What
was it?

    a) wine making

    b) farming

    c) banking

    d) horse breeding

7. Match the slogan to the brand of beer:

    a) 50                 i) Hey Mabel, _____.

    b) Canadian       ii) ____ says it all.

    c) Budweiser      iii) Me and the boys and our ___.

    d) Black Label     iv) I am _____!

    e) Ex               v) _____, the King of Beers

8. When George Sleeman ran the Sleeman Brewery in the late
19th century, it was said that the driveway leading up to his
manor was inlaid with what?

    a) beer caps

    b) bottle openers

    c) beer barrels

    d) upturned beer bottles

9. In what city is Spinnakers IPA microbrewed?

   a) Halifax
   b) Victoria
   c) St. John's
   d) Charlottetown

10. What do the letters IPA stand for?

11. In the early 1980s, Canada's brewers abandoned stubby bottles in favour of "long neck" bottles because stubbies:

    a) broke easily
    b) fell out of fashion
    c) could not keep beer fresh for more than a week
    d) could not accommodate screw-off caps

12. Where was the first Canadian beer bottle produced?

    a) Toronto, Ontario
    b) Sherbrooke, Quebec
    c) Mallorytown, Ontario
    d) Halifax, Nova Scotia

13. In 1968, a regulation was passed in Manitoba that allowed patrons of beverage rooms to:

    a) drink beer without meals
    b) stand up while drinking beer
    c) drink beer on outdoor patios
    d) purchase cases of beer on site for use at home

14. When John Molson began brewing beer in Montreal in 1786, what did a bottle of his ale cost?

    a) five cents
    b) seven cents

c) 10 cents

d) 12 cents

15. Besides brewing, which of the following businesses has the Molson family been involved in over the years?

    a) banking
    b) chemicals
    c) building supplies
    d) railway
    e) all of the above

16. What was the Labatt Streamliner?

    a) a sleek beer bottle introduced in the 1970s by Labatt
    b) a championship speedboat sponsored by the brewery
    c) the name of Labatt's beer delivery trucks
    d) the name of Labatt's corporate jet

17. Match the brewery with the province:

    a) Creemore Springs Brewery Ltd.          i) Alberta
    b) Moosehead Brewing Company               ii) Saskatchewan
    c) Great Western Brewing Company Ltd.   iii) Ontario
    d) Big Rock Brewery Ltd.                        iv) New Brunswick

18. What is mixed with beer to make a Twist Shandy?

a) tomato juice
b) lemon lime
c) orange juice
d) soda water

19. What was the name of Canada's first "light" beer?

    a) Amstel Light
    b) Carlsberg Light

c) Labatt's Cool Light
d) Oland's Lite

20. What was unique about Heidelberg beer?

   a) the shape of the bottle
   b) it was imported from Germany
   c) it contained twice the alcohol content of most beers
   d) it was the first Canadian beer with a label painted onto the bottle

➥ **Answers on pages 368–369**

# CHAPTER 22
# The Olympians

## 🏅 Our First Gold Medal: Still a Mystery

George Orton of Strathroy, Ontario, was a premier track athlete in Canada and beyond during the 1890s. But when he entered the 1900 Olympic Games in Paris, France, he was representing his American university team. Canada did not send an official team to the Olympics until 1904, which left Orton with the only option of competing for his adopted home south of the border.

Orton, who had previously attended the University of Toronto, later became a successful runner at the University of Pennsylvania, where he was working on his graduate degree. Although he received his PhD in 1896, he remained an active athlete, and apparently his mile time of 4:21.8 stood as a Canadian record for 30 years. At the Paris Olympics, Orton won a gold medal in the 2,500-metre steeplechase and a bronze in the 400-metre hurdles.

But whatever happened to those historic medals? Officials at Canada's Sports Hall of Fame would like to know, because they don't have them. The local museum in Orton's hometown of Strathroy is interested in finding them too. We contacted the International Centre for Olympic Studies at the University of Western Ontario in London, Ontario, and the University of Pennsylvania's athletic department, but they didn't know either.

An archivist at the University of Pennsylvania emailed to say there are about 40 to 50 items about Orton in the U. Penn. collection, but "we do not know the location of his Olympic medals." She indicated, however, that more research was being conducted into Orton's life. In the meantime, this is what she knows: Orton won national titles in Canada, the U.S., and the United Kingdom at various race lengths. He was also an outstanding athlete in other sports, playing soccer in Philadelphia and starting the hockey team at the university.

Orton was a teacher and a track coach and taught languages at various educational academies. He also founded two New Hampshire camps, Camp Tecumseh in 1902 and Camp Iroquois in 1916. Before the First World War, Orton was a co-author of *A History of Athletics in Pennsylvania* in several volumes. From 1928 to 1934 he was director of Philadelphia's Municipal Stadium.

From 1941 until his death on June 25, 1958, he made his home with his step-daughter, Doris B. Bolton, in Center Harbor, New Hampshire. Although we contacted the nearby

Meredith Historical Society, Camp Tecumseh, town officials in Center Harbor, and the historical society there, no one had information about what happened to those medals. Perhaps there are relatives who know, but we were unable to contact any descendants.

So, for now, the mystery of where Orton's medals are remains. If any reader knows of their whereabouts or has leads that might help us solve the riddle, please contact us. It's one hurdle we'd like to clear.

##  CANADA'S GREATEST OLYMPIANS

Ever since the 1904 Olympics, when Étienne Desmarteau became the first to win gold (in the 56-pound throw) while competing as a Canadian, Canada has had many Games heroes and multiple medal winners who performed at the top level when it counted or at a consistently high level in more than one Olympics. Though many more likely deserve to be acknowledged, here are our picks:

###  Summer Games
(in order)

1.  **Percy Williams:** His double gold victories in the 100-metre and 200-metre sprints in Amsterdam in 1928 have never been matched by Canadian sprinters.

2.  **Marnie McBean and Kathleen Heddle:** Canada's first triple gold medallists. They won their first two golds in pairs rowing and as part of the eights crew in Barcelona in 1992, then captured first place in a different event, double sculls, in Atlanta in 1996.

3.  **George Hodgson:** He won his two gold medals in 1912 in the 1,500-metre freestyle swim and the 400-metre freestyle, breaking world records along the way.

4.  **Donovan Bailey:** He claimed the title of "the world's fastest man" by winning gold in Atlanta in the 100-metre sprint. Then he anchored the Canadian team to another gold medal performance in the 4 x 100-metre relay.

5.  **Caroline Waldo:** In a sport that's harder than it looks, Waldo won silver in synchronized swimming in 1984, then came away from the Games in Seoul in 1988 with two gold medals.

6. **Alex Baumann:** In the 1984 Olympics in Los Angeles (which was boycotted by some Eastern European nations), he captured gold in the 400-metre individual medley swim while smashing the world record. A few days later, he won gold in the 200-metre version of the same event, also in world record time.

7. **Victor Davis:** He captured gold in the 200-metre breaststroke in 1984 in world-record time and silver in 100-metre breaststroke the same year, again beating the previous world record. He won silver in the 4 x 100-metre medley relay in 1984 and another silver in the same event in 1988.

8. **Fanny Rosenfeld:** As part of the strong Canadian women's team in the 1928 Olympics (which also included high jump gold-medallist Ethel Catherwood), Rosenfeld stood out, winning silver in the 100-metre sprint and leading her team to gold in a world-record performance in the 4 x 100-metre relay. She was named Canada's outstanding female athlete of the first 50 years of the century.

9. **Anne Ottenbrite and Mark Tewksbury (tie):** Swimmers who won a medal of each colour. Ottenbrite did it in 1984 — a gold in the 200-metre breaststroke (the first Canadian woman swimmer to ever win Olympic gold), silver in the 100-metre breaststroke, and bronze in the 4 x 100-metre medley relay, while Tewksbury captured gold in Olympic-record time in the 100-metre backstroke in 1992, silver in the 4 x 100-metre medley relay in 1988, and bronze in the same event in 1992.

10. **Phil Edwards:** He's the best example of an athlete who gave consistently strong performances over several years. He won five bronze medals at middle distance races in the Olympics from 1928 to 1936.

11. **Simon Whitfield:** Whitfield's gold medal win in the triathlon at the 2000 Games in Sydney, Australia is one

## Sports BITE!

At the 2008 Summer Olympics, Canadian show jumping champion Ian Millar competed at his ninth games, tying the record set by Hubert Raudaschl, an Austrian sailor. He has been named to 10 straight Olympic teams, but did not compete at the 1980 Summer Olympics because of the Canadian boycott. At 61 years of age, Millar won his first Olympic medal at the 2008 Beijing games, a silver in the team equestrian event, after a jump-off against the United States.

of the most memorable performances by an individual athlete ever. He followed it up with another exciting performance in Beijing in 2008, just missing out on gold in the last few metres of the race, and settling for silver instead. Both efforts were marked by incredible comebacks in the final stages of the race (the running leg). His winning time from the 2004 Games still stands (2009) as the Olympic triathlon record.

 ## Winter Games
(in order)

1. **Cindy Klassen:** A true Olympic star. At the 2006 Olympic Winter Games in Turin, Italy, the Winnipeg native, who trained in Calgary, became the first Canadian to win five medals at a single Winter Olympics. She won gold in the 1,500-metre, silver in the 1,000-metre, silver in the team pursuit, bronze in the 5,000-metre, and bronze in the 3,000-metre.

   Cindy had also captured an Olympic bronze medal in the 2002 Games making her the most decorated Canadian Olympic athlete in history, with a total of six Olympic medals.

2. **Clara Hughes:** With her bronze-medal performance in the 500-metre speed skating event at the 2002 Olympics, she became the first Canadian, and only the fourth athlete ever, to win medals at both the Winter and Summer Games. She won two cycling bronze medals at the 1996 Summer Olympics in Atlanta, in the individual road race and the individual time trial. At the 2006 Turin Winter Games, Hughes won her first gold medal in the 500-metre and added a silver in the team pursuit. Her total of five gold medals tied the total medal count records of Marc Gagnon and Phil Edwards; however her teammate Cindy Klassen won five medals that year also, giving her a total of six (a new record).

3. **Marc Gagnon:** This short-track speed skater from Chicoutimi, Quebec, with a total of five medals in three consecutive Olympic Games, was the most decorated Canadian athlete in Winter Olympic history until Klassen overtook him in 2006 with a total of six medals. In 1994, he won a bronze medal in the 100-metre event. Four years later, in Nagano, Japan, Gagnon won a gold medal with the Canadian relay team. But his best performance came during the 2002 Salt Lake City Games where he picked up three medals; a bronze in the 1,500-metre, and two golds, in the 500-metre and team relays.

4. **Gaetan Boucher:** Won silver in 1980 in the 1,000-metre speed skate in Lake Placid, New York, then two golds in the 1,000- and 1,500-metres and a bronze in the 500-metres in 1984 in Sarajevo, Yugoslavia.

5. **Myriam Bedard:** She won bronze in the 15-kilometre biathlon in Albertville, France, in 1992, and then double gold in Lillehammer, Norway, in 1994 in the 7.5-kilometre and 15-kilometre events.

6. **Nancy Greene:** The heroine of the 1968 Olympics in Grenoble, France, Greene won gold by an almost three-second margin in the giant slalom and silver in the slalom.

**They Said It!**

"The most important thing about skating is that it teaches you to do the things you should do before you do the things you want to do."

– *Olympic champion figure skater Barbara Ann Scott*

7. **Barbara Ann Scott:** She became Canada's sweetheart after following up her world championship win in 1947 by winning the gold medal in figure skating in 1948 in St. Moritz, Switzerland. Her athletic style that featured several jumps changed women's figure skating forever.

8. **Catriona Le May Doan:** She had all of Canada applauding her gold medal in the 500-metre speed skate and bronze in the 1,000-metres in Nagano, Japan, in 1998.

9. **Anne Heggtveit:** Won gold in 1960 in the slalom by a margin of more than three seconds over her nearest rival. Her victory helped inspire Nancy Greene.

**Sports BITE!**

The first Winter Olympic Games ever held in Canada took place in Calgary in 1988. Canada won no official gold medals that year. Hopefully we will fare better at the Vancouver Olympics, scheduled for 2010!

10. **The Toronto Granite Hockey Team:** In the 1924 Olympics in Chamonix, France, they dominated the sport like no other team has since. They captured gold by winning by such scores as 33–0 and 22–0 and the final over the United States 6–1. And an honourable mention goes out to all the Canadian hockey teams between 1920 and 1952 that had a 37–1–3 record and scored 403 goals with only 34 against.

# OLYMPIC SPOTLIGHTS

## Barbara Ann Scott

Prior to 2006, when speed skater Cindy Klassen won five medals at the Olympic Winter Games, 1948 may have seen the single greatest success for any Canadian athlete. That year, Barbara Ann Scott accomplished an unprecedented feat in figure skating history when she won the Canadian, North American, European, World, and Olympic titles.

Her talent on the ice and her winning smile endeared her to the hearts of Canadians, who more than 60 years later still haven't forgotten the former Ottawa champion. Scott, who married Tom King more than 50 years ago, still gets fan mail, and whenever she visits her home country she's inundated with requests for autographs, which she gladly signs. And several of those who contact her are girls born in the late 1940s and 1950s who were named Barbara after her.

Barbara Anne Scott became Canada's sweetheart after her gold medal win.

Scott, who retired with her husband to Amelia Island, Florida, in the late 1990s, said in an interview from her home that she thinks she captured the imaginations and support of Canadians because she won so soon after the Second World War. Canada was looking for positive, upbeat news, and fans in her home country were behind her throughout all her victories, she said. "I felt like I wasn't skating for myself; it was for all these kind people who were wishing me well."

The Olympic gold medal at the St. Moritz Olympics was the real capper. She had to skate outdoors on a hockey rink, but her figures and jumps were clean and precise and better than anyone else in the world.

When she came home, she was the toast of the country and a media star like none before her. Among the accolades she received was the design of a Barbara Ann Scott doll, many of which still exist and are now collector's items. Scott still has a specially made one, as well as one in the form of a bear that has the name "Bearbara" on its figure skates. She laughed at the tribute, noting that "the feet [on that doll] are enormous."

After her amateur triumphs, she skated professionally for another seven years before hanging up the blades. In her post-Olympics world, she lived in Chicago, where Tom developed a successful commercial real estate business. Barbara Ann was a professional figure skating judge for a while with fellow Olympic champion Dick Button, but she also made her name in the world of horse shows, where she won hundreds of ribbons and trophies.

Despite these accomplishments, she was hesitant to speak of her successes, letting husband Tom do the talking about that. "She was an extraordinary rider," he said. Tom added that his wife had virtually no ego, but that whenever they visit Canada "they call me Mr. Scott and I love it."

The two decided to settle in Amelia Island, near Jacksonville, after visiting it several years ago and "absolutely falling in love with the area," she said. With a condo right on the ocean, Scott enjoys the beach and games of golf. The couple also regularly visits the Jacksonville symphony as well as the island's two theatres.

The famed Canadian athlete still watches figure skating occasionally and says there have been many champions since her time that she admired, mentioning Peggy Fleming and Michelle Kwan as two of them. In 2004, the Kings established a scholarship at her former club, the Minto Skating Club in Ottawa. In 2006, she was a guest of the Canadian championships in Ottawa as well as an honorary chair of the Worlds competition in Calgary. She enjoys visiting with skaters during these sojourns to Canada and mentions how former champion Kurt Browning calls the Kings "grams and gramps." "I'm grandmother to all our champions," she said.

A member of Canada's Sports Hall of Fame, an Officer of the Order of Canada and, most recently, of the Order of Ontario (2009), Barbara Ann Scott has a legacy in this country that seemingly won't be forgotten. These days, "life is wonderful," she said, as she gazed out at the ocean and beach that are home. For the future she said she hopes to "live happily on Amelia Island and enjoy what's left of our lives."

## Anne Heggtveit: The Barbara Ann Scott of Skiing

Heading into the 1960 Winter Olympics in Squaw Valley, California, Canadian Anne Heggtveit was considered the woman to beat in slalom skiing. But her Olympic story almost ended in tragedy before the Games even got started.

Training in Switzerland before the Olympics, Heggtveit was rushing down a mountain while workers were busy packing snow on the trails. When she was about halfway down the hill, a man working near the slopes to her left hit her in the leg with his snow shovel. She didn't fall, but she sensed something was wrong.

"I thought he'd broken my leg," Heggtveit recalled more than 45 years later. But she made it to the bottom and was able to put weight on her leg. She had lunch and was getting ready to head back to train when she noticed her leg was bleeding. The shovel had cut into her tibia but had fortunately not severed a muscle. "That would have been disastrous."

Despite the setback, Heggtveit kept her eyes on the prize, something she had dreamed of since she was a child — to be the first Canadian to win a gold medal in her sport and become the Barbara Ann Scott of skiing.

The parallels between her and the 1948 Olympic skating champion were certainly there. Like Scott, Heggtveit had grown up in the Ottawa area, learning to ski at Rockliffe Park at the age of two. She started competing young too, and was winning races before she was 10. By age 14, Heggtveit was competing and winning ski competitions in Europe. Her father had been a champion cross-country skier and her uncles were also accomplished athletes, so Heggtveit was raised with the attitude that she could be a world-beater.

A broken leg in 1955 hampered her chances for a medal at the 1956 Olympics, but she was inspired by fellow Canadian Lucille Wheeler who won bronze there. Although Heggtveit didn't reach the podium in the downhill or the giant slalom in the 1960 Games, her focus had always been on the slalom.

Standing at the starting gate for that event, she had a good feeling about her chances, she recalls. "I felt really good and confident. Funny when I look at the film of that I look very nervous, but I didn't feel nervous."

Her first run was a gem, and the time she set held up by the end of the event, winning her the gold. In fact, her margin of victory is still the largest among any skiers in Olympic slalom history. But as she sat in her Vermont home in 2006, Heggtveit mentioned a bit of overlooked sporting trivia. She was also the winner of the combined skiing event, but in those days the Olympics didn't recognize that with a medal. The International Ski Federation did, however, so Heggtveit actually walked away from those Olympics with another gold medal. "It annoys me that people won't give me credit for the two gold medals."

But despite that, she, like her hero Scott from 12 years before, was the toast of Canada upon her return. Just as Scott did, Heggtveit received a ticker tape parade in Ottawa ("It was quite a homecoming") and that year won the Lou Marsh Trophy as Canada's outstanding athlete, beating out a young Russ Jackson of the Ottawa Rough Riders.

She had a couple of hills named for her, one in the Blue Mountain area of Collingwood, Ontario, and another at Camp Fortune in Quebec's Gatineau Hills, about 20 kilometres north of Ottawa. To this day, she's never seen the former and never skied the latter.

Winning the gold was how she capped her career. Once she'd achieved her lifelong goal, Heggtveit was "quite happy to pack it in." She'd seen one of her teammates die a couple of years before and knew all about injuries that plague people in the sport. "You start thinking about things like that as you get older," she said.

She did very little skiing for the next several years, but once her two children got interested, she began hitting the slopes of Quebec, where she lived for a while and worked as an instructor for Learn to Ski programs. In 1979, she and her husband, Ross Hamilton, moved to Vermont on Lake Champlain but not near the slopes. Heggtveit worked in accounting until 2000, and has since started her own photography and floral design company. Heggtveit says her knees "aren't good" these days, but she still skis occasionally if the weather and conditions are favourable.

She believes her win in 1960 helped inspire other Canadians, notably 1968 Olympic champion Nancy Greene, and she continues to watch her native country's athletes during the Olympics and in other events. Heggtveit said she thinks about her gold medal only around Olympic Games time, when media contact her for interviews, but she looks back on the glorious moment in 1960 on the podium as "pretty exciting."

## George Hungerford and Roger Jackson: Underdog Oarsmen

In the sporting pantheon of underdogs, few overcame the odds as much as rowers George Hungerford and Roger Jackson did.

The two Canadians, who started rowing as a pair only about a month before the 1964 Olympics, went to the Tokyo Games with virtually no expectations other than trying to do their best under the circumstances. It was certainly not the kind of preparation a typical Olympic athlete would follow, which is why the duo's emergence as gold medallists caught everyone, including themselves, off guard.

Both young men were rowers in Vancouver, Hungerford as part of the eights crew and Jackson in the pairs. But Hungerford suffered a bout of mononucleosis in 1964 that sapped him of his energy and put him in bed for about five weeks. It appeared his Olympic dream was over when officials substituted a spare rower in his place. Meanwhile, Jackson lost his partner, which left him up the creek without a paddle.

Hungerford managed to recover with some time to spare before the Tokyo Games, and he and Jackson were asked to pair up to see if they worked well together. The coaches told them they could go to the Olympics if the pairing was successful; their goal would be "not to embarrass Canada."

The two determined individuals decided to give it a try, even though most pairs racers at that level would normally work together for months or years to perfect their teamwork, Hungerford said. "Our challenge was to come together as a pair in every respect." Pairs racing requires the team to have a sensitive relationship that involves being matched well physically and mentally, and having so little time to work all that out was a huge task. "It wasn't easy for Roger and it wasn't easy for me either. The pair is a very temperamental boat," Hungerford recalled.

Despite the obvious challenges they faced, the two were impressive enough early on that they got their wish to compete at the Games. But while other world-class rowers were preparing mentally before the heats, Jackson and Hungerford were still practising basic physical skills that their competitors would have long ago ironed out.

What worked in the duo's favour was that few had expectations for them, and they trained with no media scrutiny. Nevertheless, Hungerford and Jackson overcame the odds and ended up with the fastest times in the heats.

Even still, when it came to the final, the Germans and the Dutch were expected to end up on top, but Hungerford remembers that with only a few other competitors to beat to get a medal the two Canadians thought "why not?" Their strategy was to go out hard and fast for the first two-thirds of the course and hope that Hungerford, who was still recovering, could hold on. Their first 25 strokes of the race "were almost perfect," said Hungerford, and the pair took the lead. They knew they had to keep pushing just to hang on, but the Dutch were closing fast. Hungerford recalled that at the end "my gas tank was empty; I'd given everything I could." But the Canadians held on for gold.

Hungerford said all of Canada was stunned by the victory, and he and Jackson weren't even interviewed by Canadian media until well after the race because the reporters had been at the main stadium watching sprinter Harry Jerome. But the duo's story and victory certainly became well appreciated shortly thereafter; Jackson and Hungerford shared the Lou Marsh Trophy as Canada's athletes of the year in 1964.

The two rowed together for another year, but illness slowed Hungerford again. Hungerford went on to study law and has worked as a lawyer ever since, most recently with the firm Fasken Martineau DuMoulin in Vancouver. He has been a governor and chairman of the B.C. division of the Olympic Trust of Canada and was a chairman of the B.C. Sports Hall of Fame for four years.

Jackson became a respected academic in the sports world and one of the leaders in the Olympic Games movement. A former director of Sport Canada, Jackson served three terms as president of the Canadian Olympic Committee and was dean of the Faculty of Kinesiology at the University of Calgary from 1978 to 1988. In 2004 he formed Roger Jackson & Associates Ltd., a private consulting practice that has seen him work on six Olympic bids, including Great Britain's successful bid for the 2012 Summer Games.

He is the chief executive officer of the Own the Podium 2010 project for the Winter Olympics in B.C., a $110-million sport technical initiative designed to help Canada win more medals at the 2010 Games than any other nation and place in the top three overall at the 2010 Paralympic Winter Games.

Both Jackson and Hungerford are members of the Canada Sports Hall of Fame and have received the Order of Canada.

Looking back at that 1964 victory, Hungerford said it gave him the confidence in life to tackle just about anything, including participation in the many community projects for which he is well known in Vancouver, such as the new rowing centre there. He and Jackson remain good friends. Hungerford said the gold medal was "an experience that was a fantastic journey. It shaped my life."

# CHAPTER 23
# They're Playing Our Song:
# The Canadian Music Scene

## THE BUSINESS OF MUSIC

###  Long & McQuade

Jack Long enjoyed a career performing alongside such musicians as Moe Koffman, Gordon Lightfoot, and Nat King Cole, but it was in the musical instrument business where he made his name across Canada.

In the 1940s, Long started playing trumpet while in Grade 9 at Toronto's Humberside Collegiate. By Grade 13 he was a member of the musician's union and played regularly with adult bands. "The other kids didn't have money back then, but I was always loaded," he says of those long-ago lucrative gigs.

Prior to opening a musical instruments shop in Toronto, Long played at Toronto's King Edward Hotel, various lounges in Montreal, and went on the road in the United States with his pianist wife, Carol, whom he met at the University of Toronto while he was earning his Bachelor of Music degree. Long obtained a franchise to sell band instruments in the Toronto area in August 1956, working out of two rooms in a house at 100 Carlton Street, just a short walk from Maple Leaf Gardens. Long continued to play gigs six nights a week for several years to make ends meet.

Soon after starting the company, his friend Jack McQuade, a top studio drummer in Toronto, came looking for space to teach. With McQuade on the premises for a few hours each week, he began selling drums, and the new partnership, Long & McQuade, was formed.

Because this was the early days of rock and roll, the two started getting requests to supply guitars and basses, and they became distributors for Fender products from their first shop located just north of Bloor and Yonge streets where Toronto's main public library now stands.

Musical giants who purchased equipment at Long & McQuade include Gordon Lightfoot; David Clayton-Thomas of Blood, Sweat and Tears; Robbie Robertson of The Band; and Neil Young.

## Music BITE!

Long once recalled playing a gig many years before with then unknown Gordon Lightfoot on drums. "He used to say he was going to be big once he got his folk act going." When the gig ended, Lightfoot, who later had such hits as "Sundown" and "The Wreck of the Edmund Fitzgerald," came by the store to buy a Martin acoustic guitar. "I couldn't understand why he wanted a guitar because to me he was a drummer."

McQuade, who wasn't as keen as Long about the business side of music, eventually phased himself out of the company, selling half his shares to Long in 1963 and the rest about three years later. By then, the Long & McQuade name was firmly established. McQuade died in 1976 of cancer.

Long & McQuade expanded from its Toronto base in the 1970s, opening stores in Vancouver, Winnipeg, and Windsor. It later added outlets in such places as Calgary, Edmonton, Regina, and Oshawa, Ontario.

Today, the company is the largest chain of musical instrument retailers in Canada with 42 Long & McQuade shops stretching from British Columbia to Newfoundland and employing more than 900 people. Long's son Steve is the company's current president. "I love hanging around the music store and talking with musicians," Jack once told us. "I always considered myself more a musician than a businessman."

## ♫ Sam the Record Man

What do Anne Murray, Tom Jones, Gordon Lightfoot, Tony Bennett, Liona Boyd, and legions of Canadian music fans have in common? All crossed paths with Sam Sniderman at one time or another.

Sniderman is the Toronto retailing icon that turned a job stocking records at his brother's radio store into the legendary 51-store Sam The Record Man chain with its landmark record emporium on Toronto's Yonge Street. Along the way, Sniderman supported a who's who of young and rising musical talents in Canada by promoting their records and concerts and fighting for more airtime for their music.

The Toronto native jumped into the record business in

## They Said It!

"Not everyone remembers me but people remember the song."
– singer-songwriter Terry Jacks about his multi-million hit "Seasons in the Sun"

1937 when he began stocking classical records in his brother Sid's store. It was a tactic to woo the woman of his dreams, Eleanor Koldofsky, and it worked: they were married five years later. When record sales outpaced radios in the mid-1950s, the Snider Radio Sales and Service sign was replaced with the much catchier Sam the Record Man marquee.

Initially, the outlet was a hangout for musicians who were lured by its stock of obscure labels and artists; soon, however, Sniderman was drawing enormous crowds of music lovers who couldn't resist his discounted loss leaders.

In 1961, Sniderman changed the face of Yonge Street when he converted a two-storey furniture outlet at 347 Yonge into his flagship store and invested $15,000 in a huge neon sign in the shape of two huge LPs. The sign was designed to trump his arch-enemy A&A records, two doors away, and back Sniderman's claim that the store had the largest selection of retail records in Canada. Over the years, many customers referred to the Yonge Street store as a madhouse, especially during Boxing Day sales when lineups often wound around the block onto Gould Street.

If you lived in Toronto, or even within driving distance during Sam's heyday, it was almost a rite of passage to visit the store. Many baby boomers fondly recall making the trip to Sam's with money ready to spend and hours to kill flipping through endless racks of albums.

In an article in the *Financial Post*, Sniderman credited much of his success to a tip from his mother, who once told him: "You'll always be dealing with the consumer and you've always got to be fair and honest if you want to stay in business." For years he personally handled complaints from his customers. It was his way of ensuring customers kept coming back.

But Sniderman, who during the 1960s smoked two packs of cigarettes and downed 25 cups of tea a day, was more than a peddlar of records, tapes, and CDs.

An Order of Canada member and recipient of the Governor General's Award for voluntarism in the performing arts, Sniderman for years lent a hand to up-and-coming Canadian artists like Anne Murray, Gordon Lightfoot, Buffy Sainte-Marie, and Joni Mitchell by hyping their records in the media and displaying and playing them in his stores. Back in the days when there was no such thing as a Canadian music industry, he had a significant hand in crafting the "CanCon" regulations that required radio stations to give airtime to more Canadian artists.

One of the highlights of his career was when Sainte-Marie received a Canadian Music Hall of Fame award. "She said that Sam the Record Man was

## They Said It!

"I often think that perhaps the reason I became a successful singer was that, as a kid, I could never do anything as well as my brothers. I wanted to do something better than they did."

– *singer Anne Murray*

**They Said It!**

"There's something romantic about being Canadian. We're a relatively unpopulated, somewhat civilized, and clean and resourceful country. I always push the fact that I'm Canadian."

– country singer, k.d. Lang

instrumental in her success … to be recognized in that fashion gave me goosebumps," he told *Profit* magazine.

Sniderman's contributions to the lives of some of Canada's most famous performers are well documented, from badgering record companies on Lightfoot's behalf to finding space on the stage at Mariposa for Mitchell. At one point a disconsolate Anne Murray told him: "Sam, if this record doesn't work, I'm going back to Nova Scotia to be a gym teacher." Murray remains his favourite Canadian singer and her song "You Needed Me," is one he listens to often.

After casting his famous shadow on the world's longest street for forty years, the world came crashing down on the Godfather of Canadian Music late in 2001 when Sam the Record Man declared bankruptcy. On June 30, 2007, the flagship store at the corner of Yonge and Gould streets in Toronto finally closed its doors. Its iconic neon sign was removed on October 8, 2008, to be restored and hopefully to find new life in the future as a reminder of a piece of the city's historic past. In 2008, Ryerson University paid nearly $40 million to buy four properties around its downtown campus, including the former Yonge Street location.

The last remnants of the Sam the Record Man retail empire are two franchise stores that remain open in Sarnia and Belleville. Sniderman, who will celebrate his 89th birthday in June 2009, lives in the Toronto area.

# ROCK GREATS: 11 CANADIANS IN THE ROCK AND ROLL HALL OF FAME

**1–4. The Band:** Four Canadians — Robbie Robertson, Rick Danko, Garth Hudson, and Richard Manuel, all from Ontario — were part of this popular and influential group, inducted into the Hall in 1994.

**5. Neil Young:** Inducted as a soloist in 1995, the singer-songwriter from Winnipeg was also a key member of Buffalo Springfield, who were inducted in 1997.

**6. Joni Mitchell:** The highly praised and successful musician from Alberta joined the Hall in 1997.

7. **Gene Cornish:** The Ottawa-born guitarist for the popular sixties group, The Young Rascals, was inducted along with his bandmates in 1997.

8–9. **Buffalo Springfield:** Besides Young, two other Canadians who were part of this important band of the late sixties, inducted into the Hall in 1997, were drummer Dewey Martin and bassist Bruce Palmer.

10. **Denny Doherty:** The smooth-voiced singer from Halifax was inducted along with fellow members of the Mamas and Papas in 1998.

11. **Leonard Cohen:** This truly gifted singer, songwriter, poet, and guitarist, who was born and raised in Montreal, was inducted into the Hall in 2008.

**They Said It!**

"I don't believe war is a way to solve problems. I think it's wrong. I don't have respect for the people that made the decisions to go on with war. I don't have that much respect for Bush. He's about war, I'm not about war — a lot of people aren't about war."

*— Canadian pop star Avril Lavigne*

## 🍁 FIRST CHUM CHART: A HIT WITH LISTENERS

**Music BITE!**

Paul Anka, with his hit song "Diana," was the first Canadian musician to top the CHUM Chart back in August 12, 1957. He was also the top Canadian in terms of songs charted, with 38. The next best Canadians were the Guess Who, who had 22 charted songs.

Rock music fans growing up in and around Toronto from the late 1950s to the early 1980s more than likely considered the weekly CHUM Chart their music bible.

Each week music buffs would pore over a listing of the top songs, which showed their position relative to the previous week and how long they'd been on the chart. In 1957, Toronto's CHUM became the first 24-hour-a-day hit parade station in Canada, and on May 27 of that year issued its first CHUM Chart. The simple folded "pocket charts" listed the top 50 songs of the week but by 1968 had reduced that to the top 30. In 1975, the pocket charts were ended and listings appeared in newspapers.

The first chart had a "white background, with black and orange highlighted areas," says Brad Jones, program director at 1050 CHUM. "The 'disc jockey cat' Clementine appears on the very first chart and every weekly chart for the next three years or so. The concept of the weekly hit parade was just an extension of the on-air presentation of the songs."

Topping the chart on May 27, 1957, was "All Shook Up" by Elvis Presley, and according to *The CHUM Chart Book* by Ron Hall, Presley would go on to have 85 charted songs by the time the station ended its listings in 1983. The last chart topper in December 1983 was "Say Say Say" by Paul McCartney, who coincidentally had the second most charted songs ever on CHUM (including his recordings with The Beatles and Wings), with 76 hits.

The station, which is playing oldies to this day, has that original CHUM Chart in its archives along with a full set of every one since. "As for how many of the original charts are out there is anybody's guess and for a value, no idea," said Jones. "An item is only worth something when someone is willing to pay for it."

# CLUBS WORTH REMEMBERING: FADING TO SILENCE

Every generation has its favourite clubs and bars for hanging out, drinking, and listening to great tunes from musicians on their way up or who have attained some level of stardom. For those of us lucky enough to have heard great music from the 1960s and 1970s in the following venues, the memories linger even if the clubs do not.

 ## The Cave

A Vancouver fixture in the 1950s, 1960s, and 1970s, the Cave featured a wealth of American and Canadian talent. The Righteous Brothers, the Supremes, Duke Ellington, Eric Burdon and the Animals, and James Brown, to name a few, played there. Today nothing is listed in the Vancouver city directory for the 626 Hornby Street location just west of Georgia, but the HSBC bank office tower occupies the place where that address used to be. In the area is the entrance to the underground parking lot of the HSBC building — a cave of a different kind, perhaps.

## The Esquire Show Bar

One of Montreal's hottest spots in the 1960s for jazz and blues musicians. Some of the biggest names in the biz, such as Wilson Pickett, performed there. Today, the Esquire's old Stanley Street location, just south of Ste-Catherine, houses a strip club called Chez Paree.

 ## The Hawk's Nest

Upstairs from the equally legendary Le Coq d'Or on the Yonge Street strip in Toronto, this rocking club was home to Rompin' Ronnie Hawkins and his many band members. Dancing go-go girls and some of the greatest music from the 1960s were featured here. These days the 333 Yonge Street address is home to the main HMV music store in Toronto.

**They Said It!**

On the Cave: "It was my dream to perform in the club one day, and I eventually did in the early 70s. It closed down a few years later as nightclubs became less in vogue but people still talk about the Cave and remember the multitude of wonderful performers who came through. In my opinion, there hasn't been a place since that offers the same variety and quality of good entertainment."

*– Susan Jacks, multi-hit singer with The Poppy Family and as a soloist.*

 ## Le Hibou

Le Hibou, Ottawa's legendary Ottawa coffee house, is an integral part of Canadian folk music history. And according to one of its former owners, the club played a role in the formation of one of America's supergroups.

Le Hibou opened in 1961 on the second floor of a two-storey house at 544 Rideau Street, serving coffee and French pastries to customers who took part in chess tournaments, poetry readings, and hootenannies. A year later, co-owner Denis Faulkner moved the club to a commercial building at 248 Bank Street above a paint store where there was more space for entertainment and room to serve more elaborate meals.

It remained there for three years before moving to 521 Sussex Drive, a short stroll east of the Parliament Buildings.

Before Le Hibou closed in 1975, the Sussex Drive location was the gathering place for live music in Ottawa and attracted some of Canada's folk greats, including Joni Mitchell,

Ian and Sylvia, Gordon Lightfoot, and Buffy St. Marie. Many American music legends, including John Prine, T-Bone Walker, and Ritchie Havens, also performed at the club.

**They Said It!**

On Le Hibou: "Before The Beatles there were several young fellas at high school who had long hair, not real long, just slightly over the ears. One of the lads was Sandy Crawley, a folkie guitarist. He was also responsible for DRAGGING me to the Le Hibou Coffee House on Bank Street in Ottawa. It changed my life forever, not the drugs, but the music, with lyrics that told stories, none of this moon in June stuff. It was serious."

*— Richard Patterson, drummer,*
*The Esquires and 3's A Crowd*

Harvey Glatt, who co-owned Le Hibou when it was located on Bank Street and Sussex Drive, says Ottawa and Le Hibou were at the genesis of American band Crosby, Stills and Nash.

In 1966, Graham Nash and his English pop group the Hollies were appearing at the Capitol Theatre in Ottawa. After their show, Glatt took Nash to Le Hibou, where Joni Mitchell was performing. Later, Glatt, Nash, and Bruce Cockburn visited Mitchell at her Château Laurier hotel room, where the three musicians talked into the night and swapped songs.

"It was clear something was happening between Graham and Joni … there were sparks, so Bruce and I left," recalled Glatt.

Shortly after, Nash left the Hollies, moved to California, and continued his relationship with Mitchell, who introduced him to her good friend David Crosby. Nash and former Byrds member Crosby hit it off, and the rest is history.

"That's how it all started for Crosby, Stills and Nash," said Glatt.

Le Hibou's original Rideau Street location is now an Indian restaurant. The Bank Street venue is a hairdressing salon above a submarine sandwich outlet, and the Sussex Drive location is a clothing store.

##  The Riverboat

Located at 134 Yorkville Avenue in Toronto, the Riverboat was arguably the best-known coffeehouse in Canada. During its years of operation from 1964 to the late 1970s, the Riverboat featured a who's who of folk music stars, including Gordon Lightfoot, Bruce Cockburn, Joni Mitchell, and Murray McLauchlan. Legend has it that Mitchell's "Clouds" and Phil

Ochs's "Changes" were composed in the club's backroom.

The Riverboat is now long gone and is the site of the Hazelton Hotel and Private Residences, 18 condominium units above a five-star hotel. Before construction began in October 2004, this location was a series of brownstone buildings made up mainly of shops.

#  The River Heights Community Club

Located on Grosvenor Avenue at Oak Street in the upper-middle-class south Winnipeg neighbourhood of River Heights, this popular music venue opened in the early 1950s and served as a weekend dance hall until the late 1970s.

It was one of about 50 community clubs throughout the city but was seen as the "plum gig" for budding and big-time acts, said John Einarson, a Winnipeg author, broadcaster, and music historian.

Marquis events were always held on Saturdays, often featuring bands like Chad Allan & the Reflections (later The Guess Who, who also performed at River Heights), The Deverons with Burton Cummings, The Fifth, The Sugar & Spice, Neil Young & the Squires, and Gettysbyrg Address.

Lineups often formed at five o'clock for a dance that would start three hours later, hosted by such popular deejays as Doc Steen, Ron Legge, Jim Christie, and Bob Burns, host of the TV program *Teen Dance Party*.

**They Said It!**

On the Riverboat: "It's why I'm in Toronto to this day. [Music producer and Riverboat manager] Bernie Fielder hired us sight unseen and we came in '65 to play the Riverboat, we got the bug, went home, got our stuff and that was it. The Riverboat in this region was the Mecca."

*– Brent Titcomb, folksinger and actor*

**They Said It!**

On Neil Young performing at the River Heights Community Club: "The Squires were one of the most popular bands at River Heights. Neil didn't move around much on stage. His best friend was his amplifier, which he kept close by ... you could tell Neil had confidence in himself as a musician. It wasn't ego or contrived, he was very into the music."

*– Diane Halter, a member of the teen council that booked dances at the River Heights Community Club (taken from* Neil Young: Don't Be Denied – The Canadian Years *by John Einarson.)*

The club's capacity was 400 people but more than 500 sweaty teens would often be shoe-horned into the place.

The club also had indoor and outdoor hockey rinks, soccer pitches, baseball diamonds, a football field, and a playground area.

Still in operation today as the River Heights Community Centre, the facility is used for socials and pre-teen dances and a variety of other community-related activities.

##  Smales Pace

Known in its final incarnation as the Change of Pace, the renowned folk club in London, Ontario, began inauspiciously in the early 1970s as Smales Pace in a converted Bell Canada garage at 436 Clarence Street between Dundas Street and Queens Avenue. Founded by John Smale, the Pace quickly developed a reputation for entertainment and fine food. Several folk musicians such as Stan Rogers, David Wiffen, Doug McArthur, David Bradstreet, and others made their mark there. Rogers was supposed to have written a few songs at the club. In 1976, Smales Pace moved to an upstairs location at 355 Talbot Street, eventually modifying its name to Change of Pace. As of 2009 the original location was the site of Nooner's restaurant while the Talbot Street spot was a beauty salon.

### They Said It!

On Smales: "I was no stranger to intimate, outspoken audiences. But Smales Pace was special. The performers were always treated to appreciative audiences and for that, we would have virtually played for nothing, but we always were paid well. It was like coming home each time I was privileged to play there."

— *David Bradstreet,*
*Juno Award–winning*
*singer-songwriter*

# CHAPTER 24
# The Urban Landscape: Canada's Cities

 CITY SAMPLER

- The city of Halifax not only boasts Canada's first newspaper, post office, and Protestant church, but also has the largest concentration of bars and nightclubs per capita than any other city in the country. And Halifax harbour is the second largest natural ice free harbour in the world.

- Quebec City holds the distinction of building the first covered ice rink in the world in 1852. Natural ice was used in these early arenas; artificial ice rinks started in British Columbia in 1911–12.

**City BITE!**

In 1785, Fleury Mesplet published the first edition of the *Montreal Gazette*, the oldest newspaper still in existence in Canada.

- The first Canadian city to have electric street lighting was Hamilton, Ontario, home of Canada's steel industry. Public electric lights were installed there in 1883, one year before Montreal and Toronto got them.

- During the First World War, the Ontario community of Berlin changed its name to Kitchener when the loyalty of its large German-Canadian population was questioned. The new moniker was in honour of Lord Horatio Kitchener, a British war hero who at the start of the war was appointed Secretary for War by the British government. Kitchener died in 1916 when his ship was sunk.

**They Said It!**

"Toronto is a kind of New York operated by the Swiss."

– Peter Ustinov, English actor and writer

- Kingston, Ontario, was first known as King's Town. Following the American Revolution in 1785, an influx of United Empire Loyalists settled in what was then known as Cataraqui. They renamed it King's Town, which eventually evolved to Kingston. It officially became a town in 1838, and in 1841 it served as the first capital of the United Canadas.

 **SNAPSHOT**

**Ten Biggest Cities by Population in 1901**

| | | |
|---|---|---|
| 1. | Montreal | 266,826 |
| 2. | Toronto | 207,971 |
| 3. | Quebec City | 68,834 |
| 4. | Ottawa | 59,902 |
| 5. | Hamilton | 52,550 |
| 6. | Winnipeg | 42,336 |
| 7. | Halifax | 40,787 |
| 8. | Saint John | 40,711 |
| 9. | London | 37,983 |
| 10. | Vancouver | 26,196 |

*Statistics Canada*

 **SNAPSHOT**

**Ten Biggest Cities by Population in 2007**

| | | |
|---|---|---|
| 1. | Toronto | 5,509,874 |
| 2. | Montreal | 3,695,790 |
| 3. | Vancouver | 2,285,893 |
| 4. | Ottawa | 1,168,788 |
| 5. | Calgary | 1,139,126 |
| 6. | Edmonton | 1,081,275 |
| 7. | Quebec City | 728,924 |
| 8. | Hamilton | 720,426 |
| 9. | Winnipeg | 712,671 |
| 10. | London | 469,714 |

*Statistics Canada*

- Melville, Saskatchewan, 130 kilometres northeast of Regina, was named after Sir Charles Melville Hays, a former president of the Grand Trunk Pacific Railway who died aboard the *Titanic* when it sunk near Newfoundland in April 1912.

- Lethbridge, Alberta, was first called Fort Whoop-Up by European settlers and then renamed Coal Banks after the discovery of the mineral of the same name in the area. The town boomed with the opening of the North Western Coal and Navigation Company and was renamed in 1885 in honour of the firm's president, William Lethbridge.

- Edmonton was the first city in North America with a population under 1 million to build a light rapid transit system, which opened to the public in April 1978.

- The origin of the name "Calgary" seems to be in dispute. While scholars agree that it's a Gaelic word, some say it means "bay farm," others argue that it means "clear running water," while still others contend that it's defined as "the haven by the wall."

- Alert, a small village in Nunavut, is the most northerly permanent settlement in the world. It was set up as a weather station in 1950 and was taken over by the military in 1958.

- Canada's overall population density is about 3.2 people per square kilometre, but more than 85 percent of Canadians live within a 300-kilometre strip along the Canada-United States border. In this area, the density is approximately 25 persons per square kilometre, about the same as in the U.S.

 Q AND A

**Q: If Toronto's CN Tower were to fall over, how far would it reach?**

**A:** Unless you live within its shadow, you probably don't have to cower in fear. However, the world's second-largest freestanding structure (surpassed in 2007 by the Burj Dubai in Dubai, United Arab Emirates) rises 1,815 feet, 5 inches (553.3 metres), or about one-third of a mile, above downtown Toronto near the corner of Front and John streets.

Photo by Mark Kearney.

**Where would it fall?**

The tower was built with reinforced steel and concrete to withstand winds of more than 200 miles per hour. If it ever did topple over to the south, however, it would crash through the Gardiner Expressway and reach into Lake Ontario. If it fell north, it would squash the city's Convention Centre and fall about four city blocks to King Street. Toppling east, it would cover about three and a half blocks, almost touching Union Station, while pitching over to the west the tower would slice a path through the Rogers Centre, home to Major League Baseball's Toronto Blue Jays and the Canadian Football League's Toronto Argonauts and reach to Spadina Avenue.

It is not likely to happen, but the scenario does make a good plot for a trashy B-movie horror flick.

**Q:** *Why is someone from Calgary called a Calgarian? Is there a formula that determines how to refer to a resident of a particular town or city?*

**A:** In his book *Speaking Canadian English* (1970), lawyer and linguist Mark M. Orkin gives some general rules governing the designation of a community's residents.

Orkin's formula is as follows:

If the name ends in *a*, add an *n*. That makes an Ottawa resident an Ottawan. If the name of your city ends in *ia*, also add an *n*. An Orillia resident is an Orillian. If the name ends in a *y*, like Calgary, for instance, change the *y* to an *i*, add *an* and become a Calgarian.

If a community's name ends in *on*, add *ian*. Edmonton folks, then, are Edmontonians. If the name ends in *outh*, such as Dartmouth, add *ian*, for Dartmouthian. If a name ends with a vowel other than *a*, add *ite*, sometimes with a hyphen, sometimes without; so we have Barrie-ites and Nanaimoites. And if a name ends with a consonant, in some cases, add *er*, to make Londoner. In other cases add *ite*, such as in Windsorite or Markhamite.

There are, of course, exceptions. People in Oakville, for example, probably refer to themselves as Oakvillians, says a spokesperson for the town. Toronto ends in a vowel other than an *a*, but Toronto residents are known as Torontonians, not Torontoites. And the residents of Woodstock, Ontario, who should be called Woodstockers or Woodstockites according to Orkin's formula, are in reality known as Woodstonians. And people from Halifax are called Haligonians.

# CHAPTER 25
# Cash and Carry: Business, Finance, and Trade

 MONETARY MILESTONES OF THE 20TH CENTURY

1. **1908:** A branch of the Royal Mint was established in Ottawa. For the first time Canada's official coinage was struck in Canada.

2. **1911:** The last Dominion of Canada four-dollar notes were issued. They were replaced by Dominion of Canada five-dollar notes in 1912. Legislation was passed authorizing the striking of the silver dollar. Canada's first dollar coin and two patterns for 1911 dollars were struck in silver.

3. **1912–1914:** The mint struck the first decimal gold coins for general circulation. They were five-dollar and ten-dollar coins.

4. **1914:** Canada went off the gold standard. This meant Canadian bank notes were no longer redeemable for gold.

5. **1920:** The size of the cent was reduced from 25.4 millimetres to 19.05 millimetres in diameter.

6. **1922:** The mint replaced the small, inconvenient silver five-cent piece with one made out of nickel. These quickly became known as "nickels."

7. **1931:** The mint became the Royal Canadian Mint rather than a branch of the Royal Mint in England. The last twenty-five-cent note or "shinplaster" was issued for circulation.

8. **1935:** On March 11, 1935, the Bank of Canada opened with a mandate to be the sole issuer of Canadian bank notes. The first issue of bank notes was unilingual English or French. The mint struck Canada's first silver dollar to commemorate King George V's silver jubilee and also issued a $25 note to commemorate the occasion.

9.  **1937:** Bank of Canada notes became bilingual.

10. **1968:** The rising price of silver forced the mint to replace the 10-, 25-, 50-cent pieces and the dollar coin with coins made out of nickel.

11. **1989:** The Bank of Canada issues the last one-dollar notes on June 30. (The Canadian one-dollar coin, commonly called the Loonie, had been introduced in 1987.)

12. **1996:** The two-dollar note is withdrawn and replaced on February 19 by a bi-metallic coin consisting of an outer ring made out of nickel and an inner core made of aluminum-bronze.

> **They Said It!**
>
> "Canadian money is also called the loonie. How can you take an economic crisis seriously?"
>
> —*comedian Robin Williams*

*List prepared by J. Graham Esler, former chief curator and head of the Currency Museum, Bank of Canada.*

#  TRADE TRENDS

## Canada's Eight Leading Trade Partners in 1902

1.  United States $192 million

2.  Great Britain $166.5 million

3.  Germany $13.5 million

4.  France $8 million

5.  West Indies $5.4 million

6.  Belgium $4.1 million

7. Newfoundland $3.5 million

8. South America $3.4 million
(China was ninth with $2.5 million)

# Canada's Eight Leading Trade Partners in 1997

1. United States $245 billion

2. Japan $11 billion

3. United Kingdom $3.8 billion

4. South Korea $2.9 billion

5. Germany $2.7 billion

6. People's Republic of China $2.37 billion

7. Hong Kong $1.7 billion

8. France $1.67 billion

# Canada's Eight Leading Trade Partners in 2007

1. United States $574.6 billion

2. China $47.6 billion

3. Japan $24.6 billion

4. United Kingdom $24.4 billion

5. Mexico $22.1 billion

6. Norway $9.0 billion

7. The Netherlands $5.8 billion

8. India $3.8 billion

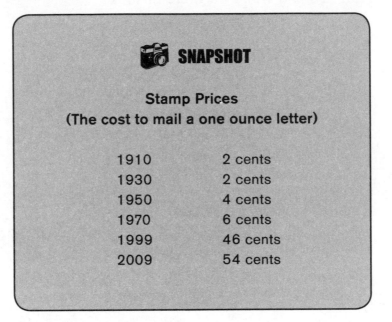

**📷 SNAPSHOT**

**Stamp Prices**
**(The cost to mail a one ounce letter)**

| 1910 | 2 cents |
|------|---------|
| 1930 | 2 cents |
| 1950 | 4 cents |
| 1970 | 6 cents |
| 1999 | 46 cents |
| 2009 | 54 cents |

 **BIZ QUIZ**

1. In the early 1900s, J.J. McLaughlin, a member of Oshawa, Ontario's famous automobile family, made a name for himself outside of the car industry. Did he:

   a) invent and manufacture Canada Dry Ginger Ale
   b) play for the Toronto Maple Leafs

      c) represent Oshawa in the House of Commons

      d) marry an American movie star

2.     Whose picture is featured on the now-defunct $1,000 bill?

3.     Air Canada was the first North American airline to ban *this* from its flights in 1986. What was it?

      a) firearms in baggage

      b) metal cutlery

      c) smoking

      d) music played without headphones

4.     CCM, once an automobile manufacturer, is the world's leading maker of hockey equipment. What do the initials CCM stand for?

      a) Canada Cycle and Motor Company

      b) Canadian Car Manufacturing Limited

      c) Cycles Cars and Motors Limited

5.     The first recorded distillery in Canada was set up in what city in 1769?

      a) Quebec City

      b) Montreal

      c) Halifax

      d) Saint John

      e) Summerside

**6.** What was hockey player and budding doughnut magnate Tim Horton's first business venture?

       a) a service station and car dealership
       b) a hockey school
       c) a chain of pizza outlets
       d) a men's clothing store

**7.** Who is the elderly character pictured on Canadian Tire money?

       a) Sandy McTire
       b) Scotty Canadian
       c) Douglas MacAuto
       d) Thomas O'Tool

➡ **Answers on page 370**

### Biz BITE!

The first financial institution in Canada to have an operational automated banking machine was the Sherwood Credit Union in Regina. The year: 1977.

# CANADA TIMELINE

**1497**    Italian-born navigator John Cabot reaches the coasts of Newfoundland and Cape Breton.

**1534**    Sailing for France, Jacques Cartier explores the St. Lawrence River and claims the shores of the Gulf of St. Lawrence for his country.

**1583**    Newfoundland becomes England's first overseas colony.

**1608**    Quebec City founded by Samuel de Champlain.

**1627**    Company of New France established to govern and exploit New France, France's North American colonies.

**1642**    Montreal founded by the French.

**1670**    Hudson's Bay Company is established by London traders.

**1756**    Seven Years' War begins between New France and the larger and economically-stronger British colonies. After early French successes, the settlement of Quebec City falls in 1759 and the British advance on Montreal.

**1763**    Britain acquires all French colonies east of the Mississippi River, including New France, under the Treaty of Paris. The new British colony is named Quebec.

**1774**    The Quebec Act recognizes the French language and the Roman Catholic religion in the colony.

**1775** The American Revolution begins. Americans invade Quebec but are eventually repulsed.

**1776** Loyalist refugees from the American War of Independence settle in Nova Scotia, Prince Edward Island, Quebec, and Ontario.

**1783** Treaty of Paris ends the American Revolution. Fur traders in Montreal set up the North West Company. The company builds up a network of trading posts across the west and north and its expeditions reach the Pacific coast.

**1791** Quebec is divided into Lower Canada (today's Quebec) and Upper Canada (today's Ontario).

**1812** The War of 1812 begins between the United States and Britain largely over the effects on the United States of British blockades of French ports. Action includes naval battles in the Great Lakes and a U.S. attack on York (now Toronto). But the United States fails to accomplish its plans to conquer Canada. The war ends in December 1814, although one last battle is fought in January 1815 at New Orleans.

**1821** Hudson's Bay Company and North West Company merge after years of rivalry descend into bloodshed.

**1837** Armed rebellions in Upper and Lower Canada erupt, caused by discontent with the ruling elites, poverty, and social divisions. Rebellions continue into 1838.

**1841** Formation of the United Province of Canada reunites Canada East (Lower) and Canada West (Upper).

**1867** British North America Act unites Ontario, Quebec, Nova Scotia, and New Brunswick in the Dominion of Canada. The Conservative Party's John A. Macdonald becomes Canada's first prime minister.

**1869**   Red River Rebellion led by Louis Riel begins in what will become Manitoba. The following year Colonel Garnet Wolseley puts down the rebellion and Riel flees.

**1870**   Louis Riel's rebellion leads to Manitoba becoming the fifth Canadian province, followed by British Columbia (1873) and Prince Edward Island (1873).

**1885**   The Last Spike is driven, signifying the completion of the Canadian Pacific Railway, which actually opens for business in June 1886. North-West Rebellion led by the Métis Louis Riel and Gabriel Dumont and Native chiefs such as Poundmaker breaks out and is quickly suppressed by the newly formed North-West Mounted Police (later the Royal Canadian Mounted Police) and army and militia units.

**1898**   Gold rush along the upper Yukon River; Yukon Territory given separate status.

**1899**   Boer War between Britain and the Boers, or Afrikaners, in South Africa begins, ending in 1902. Canada plays a major part.

**1905**   Alberta and Saskatchewan become the eight and ninth provinces of Canada.

**1914**   Outbreak of the First World War, which lasts until 1918. Canada fights on the side of Britain and France (and later the Americans).

**1917**   Conscription riots in Quebec as French Canadians protest the war draft.

**1919**   Winnipeg General Strike, caused by massive unemployment and inflation after the First World War.

**1931**   Statute of Westminster grants British dominions complete autonomy.

**1939**   Outbreak of the Second World War, which lasts until 1945.

**1945**     Canada becomes a charter member of the United Nations.

**1949**     Canada becomes a founding member of the North Atlantic Treaty Organization (NATO). Newfoundland, until then a British dominion, becomes the tenth Canadian province.

**1950**     War breaks out between North and South Korea. Canadian forces participate in the United Nations war effort. War ends in 1953.

**1959**     A.V. Roe's Avro Arrow jet fighter cancelled by Prime Minister John Diefenbaker's Progressive Conservative government.

**1960**     Canadian Bill of Rights enacted by Prime Minister Diefenbaker's government.

**1965**     The current Canadian flag is adopted by Prime Minister Lester B. Pearson's Liberal government.

**1967**     Expo 67 in Montreal invigorates Canadian national identity. French president Charles de Gaulle visits the world's fair and declares *"Vive le Quebec libre"* ("Long live free Quebec").

**1968**     "Trudeaumania" seizes Canada as Pierre Elliott Trudeau of the Liberal Party wins the federal election. Parti Québécois is formed to push for complete independence of Quebec.

**1970**     Members of a radical Quebec separatist group, the Front de libération du Québec, kidnap James Cross, a British trade official, and murder Pierre Laporte, a Quebec cabinet minister.

**1976**     Parti Québécois wins election in Quebec.

**1980**     A referendum on the separation of Quebec is defeated.

**1982**     The United Kingdom transfers final legal powers over Canada. Canada is now completely free. The country adopts its new Constitution, which includes a Charter of Rights, though Quebec refuses to be part of the Constitution.

**1984**     Pierre Trudeau retires. The Progressive Conservative Party wins under Brian Mulroney. Mulroney realigns foreign policy toward Europe and the United States.

**1985**     Three hundred and twenty-nine people, including 280 Canadians, are killed in a bomb attack on an Air India jet travelling between Montreal and London, England.

**1989**     Canada and the United States agree to establish free trade.

**1990**     Meech Lake Accord, an attempt to bring Quebec back into the constitutional fold, is defeated.

**1991**     Canadian forces participate in the Gulf War, following Iraq's invasion of Kuwait.

**1992**     Canada, the United States, and Mexico finalize the terms of the North American Free Trade Agreement (NAFTA). Charlottetown Accord, another attempt to bring Quebec into the constitutional fold, is defeated.

**1993**     Brian Mulroney resigns as leader of the Progressive Conservatives in February but remains prime minister until June. He is succeeded by Kim Campbell, Canada's first female prime minister. The Canadian Parliament ratifies NAFTA. Campbell calls an election in October, but her party suffers a humiliating defeat, winning only two seats when previously it had held 169. Campbell resigns. Jean Chrétien of the Liberals becomes prime minister.

**1995**     A referendum in Quebec rejects independence by a margin of only 1 percent.

**1997**     Jean Chrétien is re-elected prime minister with a reduced majority.

**1998**     The Canadian Supreme Court rules that if Quebec votes to secede it can only carry out separation with the federal government's consent. For its part the federal government is obliged to negotiate on secession if a majority of Quebec's citizens chooses separation.

**1999**     The Territory of Nunavut is formed in Canada's Far North. It is the first territory in Canada to have a majority indigenous population.

**2000**     Jean Chrétien is again elected prime minister. His Liberal Party picks up votes in Quebec, weakening support for Quebec separatists.

**2001**     The leaders of countries from across the Americas meet in Canada at the Summit of the Americas. They reaffirm their commitment to setting up the world's largest free trade zone by 2005. After the terrorist attacks on the World Trade Center and the U.S. Pentagon, the United States invades Afghanistan, and Canada soon joins the NATO mission there, at first with special operations forces and later with regular troops.

**2003**     Canada opts not to join the U.S.-led coalition against Iraq. Toronto is hit by the biggest outbreak of the flu-like SARS virus outside Asia. The Liberal Party beats the Parti Québécois in provincial elections in Quebec, ending nine years of rule by the pro-independence party. The biggest power cut in North American history shuts down Toronto, Ottawa, and other parts of Ontario as well as cities in the United States. Former finance minister Paul Martin is sworn in as prime minister. Chrétien retires after a decade in office.

**2004**     Scandal erupts over the misuse of Liberal Party government money intended for advertising and sponsorship. Prime Minister Paul Martin orders an inquiry. Martin is returned to power in the general elections, but his Liberal Party is stripped of its majority.

**2005**     Paul Martin's Liberal government wins a confidence motion in parliament by just one vote. The Canadian Senate approves a bill to legalize same-sex marriages. Canada has a dispute with Denmark over an uninhabited Arctic Ocean island. A commission set up to investigate the scandal involving misspent government money exonerates Prime Minister Martin but criticizes his predecessor Jean Chrétien. Martin's minority Liberal government is brought down in a no confidence vote.

**2006**    Stephen Harper's Conservatives defeat Paul Martin in the general election, ending 12 years of Liberal government. MPs vote by a narrow margin to extend Canada's military deployment in Afghanistan until 2009. Later the mission is extended until 2011. In a major anti-terrorist operation, 17 people are arrested in Toronto on suspicion of planning attacks. Parliament agrees that the Québécois should be considered a "nation" within Canada.

**2008**    The Canadian government apologizes for its earlier policy of forcing aboriginal children to attend boarding schools aimed at assimilating them. Most of the schools were closed in the 1970s. The Conservatives improve their standing in the general election but still fall short of gaining an overall majority.

**2009**    The Canadian economy, like its counterparts around the globe, is hobbled by a recession that cost the country more than 130,000 jobs in the first three months of the year, severely reduced manufacturing activity and new home construction and saw the TSE Composite Index at times tumble below 8,000 points. Many Canadians' retirement savings were in tatters. On a bright note, interest rates were at record lows, with the prime rate early in the year sitting at 2.5 percent and five-year closed mortgages hovering around the 4 percent range. The federal government unveiled a $40 billion economic recovery package designed to deal primarily with job losses.

# QUIZ ANSWERS

## CHAPTER 1: BLAST FROM THE PAST

### Answers to History Quiz: The Red and White Forever

1. c) 1925, when a committee of the Privy Council began to research possible designs for a national flag but never completed its work.

2. The Union Jack.

3. b) The flags were flown upside down.

4. b) Lawren Harris.

5. b) Royal Canadian Legion.

6. c) three.

7. d) all of the above.

8. e) all of the above.

9. Jean Chrétien, on February 15, 1996.

10. c) Two points were removed from the base of the maple leaf, reducing the number of points to 11 from 13.

11. d) He was dean of the arts at Royal Military College.

12. d) The governor general's standard.

13. a) The Canadian flag, and c) the Red Ensign.

14. b) A flag no longer suitable for use should be destroyed "in a dignified way by burning it privately," according to the Department of Canadian Heritage.

15. b) Ontario, Manitoba, British Columbia, and Newfoundland, which has a stylized version of the Union Jack.

16. a) The national coat of arms, and b) the Great Seal of Canada.

# CHAPTER 4: CAN CON CULTURE: LITERATURE AND THE ARTS

## Answers to Literary Quiz

1. c) Service in the 1942 film *The Spoilers*.

2. b) Margaret Atwood. She has only won twice; for *The Handmaid's Tale*, and for *The Circle Game*.

3. b) *The Manticore*.

4. Margaret Laurence.

5. a) Manawaka.

6. b) *Fraggle Rock*.

7. Margaret Atwood, George Bowering, Michael Ondaatje.

8. Mavis Gallant.

9. *The Acrobats*, published in 1954.

10. d) three.

11. e) all of them.

12. c) carpentry.

# CHAPTER 5: CELEBRATING, CANADIAN STYLE

## Answers to Labour Day Quiz

1.  b) 12.

2.  c) Toronto, partly as a demonstration demanding the release of union leaders who had been imprisoned for striking to gain a nine-hour working day. A few months later a similar parade took place in Ottawa.

3.  a) iii
    b) iv
    c) i
    d) ii

4.  True. James S. Woodsworth, a Manitoba Labour MP, put forth a motion in 1923 to disband the RCMP. The motion failed but several politicians were unhappy with the Mounties at the time, blaming them for the violence in the 1919 strike.

5.  b) 1961.

6.  The Rand Formula. It was named for a decision handed down on January 26, 1946 by Mr. Justice Ivan Rand of the Supreme Court of Canada while he was arbitrating a strike at Windsor, Ontario, the Ford of Canada strike.

7.  d) National Union of Public and General Employees, a family of 12 component unions that is the second largest union in Canada. Most of NUPGE's 340,000 members deliver public services of every kind to the citizens of their home provinces.

8. c) White moved to Canada from Ireland at age 14, and while working at a wood factory in the southwestern Ontario city of Woodstock he became a member of the United Auto Workers union. Eventually he become UAW Director for Canada and in 1985 was acclaimed president of Canadian Auto Workers-Canada after Canadian autoworkers pulled out of the UAW.

## Answers to Victoria Day Quiz

1. c) John Labatt. According to company history, Labatt introduced the idea while he was a councillor in London, Ontario, and other cities followed suit until it became a national celebration.

2. a) Calgary, at the Calgary Stampede, says Victoria parade chairman Ron Butlin. Victoria's 2009 event was to be the 111th consecutive Victoria Day parade and would take about two hours to pass a given point.

3. b) nine. Her eldest son later became King Edward VII.

4. d) The Kinks scored big with "Victoria" in March 1970.

5. a) Drina. Her name was Alexandrina Victoria.

6. False. Ricketts, a 17-year-old, who received his medal in 1918 for volunteering to run 100 yards across a fire-swept open field for ammunition and supplies before helping to capture eight guns and eight Germans, was from Newfoundland.

**7.** b) William IV, her uncle.

**8.** c) Laurier.

**9.** b) 1952.

## Answers to Rideau Canal Quiz

**1.** Skating on the canal. The NCC opened the Rideau Canal Skateway in January 1971. The first Winterlude was held in 1979.

**2.** e) all of them.

**3.** d) one metre in most areas; four metres deep at Dows Lake.

**4.** c) Mr. Fullerton was Chairman of the NCC from 1969 to 1973.

**5.** d) 25 centimetres. In a very cold winter, the ice can be as thick as 90 centimetres.

**6.** The Senators Alumni beat the Montreal Canadiens Alumni 14–10 in front of 1,500 fans.

**7.** a) The canal was closed to the public from 7:30 a.m. to 10:00 a.m. on February 21, 2004, when the NCC and the Ottawa Senators Hockey Club presented the Senators Hockey Day in the Capital event, as part of Hockey Day in Canada. The event saw more than 1,000 young hockey players from Canada's Capital Region play 110 simultaneous shinny hockey games.

8. c) 90.

9. Lansdowne Park is named after Sir Henry Charles Keith Petty-Fitzmaurice, fifth Marquess of Lansdowne, who was Canada's governor general from 1883–1888. Prior to his appointment as governor general, Lansdowne was a Liberal member of parliament in Britain.

10. a) beavertails.
    b) ice hogs.
    c) toques.
    d) speed skates.

# Answers to Thanksgiving Quiz

1. a) Armistice Day. From 1921 to 1930, the Armistice Day Act provided that Thanksgiving would be observed on Armistice Day, which was fixed by statute on the Monday of the week in which November 11 fell. Armistice Day was later renamed Remembrance Day.

2. c) Martin Frobisher in 1578 in what is now Newfoundland.

3.  b) April 15, 1872, to celebrate the recovery of The Prince of Wales (later King Edward VII) from a serious illness.

4.  Thursday.

5.  c) the potato was considered by many Europeans to be poisonous.

6.  b) The Cornucopia originated in ancient Greece. The original was a curved goat's horn filled to overflowing with fruit and grain. It symbolizes the horn possessed by Zeus's nurse, the Greek nymph Amalthaea, which could be filled with whatever the owner wished.

7.  True.

8.  All are varieties of turkey.

9.  a) a general election was held on the second Monday of October.

10.  Louis St. Laurent.

11.  c) 86 percent, says the Canadian Turkey Marketing Agency.

12.  d) all of the above. The name pumpkin originated from the Greek word *pepon*, which the French nasalized into *pompon*. The English changed *pompon* to *pumpion* and American colonists eventually changed *pumpion* into *pumpkin*.

## CHAPTER 6: COLOURFUL CANUCKS
## THE FAMOUS AND THE INFAMOUS

### Answers to Famous Canadians Quiz

1. Yousuf Karsh.

2. Cabot did, in 1497 (Cartier arrived in 1534, de Champlain in 1604).

3. True. It was invented by Louise Poirier.

4. The Marathon of Hope.

5. c) She was the first Canadian woman to swim the English Channel.

6. b) They were the first to drive across Canada. Although some parts of the country didn't even have roads then, the two made the trip in 52 days.

7. Sitting Bull.

8. b) Herbert.

9. b) Carnegie.

10. True.

# CHAPTER 10: GREAT WHITE NORTH

## Answers to Summer Quiz

1. d) Wasaga Beach, with 14 kilometres of sand.

2. True.

3. Lighthouse.

4. False. Several swimmers have completed the crossing, the first being Pat Budny in August 1975.

5. c) The highest temperature recorded in Canada was in Saskatchewan in July 1937, when the mercury hit 45 degrees Celsius in Midale and Yellowgrass in the southern part of the province.

6. Superior, Huron, Michigan, Erie, Ontario.

7. Prince Edward Island.

8. b) Halifax-Dartmouth in 1969.

9. True. Fifty-seven kinds of mosquitoes to be exact.

10. Hailstone. The largest one ever documented in Canada fell at Cedoux in August 1973. It weighed 290 grams and measured 114 millimetres across – about the size of a large grapefruit.

11. c) Operating a vehicle with just one tire under inflated by eight PSI can reduce the life of the tire by 15,000 kilometres and

can increase the vehicle's fuel consumption by 4 percent, says Transport Canada.

## Answers to Six to Savour Quiz

1. False. There are more than 100 species.

2. d) It was called Emerald Lake because of its greenish colour.

3. a) Ivy Lea Bridge. It does cross into the U.S. but near Gananoque.

4. b) geologist.

5. a) caribou b) badger c) coyote d) walleye

6. A blizzard.

## Answers to Coast to Coast Quiz

1. True. Mount Logan, at 5,959 metres, is Canada's highest peak.

2.   d) no one

3.   Saskatchewan and Alberta.

4.   a) Made entirely from wood, the Chateau Montebello was built using 10,000 logs from British Columbia; 500,000 hand-slit cedar roof shakes; 53 miles of plumbing and heating pipes; and 103.5 miles of wooden moulding. It is also known as the world's largest cabin.

5.   The Mackenzie, which flows 4,241 kilometres through the Northwest Territories. The St. Lawrence is 3,058 kilometres long.

## CHAPTER 11: HOLLYWOOD NORTH

### Answers to Academy Awards Quiz

1.   Manitoba.

2.   Angelica Huston.

3.   b) 1941 for the documentary *Churchill's Island*.

4.   False. Denys Arcand's *The Barbarian Invasions* won in 2004.

5.   d) Cameron.

6.   *South Park: Bigger, Louder and Uncut.*

7.   c) *Mon oncle Antoine.*

8.   *Million Dollar Baby*, directed by Clint Eastwood and *Crash*, which he co-wrote and directed himself. He did not, however, pick up the statue for Best Director, which went to Ang Lee for *Brokeback Mountain*.

## CHAPTER 12: HOW WE GET AROUND

### Answers to Quiz: You Auto Know

1. b) Imperial Oil.

2. True.

3. d) He made the trip in three hours and 20 minutes.

4. c) Winnipeg hosted Canada's first automobile race in 1901.

5. a) He was NASCAR's rookie of the year in 1974.

6. b) "Keeps pecking."

7. The Icefields Parkway.

8. False. Quebec's DOH was created in 1914. Ontario followed suit in 1916.

9. c) On July 3, 1991, the company sold its first shares to Canadians.

10. Thunderbird.

## CHAPTER 15: MY GENERATION FROM BOOMERS TO GEN X

## Answers to Quiz 1: The 1980s

1. *Family Ties.*

2. i) Quiche ii) Bonfire iii) Brief iv) Present.

3. a) Ferraro, who was the first woman nominated for that position by a major party.

4. c) *Places in the Heart.* She won Best Actress in 1979 for *Norma Rae.*

5. d) The 49ers won in 1982, 1985, and 1989.

6. e) Madonna.

7. Chrysler. The model Sinatra promoted was the Imperial.

8. c) 1986.

9. Cabbage Patch Dolls.

10. d) *Cats.* Music by Andrew Lloyd Webber and based on the poetry of T.S. Eliot.

11. The American hockey team's gold-medal win in February 1980 at Lake Placid, New York. Seeded seventh out of 12, the U.S. team knocked off the heavily favoured Soviet Union in the semi-finals before beating Finland 4-2 in the final.

**12.** b) *The Color Purple.*

**Scoring:**

| | |
|---|---|
| Ten and above – | Like, totally awesome |
| Five to nine – | Bitchin', fer sure |
| Under five – | Gag me |

## Answers to Quiz 2: The Oscar/Grammy Quiz

**1.** d) Simon and Garfunkel.

**2.** b) *On The Waterfront.* He accepted his award that time.

**3.** True.

**4.** c) Randy Traywick. However, in the early 1980s his stage name was Randy Ray, before he changed it to Randy Travis.

**5.** b) The Staples office-supply company, one of the centre's corporate sponsors.

**6.** c) Bono.

**7.** a) Pacino for *Serpico*, *Godfather II*, and *Dog Day Afternoon* respectively.

**8.** c) for the movie *Heaven Can Wait.*

**9.** b) Carson was host four times in that decade.

**Scoring:**

| | |
|---|---|
| 8 and above – | We expect to see you on the red carpet |
| 5 to 8 – | Movie and music buff |
| below 5 – | Boomer bookworm |

# Answers to Quiz 3: Advertising

**1.** a) Chiffon.

**2.** c) Maxwell House was good to the last drop.

**3.** Brylcreem.

**4.** b) Calvin Klein.

**5.** d) Mariette Hartley.

**6.** b) Rolaids.

**7.** Charlie.

**8.** a) Palmolive.

**9.** d) American Express

**10.** a) squeeze b) filling c) upper d) eat

**Scoring:**

Eight and above –    All those hours in front of the TV finally pay off

Five to 8 –    Commercially challenged

Below 5 –    What, you were out in the kitchen getting a beer and a sandwich?

# Answers to Quiz 4: Holidays

**1.**    b) 1972.

**2.**    a) ii
      b) iv
      c) i
      d) iii

**3.**    Festivus.

**4.**    d) Teenage Mutant Ninja Turtles, the "Heroes in the Half Shell" who lived in sewers and ate pizza.

**5.**    a) iv
      b) i
      c) ii
      d) iii.

**6.** b) Ray Walston, the actor best known as the star of the TV show *My Favorite Martian* and later *Picket Fences*, died on January 1, 2001, at age eighty-six. Dean Martin passed away on Christmas Day, 1995; Charlie Chaplin died on December 25, 1977, and James Brown died on Christmas Day, 2006.

**7.** c) Ross dresses up as the "Holiday Armadillo."

**8.** d) David Bowie.

**9.** a) all share a Christmas Day birthday.

**10.** a) the Chiefs, who lost by a score of 27 to 24.

**Scoring:**

Eight and above –   A holiday toast to you.
Five to eight –   Naughty or nice?
Below five –   Bah, humbug!

# Answers to Quiz 5: Music

**1.** a) iii
b) iv
c) ii
d) i.

2.  c) "Philadelphia Freedom" stayed at number one for two weeks in 1975. Other number ones for John in the 70s were "Crocodile Rock," "Bennie and the Jets," and "Lucy in the Sky with Diamonds."

3.  Bruce Springsteen.

4.  d) *Saturday Night Fever.*

5.  Sonny and Cher.

6.  a) Mr. Mister.

7.  Phil Collins.

8.  b) in 1984.

9.  b) the club was located at 84 King Street in New York City.

10. b) DJs.

11. a) Rickie Lee Jones.

**Scoring:**
Eight and above –   You still look good in glitter and platform shoes.
Five to seven –     Dy-no-mite!
Below five –        Boomer wannabe.

# Answers to Quiz 6: Music 2

1.  a) sunny
    b) shining
    c) waiting
    d) Sunday.

2.  Pina colada.

3.  Maurice. Other brother Andy was primarily a solo artist.

4.  a) his tonic and gin.

5.  c) *Paradise Theater* which was released by Styx in April 1981, and had four top forty singles, including "The Best of Times" and "Too Much Time on My Hands."

6.  "Say Say Say." "The Girl Is Mine" only reached number two.

7.  b) "You Make My Dreams."

8.  False. Ocean, born Leslie Sebastian Charles in 1950, is a native of Fyzabad, Trinidad.

9.  Burial at sea, which is usually reserved for certain members of the armed forces.

10. Supertramp

**Scoring:**

| | |
|---|---|
| Eight and above – | We know what music's on your mp3 player. |
| Five to seven – | Still an oldie but a goodie. |
| Below five – | Music memories are fading. |

## Answers to Quiz 7: Travel

1. a) The Rock and Roll Hall of Fame in Cleveland.

2. a) iii
   b) iv
   c) i
   d) ii

3. a) True. John Hertz, a native of Austria, started the Yellow Cab Company in Chicago in 1915. In the early 1920s, he began renting cars under the name Drive-Ur-Self until General Motors bought both businesses in 1925 and renamed the car rental business Hertz Rent-A-Car.

4. b) American Airlines suggests travellers put those items in their carry-on bags.

5. b) Idaho, at Sun Valley, where the world's first chairlifts were installed on Proctor and Dollar mountains.

6. Chevy Chase.

7.   c) lawyer. The Frommer series is now published by John Wiley & Sons.

8.   c) Hilton Hawaiian Village in Honolulu, which ranks as ninth largest.

9.   a) Las Vegas.

**Scoring:**

Eight or more –     Bitten by the travel bug.
Five to seven –     Weekend road warrior.
Under five –        There's no place like home for the holidays.

# Answers to Quiz 8: Trivia Hodge Podge

1.   b) 1975. He was nominated for his performance in all the others.

2.   b) Patty Hearst, who turns sixty in 2014.

3.   d) never. The highest the show ever reached was number seven in the 1972–73 season.

4.   The Harlem Globetrotters.

5.   a) iii

b) iv

c) v

d) ii

e) i

6.    c) Cernan, commander of *Apollo 17*, was the last man on the moon in December 11, 1972.

7.    Twiggy.

8.    c) The Monkees made "believers" out of everyone that year.

9.    Art Carney won Best Actor for *Harry and Tonto*.

10.    a) Robert and Linda. William and Barbara ranked number four; Richard and Carol number five; and Kenneth and Karen number fifteen, says the Social Security Administration.

**Scoring:**

| | |
|---|---|
| Eight or more – | Far out, man! |
| Five to seven – | Still able to wear your love beads proudly. |
| Below five – | Uh, what a bummer. |

## Answers to Quiz 9: Boomer Car Qiuz

1.    Originally the name was Panther but Chevy decided to continue its established pattern of using "c" names for its cars.

Camaros were released to the public in September 1966.

2.    False. "G.T.O." was a hit for Ronny & the Daytonas.

3.    a) Warner Brothers, which produced the popular *Road Runner* cartoons.

4.    True, according to a 1993 magazine article in *Mopar Muscle*.

5.    a) Duster.
       b) Gremlin.
       d) Hornet.
       d) Vega.

6.    c) The Cars.

7.    d) Vega.

8.    a) ii
       b) v
       c) iv
       d) iii
       e) i.

9.    b) American Motors, or AMC as it was also known.

**Scoring:**

| | |
|---|---|
| Eight or more – | Get your motor running, head out on the highway. |
| Five to seven – | In need of a tune-up. |
| Below five – | Time for the scrap yard. |

# CHAPTER 16: ODDS AND SODS FROM EH TO ZED

## Answers to Quick Quiz Five-Pack

1. a) Hamilton.

2. b) Scrabble was the only one invented in the United States.

Scrabble was invented by an American.

3. First World War, in April 1917.

4. a) It was the first snowmobile, invented by Armand Bombardier in 1959 in Valcourt, Quebec.

5. At 28,956 kilometres, the coastline of Newfoundland is the longest of any Canadian province. British Columbia is second with 25,725 kilometres. The distances include mainland and all significant islands.

Photo by Michele Wright.

Newfoundland has Canada's longest coastline.

# CHAPTER 17: ON THE HILL POLITICKING IN CANADA

## Answers to Political Posers Quiz

1.  Agnes Macphail.

2.  d) Sir John A. Macdonald.

3.  b) $600.

4.  b) journalist.

5.  The Golden Boy.

6.  a) firecrackers.

7.  d) Manitoba, where females won the right to vote in January 1916.

8.  c) The auditorium at the Museum of Nature, then known as the Victoria Museum.

9.  Bill Davis, Ontario's premier from 1971 to 1985.

10. c) Alexander.

## CHAPTER 18: OUR GAME
## HOCKEY HEROES

### Answers to Stanley Cup Quiz

1. b) The Dominion Hockey Challenge Cup.

2. b) $50.

3. The Montreal Canadiens in 1993, when they defeated the Los Angeles Kings to take the final, four games to one.

4. True, during the presidencies of George Bush, Bill Clinton, and George W. Bush.

5. c) They won the cup three years in a row in 1896, 1897, and 1898.

6. a) All have scored Stanley Cup-winning goals.

7. c) Sheffield, England.

8. b) The Montreal Amateur Athletic Association in 1893. The team declined to accept the Cup because of an alleged slight, but they eventually accepted the prize a year later.

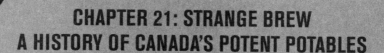

# CHAPTER 21: STRANGE BREW
# A HISTORY OF CANADA'S POTENT POTABLES

## Answers to Good For What Ales You Quiz

1.  True.

2.  d) Belgium.

3.  Brick Brewing Co. Ltd., which reintroduced Red Cap Ale.

4.  a) corn.

5.  b) Victoria Day.

6.  c) banking.

7.  a) iii,
    b) iv
    c) v
    d) i
    e) ii.

8.  d) upturned beer bottles.

9.  b) Victoria.

10. India Pale Ale.

Labatt 50, the beer that's for me and the boys.

11. b) It fell out of fashion because brewers wanted more distinctive packaging.

12.  c) Mallorytown, Ontario, at Mallorytown Glass Works, where bottles were blown by hand.

13.   b) Stand up while drinking beer and carrying a glass around the room.

14.  a) five cents.

15.  e) all of the above.

16.  c) Labatt's beer delivery truck, first unveiled in 1936.

17.  a) Alberta          iii) Big Rock Brewery Ltd.
     b) Saskatchewan    iv) Great Western Brewing Company Ltd.
     c) Ontario          ii) Creemore Springs Brewery Ltd.
     d) New Brunswick    i) Moosehead Breweries Limited.

18.  b) lemon lime.

19.  c) Cool Light, which was test marketed by Labatt's in 1972 in British Columbia and Alberta.

20.  a) It was sold in keg-shaped bottles from 1970 until 1972.

## CHAPTER 25: CASH AND CARRY BUSINESS, FINANCE, AND TRADE

### Answers to Biz Quiz

1. a) J.J. McLaughlin, a pharmacist, invented and manufactured Canada Dry Ginger Ale.

2. Queen Elizabeth's. She was also on the old one and two dollar bills, and is currently on the twenty dollar bill.

3. c) smoking. Fifteen years earlier, the carrier had introduced no-smoking sections in its aircraft.

4. a) Canada Cycle and Motor Company.

5. a) Quebec City. It was used to make rum from imported molasses.

6. a) a service station and car dealership.

Canada Dry was a druggist's creation.

7. a) Sandy McTire has been a featured character on Canadian Tire money since 1958.

# ABOUT THE AUTHORS

Mark Kearney is an award-winning journalist whose work has appeared in some 80 magazines and newspapers in North America. He has taught writing at the University of Western Ontario for the past 19 years, where he has won three awards of excellence for his teaching. Mark lives in London, Ontario, with his wife Catherine and enjoys playing clarinet and guitar, travelling, and going to as many movies as possible.

Randy Ray is a freelance writer, author, and publicist. He worked for the *London Free Press* for 13 years, including three years as Parliament Hill correspondent. He lives in Ottawa with his wife Janis, two of their three sons, and his dog Duffy. In his spare time he plays the drums, travels the province with his wife in search of quaint inns, and spends time at the cottage near Havelock, Ontario.

# Other Books by
# Mark Kearney and Randy Ray

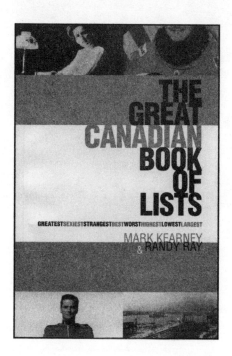

## THE GREAT CANADIAN BOOK OF LISTS

978-0-88882-213-0 / $19.99

Who were Canada's ten most romantic couples of the twentieth century? What were this country's worst disasters, its ten best beers, and its most controversial works of art in the past one hundred years?

*The Great Canadian Book of Lists* chronicles a century of achievements, trends, important and influential people, and fascinating events that have shaped this country as it heads into a new millennium. Award-winning writers Mark Kearney and Randy Ray turn the spotlight on the twentieth century to determine the best, worst, and most significant happenings in our lives.

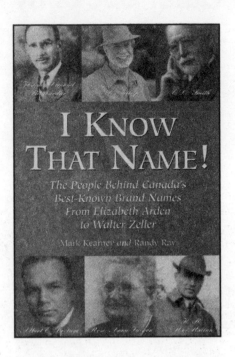

## I KNOW THAT NAME!

978-1-55002-407-4 / $22.99

Every day Canadians buy groceries at Sobeys, develop film at Black's, or grab a coffee at Tim Hortons without giving it a second thought. These brands are in our lives and in the public eye. We're familiar with the names, but what do we really know about the people who lie behind them? *I Know That Name!* will answer these questions for you. It's full of fun facts, intriguing trivia, and engrossing explorations of more than one hundred Canadian men and women who beat the odds to become household names, including Timothy Eaton, Laura Secord, and J.L. Kraft.

Available at your favourite bookseller.

# Tell us your story!

What did you think of this book?

Join the conversation at
www.definingcanada.ca/tell-your-story
by telling us what you think.